SPELLCHECKER

WITH RULES

Edwin Rankin

Acknowledgements

Firstly, I would like to thank my wife, Joan, and son, Paul, for many discussions and suggestions as the book was being written and rewritten, and my wife for some editing work. The following kindly consented to read the first complete manuscript of rules: William Ainsworth (writer), Michael Crawford (Headteacher), Pauline Crawford (Headteacher), Graham Forristalle (English Teacher). This resulted in the many useful suggestions which were incorporated into the text.

I would like to record my gratitude to the above for their help and encouragement.

For Joan and Paul

Editor: Karen Westall   Layout artist: Suzanne Ward
Cover design: Ed Gallagher

© Edwin Rankin 1999.

Every effort has been made to contact copyright holders of material used in this book. If any have been overlooked, we will be pleased to make any necessary arrangements.

British Library Cataloguing in Publication Data. A catalogue record for this book is available from the British Library.

First published 1999 by Folens Limited, Dunstable and Dublin.
Folens Limited, Albert House, Apex Business Centre, Boscombe Road, Dunstable, LU5 4RL, England.
Reprinted 2000.

ISBN 1 86202 651–3

CONTENTS

HYPHENS 201

BEGINNINGS AND ENDINGS 211

PUBLISHER'S INTRODUCTION:
Using Spellchecker with Rules

Spellchecker with Rules is a comprehensive spelling resource and should prove invaluable in helping teachers and learners with their understanding and usage of English. However, there is no getting away from the fact that the issue of spelling is difficult – and often requires specialist insight and its own vocabulary. In this context there are a number of things the reader needs to know.

1. Spellchecker

Guide words are provided at the top of each page so that spellings can be found quickly and easily. Bold letters are used within individual words to denote the problem area of the word, as dealt with by the rule listed alongside. You will not find every word in English listed here – as the author points out, this would make the text unwieldy, and be a diversion from its key function, which is to help with the problems and vagaries of spelling.

Usage of the Spellchecker is straightforward. Simply look up the problem word and then cross-reference to the rule – or rules – listed opposite. Words which have plurals dealt with in the Rules section use the abbreviation *pl*, and give the plural spelling or spellings.

2. Rules

The rules are set out according to the sections listed in the contents, from *'Vowels'* through to *'Beginnings and Endings'*. The wording of a rule is often detailed, and may use technical vocabulary when required. In cases where you are unsure of a term's meaning, such as 'cognate', use the glossary at the end of the text, which provides simple explanations. The rules themselves are numbered from 1–48, but within each one there are subsections that deal with specific categories or exceptions. These are ordered alphabetically (*14a, b, c* . . . and so on).

Finally, the rules do need to be read carefully; to absorb the variety of patterns and exceptions is not easy, but the process will be both useful and rewarding.

AUTHOR'S INTRODUCTION

This book aims to give, for all practical purposes, a *comprehensive* list of words that people find difficult to spell because a sound in the word can be represented by more than one letter combination. The first half of the book (the alphabetical list) contains at least *one form* of each word, illustrating the spelling difficulty. Alongside each word is a *reference to a rule*, and it is in the second half of the book (the Rules section) that the word can be found, under the relevant rule explanation.

An absolutely comprehensive list of words, however, would make the list too unwieldy and include many words which even poor spellers can spell. For example, there are over 1,600 words ending in *-able*. If you cannot find an *-able/-ible* word in the list, it probably ends in *-able*. The ending *-ize/-ise* presents no difficulty once you have decided which form to adopt. It is also impossible to cover all double consonants (Collins gives over 2,000 entries for *t* alone). Difficulties with prefixes and suffixes are noted. Remember that they are always written fully, often resulting in a double consonant. The main words with the endings *-ance*, *-ence*, *-ant*, *-ent*, and *-cy* are given. The thousands of entries with the common endings *-er*, *-sion* and *-tion* are not given. These endings generally pose little difficulty.

While aiming to be comprehensive, I have kept the rules as simple as possible. Homonyms and grammatical questions, which affect spelling but do not fall within the scope of the spelling rules, are not usually treated. Also usually omitted are proper names and words whose spelling can be inferred from a clear pronunciation. Apart from these omissions, as full a list of examples is given as is practicable so that the book will be useful to everyone.

The rules, especially those dealing with vowels, are full of useful material for teaching and learning reading. However, the overriding aim of this book is to teach spelling; the book is not a complete guide to pronunciation. Pronunciation is used as a guide to spelling and it is generally assumed that the reader uses the word in speech and needs to learn how to spell it. A detailed phonetic analysis of words, therefore, is beyond the remit of the book and would not cater for the wide readership envisaged. The aim of the simplified phonetic analysis described in the next paragraphs is purely pragmatic – to teach spelling, not pronunciation.

Pronunciation is indicated by using combinations of English letters between / and /, e.g. /aw/. However, it has been impossible to avoid the occasional use of the phonetic symbol schwa, /ə/. This indicates the indeterminate vowel sound of the *a* in *again*. We have no vowels that can convey this. For practical purposes, the sound of the *-ir* in *fir* is called a stressed schwa, although strictly speaking it has a different phonetic symbol, /ɜ:/. The phonetic symbols /ʌ/ (the vowel sound in '*but*') and /ʒ/ (the /zh/ sound in *treasure*) are also used.

For the purposes of the rules given in the second part of this book, a long vowel says its name (except for /u/ which is /oo/ as in *school*, not /yoo/), that is, the sound it usually has in a one-syllable word that ends with a silent *e*. Similarly, a short vowel says its sound, that is, the sound it usually has in a one-syllable word without a silent *e*. This is not the way that long and short vowel sounds are classified in the science of phonetics, but it works well in the construction of practical rules for spelling. In this simplified classification the /u/ sound in *up* and the /a/ sound in *father* are counted as short vowels.

I have also simplified phonetic diphthongs; the word *beer*, in fact, has the sound /bɪə/ (a short *i* followed by the indeterminate sound schwa – see above), but to the untrained ear the first part of the diphthong sounds like a long /e/. Where the vowels in combination are given their individual sounds, a careful pronunciation guides the spelling (e.g. *bionic*). Where the vowels produce one new sound, a careful pronunciation will not differentiate the component vowels (e.g. *boy*). Rules 4, 5 and 10 describe these vowel digraphs.

If you compare the rules on vowels I have provided plus my comments here with the chart 'Key-Words for English Phonetic Symbols' (inside the cover of the *English Pronouncing Dictionary* by Daniel Jones), you will see that all the sounds of English vowels are covered in the rules in this book. However, they are not covered to master the science of phonetics but to learn a practical way of spelling correctly. Like all good educational methods, the one adopted in this book builds on the knowledge that the child or adult already has.

Finally, the only real rule for spelling is usage. A book of this kind must be based on an ultimate authority on usage in spelling. I could have chosen any modern dictionary and it would have made little difference. However, for research purposes, I needed an electronic dictionary. The most convenient was Collins, published on CD (version 1.5) by Word Perfect. Where necessary, I extended Collins dictionary by using the Shorter Oxford English Dictionary, 3rd edition.

Like other dictionaries, Collins takes as its basic model for pronunciation what has been called 'RP' – that is, Received Pronunciation. This is the pronunciation adopted by the 'educated classes', the courts, the early BBC, and the public schools in the early part of the century. The nearest model in regional English is that which is used in the South-east, and that which is taught to second-language learners. However, Received Pronunciation is nowadays rarely used in its original form. Consequently, when using a dictionary or the rules in this book, it may be preferable to modify occasionally the pronunciation of certain words according to the modified RP in specific parts of the country.

American variations of *rules* are given in footnotes with examples. American variations of individual examples occurring elsewhere are not noted. Where the rules for American spelling differ from those of other English-speaking countries, I used the unabridged version of Webster's dictionary published by Encyclopedia Britannica in 1986.

Edwin Rankin

PART ONE

Spellchecker

'Learning about the predictable links between spelling and pronunciation is the key to understanding the spelling system. It is never enough to rely on the written language alone. An integrated approach can then act as a framework for the task of mastering the exceptions that history has imposed on the language – but this task seems less formidable once it is accompanied by understanding. If there is a daily battle being fought over spelling in our classrooms, as some suggest, it will be won only if children learn (as wartime generals did) to "know their enemy".'

David Crystal
The Cambridge Encyclopedia of the English Language (p. 272)

acoustics (sing.)	20a	adjut**ant**	31
acqu**ai**nt	4a	administrat**or**	40c
acquaintance	14b	admiral	1
acquaint**ance**	30c	admir**al**	3b
acquiesce	14b	adm**ire**	4c
acquire	14b	admiss**ible**	28f, 28h
acquisition	14b	admi**ssion**	14b
acquit	14b	admit	14b
acquittal	14b	admitt**ance**	30c
acquitt**ance**	30c	admonit**ory**	33c
ac**re**	1c	adolesc**ence**	30b, 30c
ac**re**	9c, 40d	ad**opt**ed	24
acre**age**	11	adren**al**	3b
acreage	23	adr**oit**	5b
acron**ym**	8a	adulterat**or**	40c
acro**ss**	14a	adv**ance**	30
activat**or**	40c	advant**age**	11
act**or**	9c	ad**vent**	31
actua**lly**	46a	adven**ture**	40f
actuary *pl* -r**ies**	19	adversary *pl* -r**ies**	19
ad**age**	11	adversity *pl* -t**ies**	19
adagi**os**	18b	advert**ise**	45
ada**mant**	31	advertisement	36
adapt**er** or adapt**or**	40c	adv**ice** n.	34
a**dd**	14a	adv**ise** vb.	34
a**dd**	14b	ad**vise**	45
addendum	14b	advis**er**	33c
adder	1	advis**er** or advis**or**	40c
adder	14b	advis**ory**	33c
addict	14b	advoca**cy**	34
addition	14b	**aer**ial	29
addition**al**	3b	aeron**au**tical	5a
additive	14b	**aero**plane	29
ad**dle**	3b	**aes**thetic	10
ad**dle**	14b	aestheti**cism**	25b
add-on	14b	**aff**able	14b
addre**ss**	14a	aff**able**	28b
address	14b	aff**air**	4a
addre**ss**er or addre**ss**or	40c	**aff**air	14b
adduce	14b	**aff**ect	14b
addu**cible** or addu**ceable**	28g	**aff**erent	14b
aden**oid**	5b	affer**ent**	31
adenoid**al**	3b	**aff**idavit	14b
adequa**cy**	34	**aff**iliate	14b
adher**ence**	30c	**aff**inity	14b
adher**ent**	31	**aff**irm	14b
adjec**tive**	3d	affir**mant**	31
ad**jective**	12	**aff**ix	14b
adj**oin**	5b	**aff**latus	14b

afflict	14b	albatross	14a
affluent	14b	albinos	18b
affluent	31	alcoholicity	25b
afford	14b	alga pl -ae	22d
afforestation	14b	alight	4c
affranchise	14b	align	4c
affray	14b	alimentary	33a
affricative	14b	alkaloid	5b
affright	14b	alky or -ie	8d
affront	14b	allay	4a
afloat	4d	allay	14b
afraid	4a	allayed	26
afterwards	40e	allegation	14b
again	2b, 2e	allege	14b
against	2b	allegiance	14b
ageing	23	allegiance	30c
agency pl -cies	19	allegorical	14b
agent	12	allegory pl -ries	19
agglomeration	14b	allegory	33c
aggradation	14b	alleluia	14b
aggrandizement	14b	allergic	14b
aggravate	14b	allergy pl -gies	19
aggregate	14b	alleviate	14b
aggression	14b	alleviator	40c
aggressive	14b	alley	14b
aggressor	40c	alleys	19
aggrieve	4b, 6a	alliance	14b
aggrieved	14b	alliance	30c
aggro	14b	alligator	14b
agilely	46a	alliteration	14b
agility	12	allocution	14b
aglow	4d	all-over	27f
agnosticism	25b	allow	5c
agony pl -nies	19	allow	14b
agoraphobia	15a	alloy	5b
agree	4b	allude	14b
agriculture	40f	allure	14b
aground	5c	allusion	14b
ague	15	alluvial	14b
ahead	2b	ally	14b
ahoy	5b	almond	15
aid	4a	almost	1a
ail	4a	almost	14a
aim	4a	aloes	4d
air	4a	aloud	5c
air-cooled	27f	alphabet	15a
airy	4a	already	14a
aisle	3b	alright	4c
aisle	15	altar	2d

altar	40e	anew	4e
alter	2d	angel	1e
alteration	2d	angel	3b
altercation	2d	anger	1e
alternate	2d	angle	3b
alternator	40c	angler	40b
although	15b	Anglicism	25b
altogether	14a	anglicize	25b
alumna *pl* -ae	22d	anguish	8e
alumnus *pl* -ni	22d	angular	40e
always	14a	animal	3b
amass	14a	ankle	3b
ambassador	40c	annal	3b
ambience or ambiance	30c	annal	14b
ambient	31	anneal	4b
ambitious	13	anneal	14b
ambivalence	30c	annex	14b
ambivalent	31	annihilate	14b
ambulance	30c	annihilator	40c
amenity *pl* -ties	19	anniversary	14b
amiss	14a	anniversary *pl* -ries	19
amnesty *pl* -ties	19	anniversary	33a
amoeba *pl* -ae or -as	22d	annotate	14b
among	2c	annotator	40c
amoral	3b	announce	5c
amorphous	15a	announce	14b
amount	5c	annoy	5b
amphibious	15a	annoy	14b
amphitheatre	15a	annual	3b
amphora	15a	annual	14b
amphora *pl* -ae or -as	22d	annuitant	31
ample	3b	annuity	14b
amputator	40c	annuity *pl* -ties	19
anaesthetize	10	annul	14a, 14c
anal	3b	annul	14b
analogue	15	annular	40e
analyse	45	annunciation	14b
analysis	8a	anodyne	8a
analysis *pl* -yses	22d	anoint	5b
ancestor	40c	anonymity	8a
anchor	40c	anonymous	8a
anchorage	11	another	2c
anchovy *pl* -vies	19	answer	15
ancient	13	antecede	35
ancillary	33a	antecedence	30c
android	5b	antecedent	32
anecdotal	3b	antecedent	31
anemone	3a	antechamber	32
aneroid	5b	antedate	32

antediluvian	32	anxious	13d
antemeridian	32	anybody	42
antenatal	32	anyhow	5c
antependium *pl* -dia	22d	any one	42
antependium	32	anyone	42
antepenultimate	32	anyway	4a
anteposition	32	apathy *pl* -thies	19
anteroom	32	aperient	31
anthology *pl* -gies	19	aphid	15a
anthropoid	5b	aphorism	15a
anthropomorphic	15a	aphrodisiac	15a
antibacterial	32	apiary	33a
antibiotic	32	aplomb	15
antibody	32	apocalypse	8a
anticipant	31	apocalyptic	8a
anticipator	40c	apocrypha	15a
antics (pl.)	20b	apocryphal	3b
anticyclone	8a	apocryphal	8a
anti-icer	27b	apodosis *pl* -oses	22d
anti-imperialism	27b	apologize	45
anti-imperialist	27b	apostasy *pl* -sies	19
anti-inflammatory	27b	apostasy	34
anti-inflationary	27b	apostle	3b
antilock	32	apostle	15
antioxidant	31	apostrophe	15a
antipastos	18b	apothecary *pl* -ries	19
antipathy pl -thies	19	apothecary	33a
antipathy	32	appal	14a, 14c
antiphon	15a	appalled	24b
antiphonal	3b	appalling	14b
antipodean	32	appalling	24b
antiquarian	9a	apparatus	14b
antiquary	9a	apparatus *pl* -tus or -tuses	22d
antiquary *pl* -ries	19	apparel	14b
antique	4b	apparelled	24b
antique	8e	apparent	14b
antiquity *pl* -ties	19	apparent	31
antirrhinum	15a	apparently	14b
antiseptic	32	apparitor	14b
antistatic	32	apparitor	40c
antithesis *pl* -eses	22d	appeal	4b
antithesis	32	appeal	14b
antitoxic	32	appear	4b
antitype	8a	appearance	14b
antitype	32	appearance	30c
antiwar	32	appease	4b
antonym	8a	appease	14b
antrum *pl* -tra	22d	appellant	14b
anxiety *pl* -ties	19	appellant	31

appendage	11	arable	28b
appendage	14b	Aramaic	4a
appendant	31	arbitrary	33a
appendicitis	14b	arbitrator	40c
appendix	14b	arboretum pl -ta or -tums	22d
appendix pl -dixes or -dices	22d	arbour	40e
appertain	14b	archaeology or archeology	10
appetite	14b	archaic	4a
applaud	5a	archer	40f
applaud	14b	archery	33b
applause	14b	archetype	8a
apple	3b	archipelagos or archipelagoes	18b
apple	14b	archipelagos or -oes	18c
appliance	14b	architecture	40f
applicant	14b	ardent	31
applicator	40c	ardour	40e
applied	26	are	3a
apply	14b	area	4b
applying	26	argue	36
appoint	5b	argue	4e
appoint	14b	arguor	4e
apportion	14b	argument	36
apposite	14b	ariel	3b
appraise	14b	aright	4c
appreciable	23	arise	45
appreciable	28c	aristocracy	34
appreciate	13	arithmetic	25b
appreciate	14b	arithmetician	25b
appreciator	40c	armadillos	18b
apprehend	14b	armature	40f
apprehensible	14b	armillary	33a
apprehensible	28h	armour	40e
apprehensive	14b	armoury pl -ries	19
apprentice	12	army pl -mies	19
apprentice	14b	aromaticity	25b
apprise	14b	around	5c
apprise	45	arouse	5c
approach	4o	arraign	14b
approach	14b	arraign	15a
approbation	14b	arrange	1e
appropriate	1c	arrange	14b
appropriate	14b	arrant	14b
appropriator	40c	arrant	31
approve	2c	array	4a
approve	14b	array	14b
approximate	14b	arrears	4b
aqua pl -ae or -as	22d	arrears	14b
aquarium	9a	arrest	14b
aquarium pl -riums or -ria	22d	arrive	14b

arrogance	30c	assistance	14b
arrogant	14b	assistance	31, 30c
arrogate	14b	assistant	31
arrow	4d	assizes	14b
arrow	14b	associate	14b
arsenal	3b	associate	13
artery *pl* -ries	19	assonance	14b
article	3b	assortment	14b
artifice	12	assuage	14b
ascend	15	assume	14b
ascertain	4a	assurance	30c
asceticism	25b	assure	4e
ascribe	14b	assure	14b
ashore	4d	assure	13
Asian	13d	astern	14b
asinine	3a	asteroid	5b
askance	30	astral	3b
askew	4e	astray	4a
asleep	4b	astronaut	5a
asphalt	15a	asymmetric	8a
asphyxiate	8a	asymmetry	8a
asphyxiate	15a	ate	2b
aspirant	31	athenaeum	10
aspirator	40c	athleticism	25b
aspire	14b	athwart	9a
ass	14a	atmosphere	15a
assail	4a	atoll	14a
assailant	14b	atom	1e
assailant	31	atonable or atoneable	28e
assassin	1e	atonal	3b
assassin	14b	atrium *pl* -tria	22d
assault	14b	atrocious	13
assay	4a	atrophy	15a
assayed	26	attach	11
assayer	14b	attach	14b
assemble	14b	attacher	40f
assent	14b	attack	14b
assert	14b	attain	4a
assertible	28h	attain	14b
assess	14a	attempt	14b
assess	14b	attend	14b
assessor	14b	attendance	30c
assessor	40c	attendant	31
asset	14b	attention	14b
assiduous	14b	attenuate	14b
assign	4c, 15a	attest	14b
assign	14b	attestor	40c
assimilate	14b	attic	14b
assimilator	40c	attire	14b

attitude	14b
attorney	14b
attract	14b
attractor or attracter	40c
attribute	14b
attributer or attributor	40c
attrition	14b
attune	14b
aubergine	4b
auburn	5a
auction	5a
audacious	5a
audacious	13
audible	5a
audible	28h
audience	5a
audience	30c
audio-	5a
auditor	40c
auditorium	5a
auditorium pl -riums or ria	22d
auditory	33c
aught	5a
augment	5a
augur	5a
August	5a
auntie or -y	8d
aunty pl -ties	19
aural	3b
aural	5a
auricular	40c
aurora	5a
auspices	5a
auspicious	5a
Aussie	8d
austere	2d, 5a
austerity pl -ties	19
Australia	2d
Austria	2d
authenticity	25b
author	5a
author	40c
authority	5a
auto-	5a
autobiography	15a
autograph	15a
autolyse	45
automatic	5a
automaton pl -tons or -ta	22d
autopsy	5a
autopsy pl -sies	19
autumn	15
autumnal	3b
auxiliary	5a
avail	4a
avalanche	13e
avarice	12
avenue	3d
aver	1e
average	11
avertible or avertable	28h
aviary pl -ries	19
aviary	33a
aviator	40c
avocados	18b
avoid	5b
avoidance	30c
await	4a
award	9a
away	4a
awe	5a
awesome	5a
awful	5a
awkward	5a
awkward	8e
awl	5a
awning	5a
axe	3a
axis pl -xes	22d
axle	3b
axseed	12
aye	4c
azure	40g

B

babble	3b
baby *pl* -bies	19
baby-minder	27e
baby-sitter	27e
bachelor	40c
bacillus *pl* -li	22d
background	5c
backpacker	27e
backup	27a
backward	8e
backwards	40e
bacterium *pl* -ria	22d
baddie or -y	8d
bade	3a
badge	11
badger	11
baffle	3b
bagel or beigel	3b
baggage	11
bail	4a
bailiff	14a
bait	4a
baker	9c, 40b
bakery *pl* -ries	19
bakery	33b
balanceable	28d
balcony *pl* -nies	19
balk	15
ballerina	4b
ballet	4a
balloon	4e
ballplayer	27e
balsa	2d
bambino *pl* -s or -ni	22c
bambinos	18b
bamboo	4e
bamboozle	3b
banal	3b
bandage	11
bandeau *pl* -x	22a
banger	1e
bangle	3b
banister	1e

banjos or -oes	18c
banquet	7
baptismal	3b
baptistry *pl* -ries	19
barber	40b
bare	4a
bargain	2e
barge	12
barrel	3b
barrelled	24b
barrelling	24b
barrenness	14b
barrier	1e
barrow	4d
barysphere	8a
bases	16, 22
bashful	14a
basil	3b
basis *pl* -ases	22d
basket	7
bass	14a
bassoon	4e
baste	3a
batch	11
bathe	1c
bathysphere	8a
battalion	1e, 14d
battery *pl* -ries	19
battle	3b
battle	14d
bauble	3b
baulk	5a
bawdy	5a
bawl	5a
bay	4a
bayonet	4a
bayou	4e
bays	19
beach (sea)	4b
beacon	4b
bead	4b
beagle	3b
beak	4b
beaker	4b
beam	4b
bean	4b
bear	4a
beard	4b
beast	4b

beat (hit)	4b	beige	4a, 6b
beatnik	25b	bejewel	4e
beau pl -s or -x	4d, 22a	bejewel	7
beautician	13	belabour	7
beautician	25b	belabour	40e
beautiful	14a	belated	7
because	7	belayed	26
become	2c	belfry	14a
become	7	beliefs	17
bedeck	7	believe	4b, 6a
bedevil	7	believe	7
bedew	4e	belligerence	30c
bedew	7	bellow	4d
bedraggle	7	bell-ringer	27e
bee	4b	belly pl -llies	19
beech (tree)	4b	bellyful	8c
beef	4b	belong	7
been	4b	beloved	2c
beer	4b	beloved	7
beet (vegetable)	4b	below	4d
beetle	3b	bemoan	4d
beetle	4b	bemoan	7
beeves	17	bemuse	7
befit	7	bencher	40f
before	7	beneath	4b
befriend	7	beneath	7
began	7	benefice	12
beget	7	beneficiary pl -ries	19
beggar	9c, 40e	benevolence	30c
begin	7	benevolent	31
begin	12	benign	4c, 15a
beginning	24b	benzol	3b
begonia	7	bequeath	7
begrudge	7	bereaved	4b
beguile	7	bereaved	39
begun	7	bereft adj.	39
behalf	7	beret	4a
behave	7	berry	1e
behaviour	7	berth	9c
behaviour	40e	beryl	8a
behavioural	3b	beside	7
behead	7	besiege	6a
beheld	7	bestow	4d
behest	7	bestow	7
behind	1a	betray	4a
behind	7	betray	7
behold	1a	betroth	7
behold	7	betrothal	3b
behove	7	between	4b

between	7	bistros	18b
betweentimes	27h	bitch	11
betweenwhiles	27h	bivalent	31
betwixt	7	bivouacked	25a
bevel	3b	biyearly	8d
bevelled	24b	blackmail	4a
bevelling	24b	blackout n.	27a
beverage	11	black out vb.	27a
bewail	4a	blamable or blameable	28e
beware	7	blancmange	1e
bewildered	7	blanket	7
bewitched	7	blaspheme	15a
beyond	7	blast off vb.	27a
bezel	3b	blastoff n.	27a
biased or biassed	24b	blatant	31
biases or biasses	24b	bleach	4b
biasing or biassing	24b	bleacher	40f
biblicist	25b	bleak	4b
bibliography pl -phies	19	bleary	4b
bibliophile	15a	bleat	4b
bicycle	3b	bleed	4b
bicycle	8a	bleep	4b
bier	4b	bless	14a
bilateral	3b	blew	4e
bile	14d	blight	4c
bilingual	8e	blind	1a
bilious	1e, 14d	blinder	1a
billet	7	blindfold	1a
billiards	1e	bliss	14a
billow	4d	blister	40b
billposter	27e	blizzard	40e
bimbos or -oes	18c	bloat	4d
binal	3b	blood	2c
binary	33a	bloom	4e
bind	1a	blossom	1e
bindery	33b	blotch	11
bindweed	1a	blotter	40b
bingos or -oes	18c	blouse	5c
binocular	40e	blow	4d
bio-	4c	blow-up	27a
biographer	40b	blowzy	5c
bionic	4c	bludgeon	11
birch	9c	blue	47
bird	9c	blue	4e
birdie	8d	bluebottle	3b
birdlike	27c	bluely	47
Biros	18b	bluey	23
birth	9c	blunderbuss	14a
biscuit	15	blur	9c

blurb	9c	bouffant	31
boar	4d, 9d	bougainvillea	4e
board	4d, 9d	bough	5c
boast	4d	bough	15b
boat	4d	bought	15b
bobble	3b	boulder	4d
bodice	12	bounce	5c
body pl -dies	19	bouncy	23
boggle	3b	bound	5c
bogie or -y	8d	boundary pl -ries	19
boil	5b	bouquet	4a
boisterous	5b	bouquet	4e
boisterous	41	bourgeois	4e
bold	1a	bout	5c
boleros	18b	boutique	4e
bolshie or -y	8d	bow	5c
bolt	1a	bow (arrow)	4d
bomb	15	bowdlerize	4d
bondage	11	bowel	3b
bondholder	27e	bowel	5c
boneshaker	27e	bowelled	24b
bonnet	7	bowelling	24b
booby	4e	bowl	4d
boodle	3b	bowling	4d
boogie	8d	boxer	14
book	2c	boxes	16
book-keeper	27e	boxlike	27c
bookbinder	27e	boy	5b
bookie	8d	boycott	5b
boom	4e	boys	19
boon	4e	brace	12
boost	4c	bracelet	12
boot	4e	braces	12
booth	4e	bracket	7
bootie	8d	braid	4a
bootlegger	27e	Braille	4a
booty	4e	brain	4a
booze	4e	braise	4a
booze-up	27a	bramble	3b
bordellos	18b	branch	13e
borough	15b	brandy pl -dies	19
borrow	4d	brass	14a
bosom	2c	brassie	8d
boss	14a	bravadoes or -os	18c
botcher	40f	bravery	33b
both	1c	brawny	5a
bother	1c	bray	4a
bottle	3b	brazenness	14a
boudoir	4e	breach	4b

bread	2b	brochure	40g
breadth	2b	brogue	15
break	4a	broil	5b
breakage	11	broken-down	27f
breakdown n.	27a	brolly pl -llies	19
break down vb.	27a	bronchus pl -chi	22d
breakfast	2b	brooch	4d
break-out	27a	brood	4e
break-up n.	27a	brook	2c
bream	4b	broom	4e
breast	2b	brothel	3b
breath	2b	brother	2c
breathalyse	8a	brought	15b
breathalyse	45	brow	5c
breathe	4b	brown	5c
breeches	2b	brownie	8d
breed	4b	brownness	14b
breeze	4b	bruise	4e
brew	4e	brush-up n.	27a
brewery pl -ries	19	brusquely	47
brewery	33b	bubble	3b
briar or brier	40e	bubbly	46b
bribery	33b	buccaneer	1e
brickie	8d	bucket	7
bridal	3b	buckle	3b
bridesmaid	4a	budgerigar	11
bridge	11	budget	11
bridle	3b	budgetary	33a
brief	4b, 6a	budgie	11
brier	4c	budgie	8d
bright	4c	buffaloes	18a
bright-red	27f	buffet	4a
brilliance	30c	buffoonery	33b
brilliant	31	buggy pl -ggies	19
brimful or brimfull	14a	bugle	3b
brindle	3b	build	1a
bringing	12	build-up n.	27a
bristle	3b	built	15
bristle	15	bulge	12
bristly	46b	bullet	7
Britain	1e	bulletin	7
Briton	1e	bulrush	1e
Brittany	1e	bumptious	13
brittle	3b	bundle	3b
brittlely or brittly	46b	bungalow	4d
broacher	40f	bungle	3b
broad	5a	buoy	5b
broadcast	5a	buoyancy	8a
broccoli	8	buoyant	5b

C

cabbage	11
cabby *pl* -bies	19
cable	3b
cackle	3b
cactus *pl* -tuses or -ti	22d
caddice	12
caddie or -y	8d
caddy *pl* -dies	19
cadence	30c
cadency	23
cadent	31
cadge	11
cadre	40d
Caesar	10
café	1e
cafeteria	4b
caffeine	4b, 6a
cage	12
calamity *pl* -ties	19
calceiform	2b, 6b
calculator	40c
calculus *pl* -luses	22d
calendar	40e
calibrator	40c
calibre	40d
calicoes or -os	18c
caliper	40b
calix *pl* -lices	22d
callow	4d
call-up n.	27a
callus *pl* -luses	22d
calumniator	40c
calves	17
calypso	8a
calypsos	18b
camellia	1
cameos	18b
camouflage	12
campaign	4a
campaign	15a
campus *pl* -puses	22d
canary *pl* -ries	19
cancel	3b

cancel	3b
cancelled	24b
cancelling	24b
candelabrum or -bra *pl* -bra	22d
candidacy	34
candidature	40f
candle	3b
candour	40e
candy *pl* -dies	19
cannery *pl* -ries	19
cannibal	3b
canoe	4e
canonical	1e
canopy *pl* -pies	19
canter	40b
canticle	3b
cantos	18b
cantus *pl* -tus	22d
canvass vb.	14a
canyon	8a
capable	3b
capacious	13
capacitance	30c
capacitor	40c
capillary *pl* -ries	19
capillary	33a
capital	3b
capitulator	40c
capitulatory	33c
capos	18b
capricious	13
capsule	3a
captain	2e
captivator	40c
capture	40f
car	9
caramel	3b
caravel	3b
carbuncle	3b
carburettor	40c
carcass or carcase	14a
cardboard	9d
card-carrying	27f
cardie or -y	8d
cardinal	3b
cardiograph	15a
career	4b
careful	14a
caress	14a

cargoes or -os	18c	catcher	40f
carnage	11	catches	16
carnal	3b	catchment	11
carol	3b	catchword	11
carolled	24b	category pl -ries	19
carolling	24b	category	33c
carolus pl -luses or -li	22d	caterpillar	40e
carouse	5c	cathedral	3b
carousel	3b	Catholicism	25b
carpet	7	catholicity	25b
carrel	3b	catholicize	25b
carrel or carrell	14a	catlike	27c
carriage	11	cattery	33b
carrying	8d	cattle	3b
cartel	3b	Caucasian	5a
Cartesian	13d	caucus pl -cuses	22d
Carthusian	13d	caught	5a
cartilage	11	caught	15b
cartoon	4e	caul	5a
cartridge	11	cauldron	5a
cartwright	4c	cauliflower	2d
carvery	33b	caulk	5a
carve-up n.	27a	caulk	15
casein	4b, 6a	cause	5a
caseworker	27e	caustic	5a
cashew	4e	causticity	25b
cashier	4b	cauterize	5a
casinos	18b	caution	5a
casket	7	cautious	13
cassette	14	cavalier	4b
caste	3a	caviar	4c
castigator	40c	cavilled	24b
castigatory	33c	cavilling	24b
castle	3b	cavity pl -ties	19
castle	15	caw	5a
castrator	40c	cease	4b
casualty pl -ties	19	cedar	40e
cataclysm	8a	cede	35
cataclysmal	3b	ceilidh	4a, 6b
catacomb	15	ceiling	4b, 6a
catalogue	15	celebrant	31
catalyse	45	celebrator	40c
catalysis pl -yses	22d	celebratory	33c
catalyst	8a	celery	12
catalytic	8a	celibacy	34
catarrh	15a	cell	12
catarrhal	3b	cellar	40e
catastrophe	15a	cell-like	27c
catch	11	cellos	18b

cellular	40e	chancy or chancey	23, 34
celluloid	5b	chandelier	4b
Celticist	25b	chandelier	6a
cement	12	change	1e
cemetery	33b	changeover n.	27e
cenacle	3b	channel	3b
cenobite or coenobite	10	channelled	24b
censure	13	channelling	24b
censure	40g	chaos	15a
census pl -suses	22d	chapel	3b
centenary pl -ries	19	chappie	8d
centenary	33a	charge	12
centigrade	12	charlie	8d
centimetre	12	chaseable	28e
centipede	12	chassis	13e
centos	18b	chassis pl chassis	22d
central	3b	chasten	15
centre	40d	chastise	45
century pl -ries	19	chasuble	3b
-cephalic	15a	chateau	13e
cereal	12	chateau pl -x or -s	4d, 22a
cerebral	3b	chattel	3b
cerebrum pl -brums or -bra	22d	chauffeur	4d
ceremony	12	cheap	4b
cerise	45	cheapen	39a
certain	9c	cheat	4b
certainty pl -ties	19	checkup	27a
certificate	12	cheddar	40e
certify	9c	cheek	4b
certitude	9c	cheer	4b
cervix pl -vixes or -vices	22d	cheerful	4b
cession	14b	cheerio	4b
chaffinch	14	cheese	4b
chagrined	24b	chef	13e
chain	4a	chefs	17
chair	4a	cheroot	4e
chaise	13e	cherry-like	27c
chalet	13e	cherub pl -s or -im	22b
chalice	12	chess	14a
chalk	15	chew	4u
challenge	12	chicken	7
chamberlain	2e	chicory or chiccory	33c
chambre	40d	chief	4b, 6a
chameleon-like	27c	chiefs	17
chamois	5b	chiffchaff	14a
chancel	3b	chilblain	4a
chancel	3b	chilblain	14a
chancellor	40c	child	1a
chancery	33b	children	1a

childlike	27c	cinquain	4a
chillness	14a	cipher or cypher	8a
china	4	cipher	15a
chinos	18b	circle	3b
chippy or -ie	8d	circle	9c
chiropodist	15a	circuit	9c
chiropody	15a	circular	40e
chisel	3b	circulator	40c
chiselled	24b	circulatory	33c
chiselling	24b	circumcise	45
chiv	3d	circumference	30c
chlorophyll	8a	circumflexion	38
chlorophyll	14c	circumlocutory	33c
chlorophyll	14a	circumstantial	13c
chock-full	14a	circus pl -cuses	22d
chocolate	7	cirrhosis	15a
choice	5b	citable or citeable	28e
choir	4c	citadel	3b
chokeable	28e	citizen	12
choke-full	14a	city pl cities	19
choose	4e	civvy	14
choral	3b	claim	4a
chordal	3b	claimant	31
choreograph	15a	clairvoyance	30c
chortle	3b	clairvoyant	5b
chorus pl -ruses	22d	clamant	31
chosen	39a	clamour	40e
christen	15	clampdown n.	27a
Christian	15a	clamp down vb.	27a
Christmas	15a	clanger	1e
chromaticity	25b	clangour	40e
chronicity	25b	clapperboard	9d
chronicle	3b	class	14a
chronologer	40b	classicism	25b
chrysalis	8a	classicist	25b
chrysalis pl -ises or -ides	22d	classicize	25b
chrysanthemum	8a	clause	5a
chuck-full	14a	claustrophobia	5a
chuckle	3b	claustrophobia	15a
churches	16	clavicle	3b
churn	9c	clavier	4b
chypre or chipre	40d	claw	5a
ciborium pl -ria	22d	clay	4a
cigar	12	clayey	23
cigarette	12	clean	4b
cincture	40f	cleanness	14b
cinders	12	cleanser	2b
cinematography	15a	cleanup	27a
cinerator	40c	clear	4b

clearance	30c
clear-up n.	27a
cleat	4b
cleavage	11
cleave	4b
clench	13e
clerihew	4e
clerk	9a
cliche	13e
client	31
climb	15
clincher	40f
clinician	25b
clippie	8d
cliquey or cliquy	23
cloak	4d
cloister	5b
close-up n.	27a
closure	40g
cloud	5c
clout	5c
cloven	2c
clown	5c
clownery	33b
cloy	5b
clubbable or clubable	28a
club foot	27e
club-footed	27e
clue	3d, 4e
clutch	11
coach	4d
coacher	40f
coadjutor	40c
coagulant	31
coal	4d
coarse	4d, 9d
coast	4d
coat	4d
cobalt	2d
cobble	3b
cockerel	3b
cockle	3b
cocoa	4d
codeine	4b, 6a
codex pl -dices	22d
codicil	3b

coefficient	6a
coeliac	10
coercible	28g
coercible	28h
coercion	13
coexistent	31
coffee	7
cognizable	28b
cognizance	30c
cognizant	31
coherent	31
coil	5b
coin	5b
coincident	31
cold	1a
collaborator	40c
collage	13
colleague	15
collectable or collectible	28h
collector	40c
college	7
collie	8d
colliery	8
colloquy pl -quies	19
colonel	15
colony plpl -nies	19
colophon	15a
colorant	31
colossal	14
colour	40e
colourize	40e
colt	1a
coltsfoot	1a
column	15
comb	1, 4d
comb	15
combatant	31
combustible	28h
come	2c
comedown n.	27a
come down vb.	27a
comedy pl -dies	19
comestible	28h
comeuppance	30c
comfortable	2c
comforter	2c
comfrey	2c
comma	14b
command	14b

commeasure	14b	complimentary	33a
commemorate	14b	component	31
commemoratory	33c	compositor	40c
commence	14b	composure	13
commend	14b	composure	40g
commendatory	33c	compound	5c
commensurate	14b	comprehensible	28h
commentary	33a	compress	14a
commentator	40c	compressible	28h
commercial	14b	compression	14b
commercially	13	compressor	40c
commie or -y	8d	comprise	45
commiserate	14b	compromise	45
commission	14b	conceal	4b
commission	14b	concede	35
commissionaire	14b	conceit	4b, 6a
commit	14b	conceive	4b, 6a
commitment	14b	concentricity	25b
committee	14b	concertos	18b
committee	14d	concessible	28h
commodity	14b	concession	14b
commonness	14b	concessionary	33a
commonness	14b	conchie or -y	8d
communal	3b	concierge	6a
communicate	14b	conciliable	28c
communion	14b	conciliar	40e
communiqué	14b	conciliator	40c
communism	14b	concomitance	30c
company	2c	concomitant	31
company pl -nies	19	concordance	30c
comparative	3d	concordant	31
compass	2c	concrete	3a
compass	14a	concurrence	30c
compassion	14b	concurrent	31
compatible	28c	concuss	14a
compatible	28h	concussion	14b
compelled	24b	condemn	15
compelling	24b	condensable or condensible	28h
competence	30c	condense	30c
competent	31	condign	4c
competitor	40c	condign	15a
complain	4a	conditional	3b
complainant	31	condolence	30c
complaint	4a	condominium pl -niums	22d
complaisant	31	conducible	28g
complementary	33a	conductance	30c
complexion	38	conductor	40c
compliance	30c	confederacy	34
compliant	31	conference	30c

confess	14a	conspirator	40c
confession	14b	conspiratory	33c
confessional	3b	constabulary	33a
confessor	40c	constant	31
confetti	14	constituency pl -cies	19
confidant n.	31	constituent	31
confidence	30c	constitutional	3b
confident adj.	31	constrain	4a
confinable or confineable	28e	constructible	28h
confirmatory	33c	constructor or constructer	40c
conflictory	33c	construer	4e
confluent	31	consul	3b
confound	5c	consular	40e
confraternal	3b	consultancy pl -cies	19
confrontational	3b	consultant	31
congeal	4b	consulter or consultor	40c
congratulatory	33c	contain	4a
congregational	3b	contaminant	31
congress	14a	contaminator	40c
congruence	30c	contemnible	28h
congruent	31	contemporary	33a
conjectural	3b	contemptible	28h
conjecture	12	content	31
conjecture	40f	contestant	31
conjugal	3b	continence	30c
conjure	2c	continent	31
conjure	40g	contingency pl -cies	19
connectible or connectable	28h	continuance	30c
connection or connexion	38	continuer	4e
connivance	30c	continuum pl -nua or -nuums	22d
conqueror	40c	contractible	28h
conscience	13	contractor	40c
conscience	30c	contradictory	33c
conscientious	13	contraltos	18b
conscientious	13	contrariwise	45
conscious	13	contributor	40c
consequence	30c	contributory	33c
consequent	31	controlled	24b
conservatory	33c	controller	1
consign	4c	controlling	24b
consign	15a	controvertible	28h
consistent	31	contumacious	13
consistory	33c	convector	40c
consolidator	40c	convener or convenor	40c
consonance	30c	convenience	30c
consonant	31	convenient	31
consortium pl -tia	22d	convent	31
conspiracy pl -cies	19	conventional	3b
conspiracy	34	convergence	30c

conversant	31	correspondent	31
conversational	3b	corridor	14
converter or convertor	40c	corrigendum pl -da	22d
convertible	28h	corrigible	28h
conveyance	30c	corroboratory	33c
convictable or convictible	28h	corrodible	28h
convince	30d	corruptible	28h
convincible	28g	cortex pl -tices	22d
convincible	28h	cosignatory	33c
convoy	5b	cosmetician	25b
convulsant	31	cosmonaut	5a
convulse	3d	cost	1a
coo	4e	costermonger	2c
cook	2c	coterie	8
cookery	33b	coterie	6a
cool	4e	cottage	11
coolant	31	cotyledon	8a
coop	4e	couch	5c
cooperage	11	coucher	40f
cooperate or co-operate	27b	cough	15b
cooperator or co-operator	40c	could	2c
coopt or co-opt	27b	council	3b
coordinal or co-ordinal	27b	council	5c
coordinate or co-ordinate	27b	councillor	40c
coordinator or co-ordinator	40c	counsel	5c
coot	4e	counselled	24b
copper	40b	counselling	24b
coppice	12	counsellor	40c
copy pl -pies	19	count	5c
copyholder	27e	countdown n.	27a
copyright	4c	count down vb.	27a
coral	3b	countenance	5c
cord	1b	countenance	30c
cordiality	24b	counteract	5c
corduroy	5b	counterclaimant	31
corkage	11	counterfeit	5c
corkscrew	27d	counterfeit	2b, 6b
cormorant	31	counterfoil	5c
corn	9a	countersign	4c
cornet	7	countless	5c
cornice	12	country pl -ries	19
cornu	3d	county	5c
corporal	3b	county pl -ties	19
corps	15	coup	4e
corpulent	31	couple	3b
corpus pl -pora	22d	coupon	4e
corpuscle	3b	courage	11
correctable or correctible	28f, 28h	courage	9c
corrector	40c	course	4d, 9d

court	4d, 9d	creed	4b
courtesy	9c	creedal or credal	3b
courtesy	34	creek	4b
court-martial	27g	creep	4b
court martial	27e, 27g	crematorium *pl* -riums or -ria	22d
court-martialled	27e, 27g	crematory	33c
court-martials	21	crepe	4a
cousin	2c	crept	39
covenant	2c	crescendos	18b
covenant	31	crescent	15
cover	2c	cress	14a
coverage	11	crevice	12
covert	2c	crew	4e
cover-up n.	27a	cricket	7
covet	2c	crier	4c
cow	5c	criminal	3b
coward	5c	crimple	3b
cowardice	12	crimsonness	14b
cowboy	5b	cringer	12
cower	5c	cringing	12
cowherd	40e	crinkle	3b
cowl	5c	crinkly	46b
co-worker	27b	cripple	3b
cowrie	8	crisis *pl* -ises	22d
cowslip	5c	criss-cross	14a
coy	5b	criterion *pl* -ria or -rions	22d
coyote	5b	criticize	25b
coypu	3d	croak	4d
crackle	3b	crocheted	24b
crackup	27a	crocus *pl* -cuses	22d
cradle	3b	croissant	31
cram-full	14a	crook	2c
cranium *pl* -niums or -nia	22d	croon	4u
crass	14a	croquet	4a
cravenness	14b	cross	14a
crawfish	5a	crosses	16
crawl	5a	crossover n.	27e
crayfish	4a	cross section	27c
crayon	4a	cross-sectional	27c
creak	4b	cross-slide	27c
cream	4b	cross-stitch	27c
creamlike	27c	crotchet	11
crease	4b	crouch	5c
creator	40c	croup	4e
creature	4b	crouton	4e
creature	40f	crow	4d
credible	28h	crowd	5c
creditor	40c	crown	5c
credos	18b	crucible	28h

crucifixion	13d	current (water; adj.)	31
crucifixion	38	curricular	40e
cruel	3b	curriculum *pl* -la or -lums	22d
cruel	4e	curry *pl* -rries	19
cruelly	24a	cursory	33c
cruet	4e	curtail	4a
cruise	4e	curtain	9c
cruiser	4e	curvaceous	9c
crumb	15	curvature	40f
crumbly	46b	curve	9c
crumple	3b	cushion	13
crumply	46b	cuss	14a
cruncher	40f	customary	33a
crutch	11	cuticle	3b
cry *pl* cries	19	cutie	8d
crypt	8a	cutlass	14a
crystal	8a	cutout n.	27a
cubicle	3b	cut out vb.	27a
cuckoo	4e	cyan	8a
cuddle	3b	cybernetic	8a
cuddly	46b	cyberneticist	25b
cudgel	3b	cycle	3b
cudgel	11	cycle	12
cudgelled	24b	cycle	8a
cudgelling	24b	cyclone	8a
cue	4e	cygnet	8a
cueing	23	cylinder	8a
cuff	14a	cylinder-like	27c
culinary	33a	cymbal	3b
cultural	3b	cymbal	8a
culture	40f	cynic	8a
cumulus *pl* -li	22d	cynical	8a
cuneiform	2b, 6b	cynicism	25b
cuplike	27c	cypher or cipher	8a
cur	9	cypress	8a
curator	40c	cypress	14a
curdle	3b	cyst	8a
cure	4e	cystitis	8a
curfew	4e	cystoid	5b
curl	9c	cytoplasm	8a
currant (fruit)	31	cystoid	5b
currency *pl* -cies	19	cytoplasm	8a

D

da**bble**	3b
dad**oes** or **-os**	18c
daffod**il**	3b
da**i**ly	4a
d**air**y	4a
d**air**y *pl* -r**ies**	19
da**is**	4a
da**i**sy	4a
dalli**ance**	30c
dam**age**	11
damnat**ory**	33c
dams**el**	3b
dan**ceable**	28d
dan**dle**	3b
da**nge**r	1e
da**nge**rous	12
dan**gle**	3b
dap**ple**	3b
darn**el**	3b
dashb**oard**	9d
dat**able** or date**able**	28e
dat**um** *pl* -t**a**	22d
da**u**b	5a
da**u**ghter	5a
da**ugh**ter	15b
daughter-**like**	27c
da**u**nt	5a
daw**dle**	3b
da**w**dle	5a
da**w**n	5a
da**y**	4a
da**y**light	1b
day**l**ight	4c
daz**zle**	3b
de**ad**	2b
de**af**	2b
de**a**l	4b
de**a**lt	2b
dea**lt**	39
de**a**n	4b
deaner**y** *pl* -r**ies**	19
dean**ery**	33b
de**ar**	4b

dear**y** or **-ie**	8d
de**ath**	2b
debar	7
debase	7
deb**atable**	23
deb**atable** or debat**eable**	28c, 28e
debate	7
debate	23
debauch	7
debau**cher**	40f
deben**ture**	40f
debt**or**	40c
decad**ence**	30c
decad**ent**	31
de**cay**	4a
dec**eit**	4b, 6a
deceit	7
dec**eive**	4b, 6a
deceive	7
deci**bel**	3b
decide	7
deciduous	7
decim**al**	3b
decipher	7
de**ci**sion	7
de**ci**sion	12
de**ci**sive	7
de**ck**	11
decla**i**m	4a
declamat**ory**	33c
declar**ant**	31
declarat**ory**	33c
declare	7
declension	7
decline	7
declivity	7
decommi**ssion**	14b
decompre**ssion**	14b
decorate	40c
decorat**or**	40c
de**coy**	5b
decre**ase**	4b
de**cre**ase	7
de**cree**	4b
decree	7
decrepit	7
decry	7
decumbent	7
decumb**ent**	31

deduce	7	degeneracy	34
deducible	28g	degenerative	7
deducible	28h	degrade	7
deduct	7	degree	4b
deductible	28h	degree	7
deed	4b	de-ice	27b
deem	4b	deign	6b
de-emphasize	27b	deign	15a
de-energization	27b	dejected	7
de-energize	27b	dejected	12
deep	4b	delay	4a
deepen	39a	delay	7
deer	4b	delayed	26
de-escalate	27b	delegacy	34
de-escalation	27b	delete	7
deface	7	deliberate	7
defaceable	28d	deliberator	40c
defamatory	33c	delicacy pl -cies	19
defame	7	delicacy	34
default	7	delicious	/
defeat	4b	delight	4c
defeat	7	delight	7
defecate or defaecate	10	delineable	28e
defect	7	delineate	7
defector	40c	delinquent	31
defence	7	delirious	7
defence	30c	delirium pl -riums or -ria	22d
defend	7	deliver	7
defendant	31	deliverance	30c
defensible	28h	delivery pl -ries	19
defer	7	delphinium pl -niums or -nia	22d
deference	30c	delude	7
defiant	7	delusory	33c
defiant	31	demagogue	15
deficiency pl -cies	19	demand	7
deficient	6a	demean	7
deficient	7	demeanour	4b
deficient	13	demeanour	7
defile	7	demeanour	40e
define	7	dement	31
deflate	7	demented	7
deflect	7	demise	7
deflection or deflexion	38	demise	45
defoliant	31	democracy pl -cies	19
deform	7	democracy	34
defraud	7	demolish	7
defray	4a	demonstrable	23
defray	7	demonstrable	28c
defy	7	demos	18b

demure	7	deranged	1e
denarius *pl* -narii	22d	deranged	7
denial	7	deride	7
denomination	7	derisible	7
denominator	40c	derisible	28h
denote	7	derisory	7
denounce	5c	derisory	33c
dense	30c	derive	7
dentifrice	12	dermal	3b
denture	40f	derogatory	33c
denude	7	descendant n.	31
denunciate	7	descendent adj.	31
deny	7	descendible (inheritable)	28h
deodorant	31	descramble	1d
depart	7	describe	7
department	7	description	7
departure	7	desert (sand; leave)	1e
depend	7	deserve	7
dependant n.	31	desiccant	31
dependence	30c	desiccated	1e, 14d
dependency *pl* -cies	19	design	4c
dependent adj.	31	design	7
depict	7	design	15a
depilatory	33c	designator	40c
deplete	7	desire	7
depletion	7	desist	7
depletory	33c	deskill	14a
deplorable	7	despair	7
deplore	7	despatch	7
deploy	5b	despicable	7
deponent	7	despise	7
deponent	31	despise	45
deport	7	despite	7
deposit	7	despoil	5b
depositary *pl* -ries	19	despoil	7
depositary (person; store)	33a	despond	7
depositor	40c	despondent	31
depository	7	dessert (sweet)	1e
depository *pl* -ries	19	destabilize	1d
depository (store; person)	33c	destiny *pl* -nies	19
depraved	7	destroy	5b
depreciatory	33c	destroy	7
depress	7	destroy	7
depress	14a	destruct	7
depressant	31	destructible	28h
depressible	28h	desultory	33c
depression	14b	detach	7
deprive	7	detach	11
deputy *pl* -ties	19	detacher	40f

detail	4a	dialysis *pl* -yses	22d
detain	4a	diameter	7
detain	7	diamond	4c
detect	7	dianthus *pl* -thuses	22d
detectable or detectible	28f, 28h	diarrhoea	10
detective	7	diarrhoea	15a
detector	40c	diary	4c
detention	7	diary *pl* -ries	19
deter	7	dibble	3b
detergent	7	dicey	23
deteriorate	7	dicey	34
determinant	31	Dictaphone	15a
determine	7	dictator	40c
deterrence	30c	diction	38
deterrent	31	dictionary	33a
detest	7	dictum *pl* -tums or -ta	22d
detonator	40c	diddle	3b
detour	4e	didgeridoo	11
detoxicant	31	dieresis or dieraesis	10
detract	7	diesel	3b
develop	7	diesel	4b
deviance	30c	dietary	33a
deviator	40c	dietician	25b
device	7	different	31
device n.	34	diffidence	30c
devilled	24b	diffident	31
devilling	24b	diffuser or diffusor	40c
devilry *pl* -ries	19	diffusible	28h
devise	7	digestant	31
devise vb.	34	digestible	28h
devise	45	dignity *pl* -ties	19
devoid	5b	digraph	15a
devoid	7	digress	14a
devote	7	dilatant	31
devotional	3b	dilator	40c
devour	7	dilatory	33c
devour	5c	dilemma	14
devout	7	diligence	30c
devout	5c	diminuendos	18b
dew	4e	diminutive	3d
di-	4c	dimple	3b
diaeresis or dieresis *pl* -eses	22d	dimply	46b
diagonal	3b	dinghy	15
dial	4c	dingle	3b
dialled	24b	dingoes	18a
dialling	24b	dingy	12
dialogue	15	dinkie	8d
dialyse	8a	dinosaur	5a
dialyse	45	Dionysian	13d

diphthong	15a		disguise	15
diphthongal	3b		disguise	45
diplomacy	34		dishevel	3b
director	40c		dishevelled	24b
directory pl -ries	19		dishevelling	24b
directory	33c		dishonour	37
dirigible	28h		dishonour	40e
dirk	9c		disinfectant	31
dirt	9c		disintegrable	28c
disagree	4b		disjointed	5b
disallow	37		dislikable or dislikeable	28e
disappear	14		disloyal	5b
disappoint	5b		dismal	3b
disarm	37		dismay	4a
disastrous	41		dismiss	14a
disband	37		dismissible	28h
discernible or (rare) discernable	28h		disorder	37
discharge	37		dispatch	11
disciple	1c		dispatcher	40f
disciple	3b		dispensary pl -ries	19
disciplinary	33a		dispensary	33a
disclaim	4a		dispense	30c
disclosure	40g		dispenser	33a
discolour	40e		dispersant	31
discontent	37		displaceable	28d
discordant	31		display	4a
discos	18b		displeasure	2b
discount	5c		displeasure	40g
discourage	11		dispossession	14b
discourteous	37		disposure	40g
discover	2c		disprove	2c
discovery pl -ries	19		disputant	31
discreet	4b		disrupter or disruptor	40c
discrepancy pl -cies	19		dissatisfactory	33c
discrepant	31		dissatisfy	14b
discretionary	33a		dissect	14b
discriminator	40c		dissectible	28h
discriminatory	33c		dissemble	14b
discursive	9c		disseminate	14b
discus pl -scuses or -sci	22d		disseminator	40c
discuss	14a		dissent	14b
discussible	28h		dissentient	31
discussion	14b		dissertation	14b
disdain	4a		disservice	14b
disease	4b		disserviceable	28d
disfavour	40e		dissident	14b
disfigure	40g		dissident	31
disfranchise or disenfranchise	45		dissimilar	14b
disgraceful	14a		dissimulate	14b

dissipate	14b	dollar	40e
dissipater or dissipator	40c	dolly *pl* -llies	19
dissociate	14b	dolphin	15a
dissoluble	14b	dolt	1a
dissolute	14b	domesticity	25b
dissolution	14b	dominance	30c
dissolve	14b	dominant	1e
dissolvent	31	dominant	31
dissonant	14b	domineer	4b
dissonant	31	dominoes	18a
distance	30c	done	2c
distant	31	doodle	3b
distil	3b	doom	4e
distil	14a	door	9d
distillery *pl* -ries	19	doorkeeper	27e
distillery	33b	door-to-door	27f
distinguish	8e	dormant	31
distractible	28h	dormitory	33c
distraught	15b	dornick	25b
distress	14a	dosage	11
disturbance	30c	doss	14a
ditch	11	dotage	11
ditcher	40f	double	3b
ditty *pl* -tties	19	doubt	5c
diurnal	3b	doubtful	15
diurnal	4i	douche	4e
divergence	30c	dough	4d
diversionary	33a	dough	15b
divertible	28h	doughty	5c
divisible	28f, 28h	doughty	15b
divorceable	28d	dour	4e
divulgence	30c	douse	5c
do	4e	dove	2c
docilely	46a	dowdy	5c
doctor	40c	dowel	3b
doctoral	3b	dowel	5c
doctrinal	3b	doweling or dowelling	24b
doctrine	3a	dowelled	24b
documentary	33a	dowelling	24b
doddery	33b	down	5c
doddle	3b	downfall	5c
dodge	11	download	5c
dodos or -oes	18c	downright	4c
doe	4d	downright	5c
doer	4e	downstage	27h
does	2c	downstairs	27h
dog-catcher (but dog handler)	27e	downtown	27h
doggerel	3b	downwards	40e
do-gooder	27d	downwind	27h

downy	5c	drove	2c
dowry	5c	drown	5c
dowry *pl* -ries	19	drowsy	5c
doxology *pl* -gies	19	drudge	11
dozen	2c	drudgery	33b
drain	4a	druggie	8d
drainage	11	drunkenness	14b
dramatis personae	22d	dryable	8
drapable or drapeable	28e	dryad	8a
draught	15b	dryer or drier	8
draw	5a	dryest or driest	8
drawer	5a	drying	26
drawl	5a	dryly or drily	8, 8c
drawn	5a	dryness	8, 8c
dray	4a	dubitable	28b
dread	2b	ducky or -ie	8d
dreadful	2b	ductilely	46a
dream	4b	due	47
dreamt or dreamed	39	due	4e
dreary	4b	duel	3b
dredge	11	duel	4e
drencher	40f	duelled	24b
dress	14a	duelling	24b
dressmaker	27e	duet	4e
drew	4e	duffel	3b
dribble	3b	dullness or dulness	14a
dribbly	46b	dulse	3d
dried	4c	duly	47
dried	26	dumb	15
drier or dryer	8	dungeon	12
drier	4c	duplicator	40c
driest or dryest	8	duress	14a
drivable or driveable	28e	dust-up n.	27a
drivel	3b	duty	4e
drivelled	24b	duty *pl* -ties	19
drivelling	24b	duvet	2c
drizzle	3b	dwarf	9a
drizzly	46b	dwarfs or dwarves	17
drogue	15	dwindle	3b
droll	1	dyable or dyeable	28e
droll	14a	dye	4c
drollness	14a	dyeing	26
drool	4e	dyeing	23
droop	4e	dying	26
drop out vb.	27a	dynamic	8a
dropout n.	27a	dynamite	8a
dross	14a	dynamo	8a
drought	5c	dynamos	18b
drought	15b	dynasty	8a

E

each	4b	eel	4b
eager	4b	effaceable	28d
eagle	3b	effect	7
eagle	4b	effeminacy	34
ear	4b	effervescence	30c
early	9c	effervescible	28g
earn	9c	efficacious	13
earnest	9c	efficacy	34
earphone	15a	efficient	6a
earthen	39a	efficient	13
earthy	9c	effluence	30c
easel	3b	effluent	31
easel	4b	effluvium *pl* -via or -viums	22d
easily	4b	effrontery	33b
east	4b	egg	14a
Easter	4b	egghead	27e
easy	4b	egocentricity	25b
easy-going	27f	egos	18b
eat	4b	egress	14a
eaves	4b	eiderdown	4c, 6b
eavesdrop	4b	eiderdown	5c
ebb	1e	eight	6b
ebullient	31	eight	15b
eccentricity	25b	eighteen	4b
ecclesiasticism	25b	eighteen	6b
echoes	18a	eighty	6b
eclecticism	25b	eisegesis *pl* -eses	22d
eclipse	7	eisteddfod	6b
ecology *pl* -gies	19	either	4c
ecru	3d	either	6a
ecstasy	34	eject	12
ectomorph	15a	ejector	40c
ecumenical	10	elasticity	25b
ecumenism or ecumenicism	25b	elasticize	25b
edelweiss	14a	elbow	4d
edge	11	elder	40b
edible	28h	electioneer	4b
edifice	12	electoral	3b
editor	40c	electric	7
editorial	4b	electrician	7
educator	40c	electrician	25b
educatory	33c	electricity	7
educible	28g	electrolyse	45
		elegance	30c
		elegant	31
		elementary	33a
		elephant	31
		elevator	40c
		eleven	7

eligible	28h	enchiridion	15a
eliminable	28c	enclosure	13
eliminator	40c	enclosure	40g
ellipsis pl -pses	22d	encourage	11
ellipsoid	5b	encroach	4d
eloquence	30c	encroacher	40f
eloquent	31	encumbrance	30c
elusory	33c	encyclopedia or encyclopaedia	8a
elves	17	encyclopedia or encyclopaedia	10
Elysian	13d	endanger	1e
embargoes	18a	endear	4b
embarrass	14a	endeavour	40e
embassy pl -ssies	19	endemicity	25b
embezzle	3b	endomorph	15a
emboss	14a	endorser or endorsor	40c
embrace	12	endow	5c
embraceable	28d	endurance	30c
embrasure	13	endure	4e
embrasure	40g	energy pl -gies	19
embroider	5b	enfold	1a
embroil	5b	enforceable	28d
embryo	8a	enfranchise	45
embryos	18b	engine	12
emendatory	33c	engineer	4b
emergence	30c	engross	14a
emergency pl -cies	19	enjoin	5b
emigrant	31	enjoy	5b
eminence	30c	enjoyment	8
eminent	31	enlighten	4c
emissary	33a	enormous	7
emission	14b	enough	2c
emit	14b	enough	15b
emollient	31	enquiry pl -ries	19
emotional	3b	enrapture	40f
emperor	40c	enricher	40f
emphasis	15a	enrol	14a, 14c
emphasis pl -ases	22d	ensign	4c
emphatic	15a	ensign	15a
empiricism	25b	ensure	13
empiricist	25b	enterprise	45
employ	5b	entertain	4a
emporium pl -riums or -ria	22d	enthral	14a
emu	3d	enthralled	24b
emulsible	28h	enthralling	24b
enamel	3b	enthusiasm	7
enamelled	24b	entitle	3b
enamelling	24b	entrance	30c
enamour	40e	entrant	31
encephal-	3b	entreat	4b

45

entrencher or intrencher	40f	estuary	33a
entrepreneurial	4e	etcher	40f
entry *pl* -ries	19	etching	11
envoy	5b	eternal	3b
enzyme	8a	ethicist	25b
ephemeral	3b	ethicize	25b
ephemeral	15a	ethnicity	25b
epilator	40c	ethyl	14c
epilogue	15	etymology	8a
Epiphany	15a	eucalyptus	4e
episcopacy	34	eucalyptus	8a
epistle	3b	eucalyptus or eucalypt *pl* -ptuses, -pti	
epistle	15	or -pts	22d
epitaph	15a	Eucharist	4e
epochal	3b	eugenic	4e
eponymous	8a	eugenicist	25b
equal	3b	eulogy	4e
equalled	24b	eulogy *pl* -gies	19
equalling	24b	eunuch	4e
equator	40c	euphemism	4e
equilibrium *pl* -riums or -ria	22d	euphemism	15a
equipment	7	euphony	4e
equitable	28b	euphoria	4e
equity *pl* -ties	19	euphoria	15a
equivalence	30c	eurhythmic	8a
eradicator	40c	eurhythmic	15a
erasure	13	Europe	4e
erasure	40g	evaluator	40c
-erer	40b	Evanses	20b
erodent	31	eve	3d
erodible	28h	evenness	14b
eroticism	25b	event	7
errand	1e	eventuality	7
errant	31	everybody	42
erratum *pl* -ta	22d	everyone	42
error	40c	everything	27e
eruptible	28h	everywhere	15
escalator	40c	evident	31
escutcheon	11	evince	30d
Eskimos	18b	evincible	28g
esotericism	25b	ewe	4e
especially	7	ewer	4e
espouse	5c	exactor	40c
-ess	14a	exaggerate	12
essay	4a	exaggerator	40c
essayed	26	exalt	2d
estimator	40c	examine	3a
estrange	1e	example	3b
estuary *pl* -ries	19	excavator	40c

exceed	4b
exceed	12
exceed	35
excel	3b
excel	12
excel	14a
excellent	14
except	12
exceptional	3b
excess	14a
excess	12
exchange	1e
excise	12
excise	45
excite	12
exciting	12
exclaim	4a
excludable or excludible	28h
exclusionary	33a
excursion	9c
excursus pl -suses or -sus	22d
excuse	7
executor	40c
exegesis pl -eses	22d
exemplar	40e
exemplary	33a
exemplum pl -pla	22d
exercise	12
exercise	45
exhaust	5a
exhaustible	28h
exhibitor	40c
existence	13c
existence	30c
existent	31
existential	13c
exorbitant	31
exorcize	25b
exordium pl -diums or -dia	22d
exoticism	25b
expanse	30c
expectant	31
expedient	31
expeditious	13
expellant or expellent	31
expenditure	40f
expense	30c
experience	30c
experienceable	28d
experiential	13c
expiator	40c
explain	4a
exploit	5b
explosion	7
exponent	31
expositor	40c
expository	33c
exposure	13
exposure	40g
expound	5c
express	14a
expressible	28h
expression	14b
exsanguine	12
exscind	12
exsect	12
exsert	12
exsiccate	12
extendible or extendable	28h
exterminator	40c
external	3b
extinguish	8e
extol	3b
extol	14a
extolling	1
extractor	40c
extra-curricular	27f
extramural	3b
extrasensory	33c
extravagance	30c
extrusible	28h
exuberance	30c
exuberant	31
eye	4c
eye-catcher	27e
eyrie	4b

F

fable	3b
face	12
faceable	28d
facetious	13
-facient (making)	6a
facilely	46a
facilitator	40c
factious	13
factory	33c
faculty *pl* -ties	19
fade-out	27a
faeces	10
Fahrenheit	4c, 6b
fail	4a
failure	4a
failure	40g
faint	4a
fair	4a
fairly	4a
fairy	4a
fairy *pl* -ries	19
faith	4a
faithful	4a
fallacy *pl* -cies	19
fallacy	34
fallible	28h
fallow	4d
false	2d
falter	2d
falter	40b
familiar	40e
famine	3a
fanaticism	25b
fanaticize	25b
fancied	6a
fancier	6a
fancy	6a
fandangos	18b
fantasy	34
farragos or -oes	18c
farther	40b
fascia or facia	13
fascinate	12

fashion	13
fasten	15
fatality *pl* -ties	19
fathead	27e
father	40b
fatigue	15
fault	2d
faun	5a
favour	40e
favourite	9c
fawn	5a
fear	4b
feasible	28h
feast	4b
feat	4b
feather	2b
feature	4b
feature	40f
febrile	1c
fee	4b
feeble	4b
feed	4b
feel	4b
feet	4b
feign	4a, 6b
feign	15a
feint	4a, 6b
felony *pl* -nies	19
felt	39
fence	12
fender	40b
fennel	3b
feral	3b
fern	9c
ferocious	13
ferret	7
ferry *pl* -rries	19
fertile	9c
fertilely	46a
fervent	9c
fervent	31
fervour	9c
fervour	40e
fetch	11
fetcher	40f
fete	4a
fettle	3b
fetus or foetus	10
fetus or foetus *pl* -tuses	22d

feud	4e	flambeau *pl* -x or-s	22a
feudal	3b	flamboyant	5b
feudal	4e	flamencos	18b
fever	40b	flamingos or -oes	18c
few	4e	flange	1e
fiascos or -oes	18c	flannel	3b
fibre	40d	flare-up n.	27a
fibrefill	14a	flashover n.	27e
fibroid	5b	flatter	40b
fickle	3b	flatulent	31
fictional	3b	flaunt	5a
fictitious	13	flavour	40e
fiddle	3b	flaw	5a
fiddly	46b	flea (insect)	4b
fidget	11	fledgling or fledgeling	11
field	4b, 6a	flee (run)	4b
fiend	4b, 6a	fleece	4b
fierce	4b	fleet	4b
fierce	6a	fletcher	40f
fiery	4c	flew	4e
fiery	23	flexible	28h
fifteen	4b	flexion	38
fight	4c	flier	4c
figure	40g	flight	4c
filcher	40f	flincher	40f
filigree	4b	flippant	31
filleted	24b	flirtatious	13
fill-up n.	27a	float	4d
finable or fineable	28e	flock	11
final	3b	flood	2c
find	1a	floodlight	4c
finger	12	floor	9d
finish	1e, 14d	floozy or -ie or floosie	8d
Finnish	1e	floral	3b
fir	9c	floss	14a
fire	4c	flotsam	1
fireable	28e	flounce	5c
firm	9c	flour	5c
first	9c	flout	5c
fishmonger	2c	flow	4d
fishmonger	27e	flown	4d
fission	14b	flow over	27g
fissure	13	flue	4e
fissure	40g	fluent	4e
fixture	40f	fluent	31
fizzle	3b	fluxion	38
flagrant	31	flycatcher	27e
flail	4a	flyleaf	8c
flair	4a	flyless	8c

flyover n.	27e	forfeit	2b, 6b
foal	4d	forfeiture	40f
foam	4d	forgery	33b
focus *pl* -cuses or -ci	22d	forget	43
foe	4d	forgive	43
foil	5b	forgo	43
foist	5b	forgotten	24b
fold	1a	forlornness	14b
foldout	5c	formal	3b
foliage	11	formant	31
foliar	40e	formidable	28b
folios	18b	formula *pl* -as or -ae	22, 22d
folk	1	formulary *pl* -ries	19
folk	15	formulary	33a
folkie or -y	8d	fornicator	40c
follicle	3b	forsake	43
follow	4d	forsakenness	14b
fondant	31	forsook	2c
fondle	3b	forswornness	14b
food	4e	forthright	4c
foodie or -y	8d	fortnight	4c
fool	4e	fortress	14a
foolery	33b	fortunate	13e
foolish	4e	fortune	13e
foot	2c	fortune	40f
footage	11	forum *pl* -rums or -ra	22d
footgear	4b	forward	43
footsie	8d	fossil	3b
forage	11	fought	15b
forbearance	30c	foul	5c
forbid	43	found	5c
forbiddance	30c	foundry	5c
forbidden	24b	foundry *pl* -ries	19
forceable (able to be forced)	28d, 28g	fount	5c
forcible (having force)	28g	fountain	2e
forecast	43	fountain	5c
forecastle	15	four	4d, 9d
fore-edge	27b	fourteen	4b
foregone	43	fowl	5c
forehead	43	fractious	13
foreign	2b, 6b	fragilely	46a
foreign	15a	fragmentary	33a
foreignness	14b	fragrance	30c
foreman	43	fragrant	31
foresight	4c	frail	4a
forest	7	framable or frameable	28e
foretold	1a	frame-up n.	27a
forewarn	9a	franchise	45
forewarn	43	frangible	28h

frankincense	30c	fuddle	3b
fraud	5a	fudge	11
fraudulent	31	fuel	3b
fraught	5a	fuel	4e
fraught	15b	fuelled	24b
fray	4a	fuelling	24b
frazzle	3b	fugue	15
freak	4b	fulcrum *pl* -crums or -cra	22d
freckle	3b	fulfil	14a
freckly	46b	fullback	14a
free	4b	full face adj.	14a
freebie	8d	fullface advb.	14a
freedom	4b	full-length	27c
freehold	4b	fullness	14a
freestyle	4b	fulminatory	33c
freeway	4a	fulsome	14a
freeway	4b	fumigant	31
freeze	4b	fumigator	40c
freeze-up n.	27a	functionary	33a
freight	6b	funeral	3b
freight	15b	funerary	33a
frequent	31	fungal	3b
frescoes or -os	18c	fungicidal	3b
friar	40e	fungoid	5b
Friday	4a	fungus *pl* -gi or -guses	22d
fridge	11	funnel	3b
fried	4c	funnelled	24b
friend	2b, 6b	funnelling	24b
frieze	4b	fur	9c
fright	4c	furlough	15b
frightful	4c	furnace	2f
fringe	3c	furniture	40f
Frisian	13d	furrow	4d
frizzly	46b	furry	9c
frontage	11	further	9c
frost	1a	fusible	28h
frown	5c	fuss	14a
frozenness	14b	futilely	46a
frugal	3b	future	40f
fruit	4e		

G

gabble	3b
gadget	11
gaggle	3b
gaily	4a
gain	4a
gainsay	4a
gait	4a
galaxy *pl* -xies	19
gallant	31
gallery *pl* -ries	19
Gallicize	25b
galloper	24b
gambol (skip)	3b
gambolled	24b
gambolling	24b
gamekeeper	27e
gander	40b
ganglion *pl* -glia or -glions	22d
gangway	4a
gantry *pl* -tries	19
gaol	4a
garage	11
garbage	11
gargle	3b
gargoyle	5b
garlicky	25a
gateau *pl* -x	4d, 22a
gatekeeper	27e
gateway	4a
gaudy	5a
gauge	4a
gaunt	5a
gauntlet	5a
gauze	5a
gavel	3b
gawky	5a
gay	4a
gazebos or -oes	18c
gear	4b
gear	12
geese	4b
Geiger	12
Geiger counter	4c

geisha	12
geisha	6b
gelatin or gelatine	12
gelignite	12
gem	12
gender	12
gene	12
genealogy	12
general	3b
general	12
generate	12
generator	40c
generous	12
genesis	12
genesis *pl* -eses	22d
geneticist	25b
genial	4c
genial	12
genie	12
genital	12
genitive	12
genius *pl* -niuses or -nii	22d
genocide	12
genre	12
genre	40d
gent	12
genteel	4b
genteel	12
gentile	12
gentle	3b
gentle	12
gently	46b
genu	3d
genuflect	12
genuflection or genuflexion	38
genuine	12
genus	12
genus *pl* -nera or -nuses	22d
geo-	12
geodesy	34
geography	12
geology	12
geomorphic	15a
geranium	12
gerbil	3b
gerbil	9c
gerbil	12
geriatric	12
germ	9c

germ	12	girdle	3b
german	12	girl	12
German	12	girl	9c
germane	12	girlie	8d
Germanys	19	giros	18b
germicidal	3b	girt	12
germinal	3b	girth	9c
germinant	31	girth	12
gerund	12	gismo	12
gestation	12	gismos	18b
gesticulate	12	gist	12
gesture	12	givable or giveable	28e
gesture	40f	give	12
get	12	glacier	6a
ghee	4b	gladiator	40c
gherkin	15	gladiolus pl -lus, -li or -luses	22d
ghettos or -oes	18b, 18c	glamour	40c
ghost	1a	glance	30
ghoul	4e	glandular	40e
giant	12	glass	14a
giant	31	glass-maker	27e
giddy	12	glaucoma	5a
gift	12	gleam	4b
gigabyte	12	glean	4b
gigantic	12	glee	4b
giggle	3b	glisten	15
giggle	12	glitch	11
giggly	46b	gloat	4d
gigolos	18b	global	3b
gill	14a	globoid	5b
gill (fish)	12	globular	40e
gill (measure)	12	gloom	4e
gill-less	27c	gloss	14a
gill-like	27c	glossary pl -ries	19
gilt	12	glossary	33a
gimel	12	glove	2c
gimlet	12	glow	4d
gimmick	12	glue	4e
gimmick	25b	gluer	4e
gimmicky	25a	gluey	23
gin	12	gluing	23
ginger	12	glycerin	8a
gingham	12	gnarl	15a
ginnel	3b	gnat	15a
ginseng	12	gnaw	5a
Gipsy (gipsy)	12	gnaw	15a
(Gipsy) gipsy or (Gypsy) gypsy	8a	gneiss	4c, 6b
giraffe	12	gneiss	15a
gird	9c	gnome	15a

gnosis	15a	grandchild	15
gnostic	15a	granddaughter	15
Gnosticize	25b	grandfather	15
gnu	3d	grandmother	15
gnu	15a	grandson	15
goad	4d	grange	1e
goal	4d	granite	3a
goalie	8d	granny or -ie	8d
goalless	14b	granular	40e
goat	4d	-graph	15a
goatherd	40e	grapheme	15a
gobble	3b	-grapher	40b
goer	4d	grapnel	3b
goes	18a	grapple	3b
goggle	3b	grass	14a
goggly	46b	grav	3d
going	5	gravel	3b
going-over n.	27e	gravelled	24b
goitre	5b	gravelling	24b
goitre	40d	gravy pl -vies	19
gold	1a	grease	4b
gold-digger	27e	great	4a
goldenness	14b	greed	4b
gone	3a	green	4b
good	2c	greenery	33b
goodbye	4c	greenness	14b
gooey	4e	greet	4b
goolie or -y	8d	grew	4e
goon	4e	grey	4a
goose	4e	griddle	3b
gorgeous	12	grief	4b, 6a
gorilla	14	griefs (OED)	17
gospel	3b	grievance	30c
Gothicize	25b	grieve	4b
gouge	5c	grievous	6a
gourd	4e	grind	1a
gourmand	4e	gristle	3b
gout	5c	gristle	15
govern	2c	grizzle	3b
governor	40c	groan	4d
gown	5c	groat	4d
gradient	31	grocery pl -ries	19
gradually	24b	grocery	33b
Graecize	25b	groin	5b
grain	4a	groom	4e
grammar	40e	groove	4e
gramophone	15a	gross	1
granary pl -ries	19	grotesquely	47
granary	33a	grottoes or -os	18c

grouch	5c	guild	15
ground	5c	guile	15
group	4e	guilt	15
groupie	8d	guinea	15
grouse	5c	guise	15
grout	5c	guise	45
grovel	3b	guitar	15
grovelled	24b	gullible	28h
grovelling	24b	gull-like	27c
grow	4d	gunfighter	27e
growl	5c	gunwale or gunnel	3b
growth	4d	guppy pl -ppies	19
grudge	11	gurgle	3b
gruel	3b	guru	3d
gruelling	24b	guttural	3b
gruff	14a	guv	2c
grumble	3b	guv	3d
gryphon	8a	guv'nor	2c
guano	8e	guzzle	3b
guanos	18b	gymkhana	8a
guard	15	gymnasium	8a
guardian	15	gymnasium pl -siums or -sia	22d
guerilla	15	gymnast	8a
guess	15	gynaecology	10
guest	15	gynaecology	8a
guidance	15	gypsum	8a
guidance	30c	(gypsy) Gypsy	12
guide	15	(Gypsy) gypsy or (Gipsy) gipsy	8a
guild	1a	gyro-	8a

H

habit**able**	28b
habit**ant**	31
habit**us** *pl* -t**us**	22d
hac**kle**	3b
ha**e**moglobin	10
ha**e**mophilia	10
haemo**ph**ilia	15a
haemo**ph**iliac	15a
ha**e**morrhage	10
haemorrh**age**	11
haemo**rrh**age	15a
haemorrh**oids**	5b
ha**e**morrhoids	10
haemo**rrh**oids	15a
hag**gle**	3b
ha**il**	4a
h**air**	4a
h**air**y	4a
ha**jj**	12
halb**erd**	40e
hal**cy**on	8a
half-a-crown	27d
half-a-dollar	27d
half-afraid	27d
half-alive	27d
half-and-half	27d
half-anglicized	27d
half-ashamed	27d
half-asleep	27d
half-awake	27d
halfback	27d
half-baked	27d
half-ball	27d
half-barrel	27d
halfbeak	27d
half-begging	27d
half-begun	27d
half-bent	27d
half-blind	27d
half-blood	27d
half-blue	27d
half board	27d
half-boot	27d
half-bottle	27d
half-bound	27d
half-breed	27d
half-brother	27d
half-buried	27d
half-butt	27d
half-castle	27d
half-century	27d
half-circle	27d
half-civilized	27d
half-civilly	27d
half-clad	27d
half-clothed	27d
half-cock	27d
half-completed	27d
half-concealed	27d
half-conscious	27d
half-consumed	27d
half-convinced	27d
half-cooked	27d
half-covered	27d
half-crazy	27d
half-crown	27d
half-day	27d
half-dazed	27d
half-dead	27d
half-deaf	27d
half-demented	27d
half-deserted	27d
half-developed	27d
half-digested	27d
half-dollar	27d
half-done	27d
half-dozen	27d
half-dressed	27d
half-dried	27d
half-drowned	27d
half-drunk	27d
half eagle	27d
half-eaten	27d
half-educated	27d
half-empty	27d
half-English	27d
half-expectant	27d
half-famished	27d
half-filled	27d
half-forgotten	27d
half-formed	27d
half-forward	27d

half frame	27d	**half**-plate	27d
half-frozen	27d	**half**-playfully	27d
half-fulfilled	27d	**half**-pleased	27d
half-full	14a	**half**-price	27d
half-full	27d	**half**-protesting	27d
half gainer	27d	**half**-proved	27d
half-grown	27d	**half**-questioning	27d
half-hardy	27d	**half**-raw	27d
half-heard	27d	**half**-reluctant	27d
half-hearted	27d	**half**-remembered	27d
half-hitch	27d	**half**-repentant	27d
half holiday	27d	**half**-rhyme	27d
half-hoping	27d	**half**-right	27d
half-hour	27d	**half**-rotten	27d
half-human	27d	**half**-round	27d
half-inch	27d	**half**-savage	27d
half-inclined	27d	**half**-second	27d
half-informed	27d	**half**-section	27d
half-instinctive	27d	**half**-seen	27d
half-intoxicated	27d	**half**-sensed	27d
half-jack	27d	**half**-serious	27d
half-joking	27d	**half**-shut	27d
half-knowledge	27d	**half**-silvered	27d
half landing	27d	**half**-sister	27d
half-learned	27d	**half**-size	27d
half-leather	27d	**half**-slip	27d
half-length	27d	**half**-smile	27d
half-lie	27d	**half**-sole	27d
half-life	27d	**half**-starved	27d
half-light	27d	**half**-stated	27d
half-mad	27d	**half**-step	27d
half-marathon	27d	**half**-submerged	27d
half-mast	27d	**half**-tide	27d
half measure	27d	**half**-timber	27d
half-mile	27d	**half**-title	27d
half-minute	27d	**half**tone	27d
half-monthly	27d	**half**-track	27d
half-moon	27d	**half**-trained	27d
half-mourning	27d	**half**-true	27d
half-naked	27d	**half**-truth	27d
half-nelson	27d	**half**-understood	27d
half-note	27d	**half**-used	27d
half-open	27d	**half**-verified	27d
half-pagan	27d	**half** volley	27d
half-pay	27d	half**way**	4a
half-pedalling	27d	**half**way	27d
halfpenny	27d	**half**-wild	27d
half-petrified	27d	**half**witted	27d
half-pie	27d	**half**-wrong	27d

half-year	27d	head	2b
half-yearly	27d	headache	27d
hall**ow**	4d	head-banger	27e
hallucinat**or**	40c	head-hunter	27e
hal**oes** or **-os**	18c	head**light**	4c
ha**l**t	2d	headmistress**ss**ship	14b, 27c
ha**l**ter	2d	head**ph**ones	15a
ha**l**ve	15	head**quar**ters	9a
hammock	1	head**way**	4a
handful	14a	hea**l**	4b
handfuls	21	hea**l**th	2b
handkerch**ief**	4b, 6a	hea**p**	4b
han**dle**	3b	hea**r**	4b
handl**eable**	28e	hea**r**d	9c
handover n.	27e	hear**say**	4a
han**d**some	15	hear**se**	9c
hang**ar** (plane)	40e	hea**r**t	4a
h**ange**r	1e	heartbroke**nness**	14b
hang**er** (coat)	40b	hea**r**th	4a
hangover n.	27e	hea**t**	4b
hank**y** or **-ie** *pl* **-kies**	8d, 19	heat seeker	27e
ha**pp**en	14	hea**t**h	4b
ha**pp**iness	14	hea**th**en	4b
harang**ue**	15	heathe**nness**	14b
hara**ss**	1e, 14a	hea**t**her	2b
harb**our**	9c, 40e	hea**v**e	4b
harmony *pl* **-nies**	19	hea**v**en	2b
harne**ss**	14a	hea**v**y	2b
harr**ow**	4d	Hebr**aic**	4a
ha**ssle**	3b	Hebr**ew**	4e
hasten	15	hec**kle**	3b
hat**able** or hat**eable**	28e	he**dge**	11
ha**tch**	11	hee**d**	4b
ha**tch**er	40f	hee**l**	4b
ha**tch**et	11	heel**less**	14b
ha**ug**hty	5a	he**if**er	2b, 6b
h**aug**hty	15b	he**igh**t	4c, 6b
ha**u**l	5a	he**igh**t	15b
ha**u**lage	5a	he**i**nous	4b, 6b
haul**age**	11	he**ir**	4a
ha**u**nch	5a	he**ir**	6b
ha**u**nt	5a	heir apparent	27e
ha**v**e	3d	heir**ess**	14a
havo**ck**er	25a	he**i**st	4c, 6b
havo**cking**	25a	helicopt**er**	40b
ha**w**k	5a	hel**ix** *pl* **-lices** or **-lixes**	22d
ha**w**thorn	5a	he**r**	9c
ha**y**	4a	he**r**b	9c
haze**l**	3b	her**bal**	3b

herbicidal	3b	hitch	11
herbicide	9c	hitcher	40f
herd	9c	hoar	4d, 9d
herd	40e	hoard	4d, 9d
hereditary	33a	hoarse	4d, 9d
heresy pl -sies	19	hoary	4d, 9d
heresy	34	hobble	3b
heritage	11	hobby pl -bbies	19
hermit	9c	hoboes or -os	18c
hermitage	11	hodgepodge	11
heroes	18a	hoe	4d
heroine	3a	hoer	4d
heroine	3a	hoist	5b
hesitance	30c	hold	1a
hesitant	31	holdall	14a
hesitater or hesitator	40c	hold-up n.	27a
Hessian	13d	holey (hole)	23
hew	4e	holiday	4a
hexagonal	3b	hollow	4d
heyday	4a	holster	40b
hiatus pl -tuses or -tus	22d	holy (saint)	23
hibiscus pl -scuses	22d	homage	11
hiccup	14	homeopathy or homoeopathy	10
hiddenness	14b	homicidal	3b
hidebound	5c	homonym	8a
hierarchical	3b	homophobia	15a
hierarchy pl -chies	19	homophone	15a
hierocracy	34	honestly	7
hieroglyphics	4c	honey	2c
hieroglyphics	8a	honey-eater	27e
high	4c	honeycomb	15
high-handed	27f	honeysuckle	3b
highjack	27d	honorarium pl -riums or -ria	22d
high-up n.	27a	honorary	33a
highway	4a	honour	40e
hind	1a	hood	2c
hindrance	30c	hoof	4e
Hindu	3d	hook	2c
hinge	12	hooky	2c
hippie or hippy	8d	hoop	4e
hippy pl hippies	19	hooray	4a
hippos	18b	hoot	4e
hirable or hireable	28e	hooves or hoofs	17
Hispanicize	25b	hope	3a
historicism	25b	hormonal	3b
historicist	25b	horologium pl -gia	22d
historicity	25b	horrible	28h
history pl -ries	19	horsy or horsey	23
history	33c	hosiery	33b

hospice	12	hyacinth	8a
hospital	3b	hybrid	8a
host	1a	hydrangea	8a
hostage	11	hydrant	8a
hostel	3b	hydrant	31
hostilely	46a	hydrated	8a
hotchpotch	11	hydraulic	2d
hotel	3b	hydraulic	8a
hothead	27e	hydro-	8a
hound	5c	hydroelectric	8a
hour	5c	hydrogen	8a
house	5c	hydrolyse	45
household	1a	hydrometer	8a
hovel	3b	hygiene	6a
hover	2c	hygiene	8a
how	5c	hymn	8a
howl	5c	hymnal	3b
huddle	3b	hype	8a
hue	4e	hyper-	8a
huge	12	hypersensitive	8a
hull-less	27c	hyperspace	8a
humanity or humanness	14b	hyphen	8a
humble	3b	hyphen	15a
humbly	46b	hypnosis	8a
humerus pl -ri	22d	hypnotize	8a
humorous	40e	hypocaust	5a
humour	40e	hypocaust	8a
hurdle	3b	hypocrisy	8a
hurricane	3a	hypocrisy	34
hurry	14	hypocrite	8a
hurt	9c	hypotenuse	8a
hurtle	3b	hypothesis	8a
hustle	3b	hypothesis pl -eses	22d
hustle	15	hysterectomy	8a
hutch	11	hysterical	8a

-ial	4b
-ian	4b
icebreaker	27e
icicle	3b
icily	8
ictus pl -tuses or -tus	22d
icy	23, 34
idea	1b
ideal	4b
ideally	24
idiocy	34
idiom	4b
idiosyncrasy	34
idle	3b
idol	3b
idyll	8a
idyll	14a
-iferous	14d
ignitable or ignitible	28h
ignominy	8
ignominy pl -nies	19
ignorance	30c
ignorant	31
-ilia	14d
-iliate	14d
-ility	14d
illegal	3b
illegal	14b, 48b
illegible	14b, 48b
illegible	28h
illegitimacy	34
illegitimate	14b, 48b
illiberal	14b, 48b
illicit	14b, 48b
illimitable	14b, 48b
illiquid	14b, 48b
illiteracy	34
illiterate	14b, 48b
illness	14a
illogical	14b, 48b
illuminate	14b
illusion	14b
illusory	14b

illusory	33c
illustrator	40c
image	11
imagery	11
imaginary	33a
imagine	12
imbecilely	46a
imbue	4e
immaculate	14b, 48b
immanent	14b
immanent	31
immaterial	14b, 48b
immature	14b, 48b
immature	40f
immeasurable	14b, 48b
immediacy	34
immediate	14b, 48b
immedicable	48b
immemorial	14b, 48b
immense	14b, 48b
immense	30c
immerse	14b
immersible	28h
immigrant	14b
immigrant	31
immigrate	14b
imminent	14b
imminent	31
immiscible	14b, 48b
immiscible	28h
immiscible	28g
immitigable	14b
immobile	14b, 48b
immobilize	14b
immoderate	14b, 48b
immodest	14b, 48b
immolate	14b
immoral	3b
immoral	14b, 48b, 48c
immortal	14b, 48b
immotile	48b
immovable	2c
immovable	14b, 48b
immovable or immoveable	28e
immune	14b
immunisation	14b
immure	14b
immutable	48b
impartial	13c

61

impatient	13c
impeacher	40f
impedance	30c
impel	14a
impenitence	30c
imperative	3d
impersonal	3b
impersonator	40c
impertinent	31
impetus pl -tuses	22d
implausible	28h
implore	4d
importance	30c
important	31
impossible	28h
imposter	40b, 40c
imposture	40f
impotence	30c
impound	5c
impresarios	18b
impress	14a
impression	14b
improve	2c
improvise	45
imprudence	30c
impugn	15a
impulse	3d
impure	4e
inaccessible	28h
inaccuracy	34
inadequacy	34
inadmissible	28h
inadvertence	30c
inaudible	5a
inaudible	28h
inaugural	3b
inaugurator	40c
inauspicious	13
incautious	13
incendiary	33a
incense	30c
incessant	31
inch	13e
incidence	30c
incident	31
incipient	31
incise	45
includable or includible	28h
incoercible	28g
incoherence	30c
incompatible	28h
incompetence	30c
incompliant	31
inconceivable	6a
inconstant	31
incontrovertible	28h
inconvincible	28g
incorrigible	28h
increase	4b
incubus pl -bi or -buses	22d
indeed	4b
indefensible	28h
indelicacy	34
indenture	40f
index pl -dexes or -dices	22, 22d
indicate	40c
indicator	40c
indict	1
indict	15
indignant	31
indigos or -oes	18c
indiscreet	4b
indisposed	48a
indolence	30c
indolent	31
indomitable	28b
Indonesian	13d
inducible	28g
industry pl -ries	19
-ine	4b
inebriant	31
ineffable	28b
ineffaceable	28d
inefficacy	34
inevitable	28b
inexorable	28b
inexperienced	48a
infant	31
infanticidal	3b
infeasible	28h
infectious	13
infernal	3b
infernos	18b
infertilely	46a
infidel	3b
infinitesimal	3b
infirmary pl -ries	19
infirmary	33a

infixion	38	insolent	31
inflatable	23	insoluble	48c
inflatable	28c	insolvent	31
inflate	23	insouciant	31
inflationary	33a	inspector	40c
inflection or inflexion	38	install or instal	14a
influence	4e	instalment	14
informal	3b	instance	30c
informant	31	instant	31
ingenious	12	instead	2b
ingle	3b	instigator	40c
ingress	14a	instil	3b, 14a
inhabitant	31	institutional	3b
inherent	31	instructible	28h
in-house	27h	insuperable	28b
inhuman	48c	insurance	13
iniquity pl -ties	19	insurance	30c
initial	13c	insure	4e
initiate	13c	insure	13
inject	12	integral	3b
injector	40c	intelligible	28h
injudicious	13	intense	30c
injure	40g	intentional	3b
injury pl -ries	19	intercede	35
injustice	12	interchange	1e
inlay	4a	interdenominational	3b
innings (sing. & pl.)	20	interfere	4b
innocent	14	interject	12
innocuous	14d, 48b	intermediacy	34
innoxious	48b	intermediary	33a
innuendos or -oes	18c	intermezzos	18b
innumerable	48b	intermission	14b
innumeracy	34	internal	3b
innumerate	48b	international	3b
innutritious	48b	interplay	4a
inoculate	14d	interracial	14b
inordinacy	34	interregional	14b
inquiry	8e	interregnum	14b
inquiry pl -ries	19	interrelate	14b
inquisition	8e	interreligious	14b
inquisitive	8e	interrogate	14b
ins-and-outs	21	interrogator	40c
insanitary	33a	interrogatory	33c
insatiable	13c	interrupt	14b
inscrutable	28b	interview	4e
insecticidal	3b	interviewee	4b
in-service	12	intestacy	34
insignificance	30b	intestinal	3b
insistent	31	intimacy	34

in to	44	**irr**egular	48b
into	44	irrelev**ance**	30c
intoler**ant**	31	**irr**elevant	48b
intoxic**ant**	31	**irr**elievable	48b
intren**cher**	40f	**irr**eligious	48b
intrica**cy**	34	**irr**emediable	48b
intrigue	15	**irr**emissible	48b
intrigu**ing**	15	**irr**emovable	48b
introdu**ce**	12	**irr**eparable	48b
introdu**cible**	28g	irrepla**ceable**	28d
introduct**ory**	33c	**irr**eplaceable	48b
inutil**ely**	46a	**irr**epressible	48b
inv**eigh**	4a, 6b	**irr**eproachable	48b
inv**eigh**	15b	**irr**esistible	48b
inv**ei**gle	6b	**irr**esoluble	48b
invent**or**	40c	**irr**esolute	48b
inventor**y** pl -r**ies**	19	**irr**esolvable	48b
invent**ory**	33c	**irr**espective	48b
Invernes**s-s**hire	27c	**irr**espirable	48b
invetera**cy**	34	**irr**esponsible	48b
invigilat**or**	40c	**irr**esponsive	48b
invin**cible**	28h	**irr**etentive	48b
invin**cible**	28g	**irr**etrievable	48b
invis**ible**	28h	irrever**ent**	31
inv**oi**ce	5b	**irr**everent	48b
involunt**ary**	33a	irrevers**ible**	28h
irasc**ible**	28h	**irr**eversible	48b
iras**cible**	28g	**irr**evocable	48b
ire	4c	ir**rit**able	14
irenic or **eir**enic	4c	irrit**ant**	31
irides**cent**	12	ir**rit**ate	14
ironmaster	27e	i**sl**and	15
ironm**o**nger	2c	is**le**	3b
ironworker	27e	isle	15
irration**al**	3b	issu**ance**	30c
irreclaimable	48b	iss**ue**	4e
irreconcilable	48b	issu**er**	4e
irrecoverable	48b	itali**cize**	25b
irrecusable	48b	i**tch**	11
irredeemable	48b	iter**ance**	30c
irredu**cible**	28g	-it**erate**	14d
irreducible	48b	itiner**ant**	31
irreflexive	48b	itiner**ary**	33a
irrefragable	48b	ivor**y** pl -r**ies**	19
irrefutable	48b	iv**y** pl -v**ies**	19

jackal	3b	jewel	12
jackass	14a	jewelled	24b
jackdaw	5a	jewellery	33b
jacket	7	jewelling	24b
jacksie or -y	8d	jib	12
jagged	7	jibe	12
jail	4a	jiffy	12
jailless	14b	jig	12
jamb	15	jiggle	3b
jangle	3b	jiggly	46b
jarveys	19	jigsaw	5a
jaundice	12	jigsaw	12
jaunt	5a	jilt	12
jaw	5a	jingle	3b
jawbreaker	27e	jingle	12
jazz	14a	jingly	46b
jealous	2b	jingoes	18a
jealous	12	jink	12
jeans	4b	jinks	12
jeans	12	jinn	12
jeep	4b	jinx	12
jeep	12	jitter	12
jeer	4b	jive	12
jeer	12	jockeys	19
jejune	12	jocular	40e
jelly	12	joeys	19
jeopardize	12	join	5b
jeopardize	2b	joinery	33b
jeopardy	2b	joint	5b
jerk	9c	joist	5b
jerk	12	jolt	1a
jerkin	9c	Joneses	20b
jerry	12	jostle	3b
jersey	9c	jostle	15
jersey	12	journal	3b
jester	12	journal	9c
jet	12	journalist	9c
jetsam	12	journey	9c
jetty	12	joust	5c
Jew	12	jovial	4c
Jew	4e	jowl	5c
jewel	3b	joy	5b
jewel	4e	joyful	5b
		joyless	8
		joystick	5b
		judder	40b
		judgment or judgement	36
		judiciary	33a
		juggernaut	5a

juggle	3b	jungle	3b
jugular	40e	jungly	46b
juice	4e	junior	4c
juicy	34	junior	40c
jujitsu or jujutsu or jiujutsu	3d, 12	junky or -ie	8d
jumble	3b	jury pl -ries	19
jumbos	18b	justice	12
jump-off	27a	juvenile	2c
juncture	40f	juvenilely	46a

K

kaleidoscope	6b
keel	4b
keen	4b
keenness	14b
keep	4b
kennel	3b
kennelled	24b
kennellIng	24b
kept	39
kerb	9c
kernel	3b
kernel	9c
kestrel	3b
ketch	11
kettle	3b
key	4b
keyboard	4d, 9d
keyed	8
kick	11
kiddy or -ie	8d
killick	25b
kilogram	1e
kilometre	1e
kimonos	18b
kind	1a
kindle	3b
Kinross-shire	27c
kiosk	4b
kirk	9c
kitchen	11
knack	15

knapweed	15
knave	15
knavery	33b
knead	4b
knead	15
knee	15
kneel	4b
kneel	15
knell	15
knelt or kneeled	39
knew	4e
knew	15
knickers	15
knick-knack	15
knife	15
knight	4c
knight	15
knit	15
knives	17
knob	15
knock	15
knocker	15
knock-outs	21
knock-up n.	27a
knoll	1
knot	15
know	4d
know	15
knowledge	11
knowledge	15
knowledgeable or knowledgable	28d
knuckle	3b
knuckle	15
knuckly	46b
knur or knurr	15
knurl	15
kohl	3b

L

label	3b
labelled	24b
labelling	24b
laboratory *pl* -ries	19
laboratory	33c
labour	40e
labyrinth	8a
ladle	3b
lady *pl* -dies	19
lady-killer	27e
laicism	25b
laicize	25b
laid	4a
laid	8b, 26
lain	4a
lair	4a
laird	4a
lamb	15
lance	12
landfill	14a
land-holder	27e
landowner	4d
language	11
language	8e
languid	8e
languor	15
languorous	15
lantern	9c
lapidary	33a
lapsus *pl* -psus	22d
larceny *pl* -nies	19
larder	40b
large	12
largess or largesse	14a
largos	18b
larva *pl* -ae	22d
larvicidal	3b
laryngitis	8a
lash-up n.	27a
lassie	8d
lassoer	4e
latch	11
latent	31
lateral	3b
lather	40b
lattice	12
laud	5a
laudatory	33c
laugh	15b
launch	5a
launcher	40f
laundry	5a
laundry *pl* -ries	19
laurel	3b
laurelled	24b
laurelling	24b
lavatory *pl* -ries	19
lavatory	33c
lavender	40b
law	5a
lawbreaker	27e
lawn	5a
lawyer	40b
lay	4a
layer	4a
layout n.	27e
leach	4b
leacher	40f
lead n.	2b
lead vb.	4b
leaf	4b
leaf-hopper	27e
league	15
leak	4b
leakage	11
lean	4b
leanness	14b
leant	2b
leant or leaned	39
leap	4b
leapt	2b
leapt or leaped	39
learn	9c
learnt or learned	39
lease	4b
leash	4b
least	4b
leather	2b
leave	4b
leaves	17
lecher	40f
lectionary *pl* -ries	19

lectionary	33a	licence n.	30c
lecture	40f	license vb.	30c
ledge	11	licensee	4b
lee	4b	licentious	13
leek	4b	lichen	15a
leer	4b	lich gate or lych gate	8a
leeway	4b	-licity	14d
left	39	lidos	18b
leftover n.	27e	liege	6a
legacy pl -cies	19	lieu	4e
legacy	34	lieutenant	31
legal	3b	liftoff	14a
legionary	33a	ligature	40f
legislature	40f	light	4c
legitimacy	34	lightening (brighter)	23
legwarmer	9a	lightning (bolt)	23
leisure	2b, 6b	likable or likeable	28e
leisure	13	likewise	45
leisure	40g	lily	1e
loitmotiv	4c, 6b	limb	15
lenience	30c	limbos	18b
lenient	31	lime burner	27e
lentil	3b	limerick	25b
leopard	2b	linable or lineable	28e
leprosarium pl -ria	22d	linctus pl -tuses	22d
leprosy	34	lineage	23
-less	14a	line-up n.	27a
lessen (make less)	39a	lingoes	18a
lesson (teaching)	39a	linguist	8e
lethal	3b	linkage	11
lettuce	2b	linkup	27a
leukaemia	4e	linoleum	1e
leukaemia	10	lintel	3b
level	3b	lion	4c
leverage	11	liquefacient	6a
lewd	4e	liquefy	7
liability pl -ties	19	liquid	7
liable	4c	liquid	8e
liaise	4a	liquidate	8e
libel	3b	liquidator	40c
libellant	31	liquidity	8e
libelled	24b	liquidize	8e
libelling	24b	liquorice	12
liberal	3b	lisle	3b
liberator	40c	listen	15
libidos	18b	literacy	34
library pl -ries	19	literal	3b
library	33a	literary	33a
librettos or libretti	18b	literature	40f

lithogra**ph**	15a
litig**ant**	31
lit**re**	40d
lit**tle**	3b
liv**able** or liv**eable**	28e
live vb.	3a
liver	14
liver**y** pl **-ries**	19
lives	17
loa**d**	4d
loaf	4d
loa**m**	4d
loa**n**	4d
loa**th**	4d
loa**ves**	4d
loa**ves**	17
lobb**y** pl **-bbies**	19
lock**up**	27a
loc**us** pl **-ci**	22d
lo**dge**	11
lo**dge**r	11
lodgment or lodg**e**ment.	36
-log**er**	40b
log**os**	18b
loi**n**	5b
loi**ter**	5b
lol**li**pop	14
loo	4e
loo**k**	2c
loo**m**	4e
loo**n**	4e
loo**ny**	4e
loo**p**	4e
loo**py**	4e
loo**se**	4e
loo**t**	4e
loqua**cious**	13
Lord Mayor**s**	21
Lord**s** of Appeal	21
lorr**y** pl **-ries**	19
lost	1a
loth	1
Lothari**os**	18b
lotter**y** pl **-ries**	19
lotus-eater	27e
lou**d**	5c
lou**nge**	5c
lou**se**	5c
lou**t**	5c
lou**v**re	4e
lov**able** or love**able**	28e
love	2c
lo**w**	4d
low-down	27f
lower	4d
low**ly**	4d
lo**y**al	5b
loyalt**y** pl **-ties**	19
lu**ck**	11
luc**re**	40d
luder**ick**	25b
lugg**age**	11
luke**war**m	9a
lum**bar** (back)	40e
lum**ber** (jumble)	40e
lumin**ary**	33a
luna**cy**	34
lun**ar**	40e
lun**cher**	40f
lur**ch**	9c
lur**cher**	40f
lure	4e
lur**k**	9c
lus**cious**	13
lustr**al**	3b
lustre	1c
lust**re**	40d
luxuri**ance**	30c
luxuri**ant**	31
luxur**y** pl **-ries**	19
l**y**ch gate or lich gate	8a
l**ye**	4c
lying	26
lym**ph**	15a
lymph**oid**	5b
lynch	8a
lyn**cher**	40f
lynx	8a
lyre	4c
ly**re**	8a
ly**ric**	8a
lyri**cism**	25b
lyri**cist**	25b
lyse	45

M

macabre	40d
machete	11
machinable or machineable	28e
machine	3a
machine	13e
machinery	4b
machinery	33b
macho	11
mackerel	3b
made-up	27f
madrigal	3b
maestri or maestros	18b
maffick	25b
magazine	3a
magician	25b
magistral	3b
magnetos	18b
magnificence	30c
magus *pl* -gi	22d
maid	4a
maiden	4a
mail	4a
maim	4a
main	4a
mainstay	4a
maintain	4a
maintenance	30c
maize	4a
majesty	12
make-up n.	27a
malady *pl* -dies	19
Malaysian	13d
malice	12
malign	4c, 15a
malignant	31
mall	14a
malleable	28b
mallet	7
mallow	4d
malpractice	12
malt	2d
mammal	3b
mammallike	14b

mammy or -ie	8d
manacle	3b
manage	11
mandatory	33c
mange	1e
manger	1e
manger	12
mangetout	1e
mangle	3b
mangoes or -os	18c
manifestoes or -os	18c
manikin or mannikin	24b
manipulator	40c
mannequin	8e
manoeuvre	10
manor	40c
manse	30c
mantel	3b
mantle	3b
manufacture	40f
manure	1e
many	2b
maple	3b
marauder	5a
marcher	40f
mare	40c
margarine	12
marginal	3b
marigold	1a
marine	4b
market	7
mark-up n.	27a
maroon	4e
marriage	11
marshalled	24b
marshalling	24b
martial	13c
martyr	8a
marvel	3b
marvelled	24b
marvelling	24b
marvellous	24b
Marys	19
mashie or -y	8d
massacre	40d
mastiff	14a
mastoid	5b
match	11
matcher	40f

matchmaker	27e	mediocre	40d
maternal	3b	medium *pl* -dia or -diums	22d
mathematician	13	meek	4b
mathematician	25b	meet	4b
matrix *pl* -trices or -trixes	22d	melange	1e
matronal	3b	mellow	4d
mattress	1e	meltdown	5c
mature	4e	memorable	28b
mature	40f	memorandum *pl* -dums or -da	22d
matzos	18b	memos	18b
maul	5a	menace	2f
mausoleum	5a	menagerie	8
mausoleum *pl* -leums or -lea	22d	mendacious	13
mauve	4d	menial	4c
maverick	25b	meniscus *pl* -sci or -scuses	22d
maximal	3b	menservants	21
maximum *pl* -mums or -ma	22d	menu	3d
may	4a	mercantile	9c
mayor	8a	mercenary	9c
mayor	40c	mercenary *pl* -ries	19
mayoral	3b	mercenary	33a
mead	4b	merchandise	45
meadow	2b	merchant	9c
meagre	4b	merchant	31
meagre	40d	mercury	9c
meal	4b	mercy	9c
mealless	14b	meretricious	13
mealy	24	merge	9c
mean	4b	meringue	15
meanie	8d	merinos	18b
meanness	14b	meritocracy	34
meant	2b	mermaid	9c
meant	39	merriment	8
measles	4b	mesomorph	15a
measles (sing.)	20a	message	11
measure	2b	metacarpus *pl* -pi	22d
measure	13	metalled	24b
measure	40g	metalling	24b
meat	4b	metamorphosis *pl* -oses	22d
mechanical	1e	metaphoric	15a
medalled	24b	metaphysicize	25b
medalling	24b	metaphysics	8a
meddle	3b	metatarsus *pl* -si	22d
medial	4c	meteor	4b
medial	4b	methylated	8a
mediator	40c	metonym	8a
medicinal	3b	metre	40d
medicine	3a	metros	18b
medieval	10	mettle	3b

microccocus *pl* -ci	22d	misalign	4c
microphone	15a	misbehaviour	40e
micros	18b	miscellaneous	15
midday	4a	miscellany *pl* -nies	19
middle	3b	mischief	6a
midget	11	miscible	28g
midnight	4c	misdemeanour	4b
mid-off	27a	misdemeanour	40e
midriff	14a	miserable	28c
might	4c	misery *pl* -ries	19
mighty	4c	misfortune	40f
migraine	4a	misguided	15
migrant	31	misinformant	31
mild	1a	mislay	4a
mildew	4e	misogyny	8a
mileage or milage	11	misshapen	14b
mileage or milage	23	misshapenness	14b
militant	31	mission	14b
military	33a	mission	13a, b
millennium *pl* -niums or -nia	22d	missionary	33a
millinery	33b	misspell	14b
million	8d	misspend	14b
millionaire	4a	misstate	14b
mimicked	25a	mistakable or mistakeable	28e
mimicker	25a	mistaken	39a
mimicking	25a	mistakenness	14b
minable or mineable	28e	mistletoe	15
minatory	33c	mistral	3b
mince	30d	mitre	40d
mind	1a	mixture	40f
minder	1a	mix-up n.	27a
mind-reader	27e	mnemonic	15
minehunter	27e	moan	4d
miner (job)	40b	moat	4d
mineral	3b	moccasin	1e
mingle	3b	mockery *pl* -ries	19
miniature	40f	mock-up n.	27a
minimal	3b	model	3b
minimum *pl* -mums or -ma	22d	modelled	24b
ministry *pl* -ries	19	modelling	24b
minnow	4d	moderator	40c
minor (lesser)	40c	modernity or modernness	14b
minstrel	3b	modular	40e
minute (as in time)	2b	mogul	3b
minutiae	22d	moist	5b
miracle	3b	moisten	15
mirage	12	moisture	40f
mirror	40c	molar	40e
mirth	9c	molten	1a

momentary	33a	morphology	15a
momentum *pl* -ta or -tums	22d	morphosis *pl* -oses	22d
monarchal	3b	morrow	4d
monarchy *pl* -chies	19	morsel	3b
monastery *pl* -ries	19	mortar	40e
monastery	33b	mortgage	11
monasticism	25b	mortice	12
Monday	2c	mortician	25b
Monday	4a	mortuary *pl* -ries	19
monetary	2c	mortuary	33a
monetary	33a	mosaic	4a
money	2c	mosaicist	25b
moneychanger	1e	mosquitoes or -os	18c
moneymaker	27e	moss	14a
mongol	3b	moss stitch	27c
mongrel	2c	most	1a
mongrel	3b	mother	2c
monitor	40c	motherboard	9d
monk	2c	mother-in-law	27e
monkey	2c	mothers-in-law	21
monkeys	19	motor	40c
monkfish	2c	mottle	3b
monocle	3b	mould	4d
monograph	15a	moult	4d
monogynous	8a	mound	5c
monologue	15	mount	5c
monsoon	4u	mountain	2e
monstrous	4l	mourn	4d, 9d
month	2c	mouse	5c
moo	4e	moustache	13e
mooch	4e	mouth	5c
moocher	40f	movable or moveable	28e
mood	4e	move	2c
moody	4e	movie	8, 8d
moon	4e	mow	4d
moor	4e	much	11
moose	4e	muddle	3b
moot	4e	muddly	46b
moral	3b	muesli	4e
moratorium *pl* -ria or -riums	22d	muffle	3b
moratory	33c	multiple	3b
morceau *pl* -x	22a	mumble	3b
mordant (sarcastic)	31	muncher	40f
mordent (music)	31	municipal	3b
morellos	18b	mural	3b
morgue	15	murderer	40b
-morph	15a	murmur	9c
morpheme	15a	muscle	3b
morphine	15a	muscly	46b

muscular	40e	myrtle	3b
mushroom	4e	mysterious	8a
musician	25b	mystery	8a
mussel	3b	mystery *pl* -ries	19
mustachios	18b	mystery	33b
mustard	40e	mystic	8a
mutant	31	mysticism	25b
mutiny *pl* -nies	19	myth	8a
muzzle	3b	mythical	8a
myopic	8a	mythicist	25b
myriad	8a	mythicize	25b
myrrh	15a	mythology	8a

N

nacre	40d
nail	4a
naked	7
namable or nameable	28e
nanny pl -nnies	19
narcissus pl -suses or -si	22d
narrative	3d
narrator	40c
narrow	4d
nation	13
national	3b
natural	3b
nature	40f
naught	5a
naught	15b
naughty	5a
naughty	15b
nausea	5a
nautical	5a
nautilus pl -luses or -li	22d
navel	3b
navigator	40c
navvy	14
navy pl -vies	19
Neanderthal	3b
near	4b
nearly	4b
neat	4b
nebula pl -ae or -as	22d
necessary	12
necklace	12
nectar	40e
need	4b
needle	3b
neglect	7
negligence	30c
neigh	4a, 6b
neigh	15b
neighbour	4a, 6b
neighbour	15b
neighbour	40e
neither	4c, 6a, 6b
neo-orthodox	27b

nephew	4e
nerd	40e
Neros	18b
nerve	9c
-ness	14a
nestle	3b
nestle	15
nettle	3b
nettly	46b
neural	3b
neural	4e
neuritis	4e
neurology	4e
neuroses	16
neurosis	4e
neurosis pl -oses	22d
neurotic	4e
neuroticism	25b
neutral	3b
neutral	4e
neutron	4e
new	4e
newscaster	27e
newsmonger	27e
newsreader	27e
newt	1b
nexus pl -us	22d
nibble	3b
nicety pl -ties	19
nickel	3b
niece	4b
niggle	3b
niggly	46b
nigh	4c
night	4c
nightie or -y	8d
nimble	3b
nimbus pl -bi or -buses	22d
nineteen	4b
ninth	1
nipple	3b
nitrate	1c
nitre	40d
nobble	3b
noble	3b
nobody	27a, 42
nocturnal	3b
noise	5b
noisemaker	27e

nomenclature	40f	notional	3b
nominal	3b	nought	15b
nonchalance	30c	noun	5c
nonchalant	31	nourish	9c
nonchronological	27a	nouveau *pl* -x	4d, 22a
nonconstitutional	3b	novel	3b
noncontributory	33c	novice	12
none	2c	noviciate or novitiate	13, 13c
nonfiction	27a	now	5c
nonlethal	3b	noway	4a
non-national	27b	nowhere	27a
non-native	27b	nowise	45
non-natural	27b	noxious	13d
non-naturalism	27b	nozzle	3b
non-navigable	27b	nucellus *pl* -li	22d
non-negotiable	27b	nuclear	40e
non-nervous	27b	nucleus *pl* -clei or -cleuses	22d
non-nuclear	27b	nudge	11
nonobligatory	33c	nuisance	4e
nonsense	27a	numb	15
nonsense	30c	numeracy	34
noodle	3b	numeral	3b
nook	2c	nunciature	40f
nooky or -ie	8d	nunnery	33b
noon	4e	nuptial	13c
no-one or no one	27b	nursery *pl* -ries	19
no-one or no one	42	nursery	33b
noose	4e	nurture	40f
normal	3b	nutcracker	27e
north	9d	nutrient	31
notary	33a	nutritious	13
notch	11	nuzzle	3b
noteworthy	27c	nylon	8a
nothing	2c	nymph	8a
notice	12	nymph	15a
noticeable	28d	nymphal	3b

oaf	4d
oak	4d
oar	4d, 9d
oasis *pl* -ases	22d
oat	4d
oath	4d
obduracy	34
obedient	31
obeisance	4a, 6b
obeisant	31
obey	4a
obfuscatory	33c
obituary *pl* -ries	19
obituary	33a
object	12
obligatory	33c
oblige	12
obliquely	47
obliquitous	8e
oboe	4d
obscurant	31
obsequious	8e
observance	30c
observant	31
observatory *pl* -ries	19
observatory	33c
obsession	14b
obstacle	3b
obstetrician	13
obstetrician	25b
obstinacy	34
obtain	4a
occasion	14b
occasional	3b
occasionally	24b
occidental	14b
occlude	14b
occult	14b
occupant	31
occupation	14b
occupational	3b
occupied	26
occupier	4c

occupy	4c
occupy	14b
occur	9c
occur	14b
occurrence	14b
occurrence	24b
ocean	13d
o'clock	11
octangle	3b
octavos	18b
octopus *pl* -puses	22d
ocular	40e
oddity *pl* -ties	19
odour	40e
oesophagus	15a
oesophagus *pl* -gi	22d
off	14a
offal	3b
offal	14b
off-centre	27a
offence	14b
offence	30c
offend	14b
offensive	14b
offer	14b
offertory	33c
office	12
office	14b
official	14b
officiate	14b
officious	13
officious	14b
off-load	27a
off-peak	27a
off-street	27a
offshore	27a
offstage	27a
often	15
ogle	3b
ogre	40d
oil	5b
ointment	5b
old	1a
olden	1a
oldie	8d
omelette	14
omissible	28h
omission	14b
omission	14b

omit	14b	ordain	4a
omnibus *pl* -buses	22d	ordeal	4b
omnipotent	31	ordinal	3b
once	3c	ordinance	30c
once	2c	ordinary	33a
once-over n.	27e	ordure	40g
one	2c	-oriferous	40e
on foot	27h	-orific	40e
on horseback	27h	orifice	12
onion	2c	original	3b
onion	8d	-orize	40e
only	1	-orous	40e
onomatopoeia	10	orthopaedic	10
onset	27a	oscillatory	33c
onslaught	15b	ossuary *pl* -ries	19
onto	44	ossuary	33a
onus *pl* onuses	22d	ostensible	28h
ooze	4e	ostentatious	13
opal	3b	ostracize	25b
opaquely	47	other	2c
openness	14b	otherwise	45
operation	1e	ought	15b
operational	3b	ounce	5c
ophthalmic	15a	our	5c
oppilate	14b	ourselves	5c
opponent	14b	out	5c
opponent	31	outboard	9d
opportunity	14b	outclass	5c
oppose	14b	outdated	5c
opposite	14b	outer	5c
oppress	14b	outfall	5c
oppression	14b	outfit	5c
oppressor	40c	outfitter	24b
opprobrium	14b	outgoings	5c
oppugn	14b	outlandish	5c
optician	25b	outlaw	5a
optimal	3b	outlaw	5c
optimum *pl* -ma or -mums	22d	outlet	5c
optional	3b	outlook	5c
opulence	30c	outpatient	5c
opus *pl* opuses or opera	22d	outrage	5c
oracle	3b	outrange	1e
oral	3b	outreach	4b
orange	1e	outright	4c
-orate	40e	outrunner	24b
-oration	40e	outset	5c
oratorios	18b	outside	5c
oratory	33c	outsize	5c
orchestra	15a	outstanding	5c

outstay	4a	overhead	27f, 27h
outward	5c	overlay	4a
outwit	5c	overspill	14a
oval	3b	overstay	4a
ovary *pl* -ries	19	overtake	27g
ovary	33a	overture	40f
oven	2c	overturn	27g
over	2c	ovoid	5b
overanalyse	45	ovum *pl* -va	22d
overarm	27h	owe	4d
overboard	27h	owl	5c
overdrawn	5a	own	4d
overdue	4e	oxidant	31
overfill	14a	oxygen	8a
overflow	27g	oyster	5b
overfull	14a		

P

passenger	12	peat	4b
passion	14b	pebble	3b
passport	27d	pebbly	46b
pastel	3b	peccadillos or -oes	18c
paste-up n.	27a	pectoral	3b
pastoral	3b	peculiar	40e
pastry	1c	pecuniary	33a
pasturage	11	pedagogue	15
pasture	40f	pedagogy	10
patcher	40f	pedal	3b
patent	31	pedalled	24b
patentee	4b	pedalling	24b
paternal	3b	pedant	31
pathfinder	27e	peddle	3b
pathway	4a	pederast	10
patience	30c	pedestrian	4b
patient	31	pedigree	4b
patient	13c	pedlar, peddler or pedler	40e
patios	18b	peek	4b
patriarchal	3b	peel	4b
patricidal	3b	peen	4b
patrimony pl -nies	19	peep	4b
patrol	1	peer	4b
patroller	1	peerage	4b
patronage	11	peerage	11
patronal	3b	peevish	4b
pauper	5a	peewee	4b
pause	5a	peewit	4b
paw	5a	pellet	7
pawl	5a	penal	3b
pawn	5a	penance	30c
pawnbroker	5a	pence	12
pawnbroker	27e	penchant	31
pay	4a	pencil	3b
payee	4b	pencilled	24b
payor	40a	pencilling	24b
payphone	15a	pendant	31
pea	4b	penguin	8e
peace	4b	penitence	13c
peaceable	28d	penitence	30c
peacemaker	27e	penitent	31
peach	4b	penitential	13c
peacher	40f	penitentiary	33a
peak	4b	pennant	31
peal	4b	penny pl -nnies	19
pear	4a	penology	10
pearl	9c	Pentateuch	4e
peasant	31	people	3b
peashooter	27e	people	4b

perceive	4b, 6a
percher	40f
percolate	9c
percolator	40c
percuss	14a
percussion	14b
perfect	9c
perfectible	28f, 28h
perforator	40c
performance	30c
perfumery	33b
perilled	24b
perillIng	24b
period	4c
peripheral	3b
peripheral	15a
periphrasis *pl* -ases	22d
perjure	40g
perk	9c
permanent	9c
permanent	31
permeate	9c
permissible	28h
permission	14b
permit n.	9c
pernicious	13
perpendicular	40e
perpetrator	40c
perplexity *pl* -ties	19
perquisite	9c
perquisite	8e
persecute	9c
persecutor	40c
perseverance	30c
Persian	13d
persistence	30c
persistent	31
person	9c
personage	11
personal	3b
perspicacious	13
persuadable or persuasible	28h
pert	9c
pertinacious	13
pertinent	9c
pervertible	28h
pesos	18b
pessary *pl* -ries	19
pessary	33a

pestilence	30c
pestilential	13c
pestle	3b
pestle	15
petrel	3b
petrol	3b
petticoat	27e
petulance	30c
petulant	31
pew	4e
pewter	4e
phalange	1e
phallus *pl* -li or -luses	22d
phantom	15a
-phany	15a
pharaoh	15a
Pharisaic	4a
pharmaceutical	4e
pharmaceutical	15a
pharmacist	25b
pharmacy	15a
pharmacy *pl* -cies	19
pharmacy	34
pharynx	8a
pheasant	2b
pheasant	15a
pheasant	31
phenomenon	10
phenomenon *pl* -na or -nons	22d
phenyl	14c
philately	15a
-phile	15a
Philip	15a
Philippines	15a
philosophy	15a
philtre	40d
phlegm	15a
phlegmatic	15a
-phobia	15a
-phone	15a
phone	15a
phoneme	15a
phonetic	15a
phoney	15a
phonograph	15a
phony *pl* -nies	19
phooey	4e
photocopy *pl* -pies	19
photograph	15a

photos	18b
phrase	15a
phylactery	15a
phylactery	33b
physical	8a
physician	8a
physician	25b
physicist	25b
physicky	25a
physics	8a
physiognomy	8a
physiology	8a
physique	8a
piano	4b
piastre	40d
pickle	3b
pick-up n.	27a
picture	40f
picturesquely	47
piddle	3b
piece	4b, 6a
pier	4b
pierce	4b
pierce	6a
pierceable	28d
piezoelectricity	6a
piffle	3b
pigeon	12
piggery	33b
pigmentary	33a
pigmy (Pigmy) or pygmy (Pygmy)	8a
pigmy (Pigmy) or pygmy (Pygmy) *pl* -mies	19
pigsticker	27e
pilgrim	1
pilgrimage	11
pillage	11
pillar	40e
pillow	4d
pimentos	18b
pimple	3b
pimply	46b
pincers	40b
pineapple	3b
pinion	4c
pinnace	2f
pinnacle	3b
pinny *pl* -nnies	19
pint	1

pin-up n.	27a
pioneer	4c
pioneer	4b
pious	4c
pipefiller	27e
piquant	31
piracy	34
pirate	3a
pirouette	4e
pistil	3b
pistol	3b
pistolled	24b
pistolling	24b
pitch	11
pitcher	40f
pitfall	14a
pittance	30c
pituitary	33a
pixel	3b
pixie	8
place	12
placebos or -oes	18c
plague	15
plaguy or plaguey	23
plaice	4a
plaid	4a
plain	4a
plainness	14b
plait	4a
planetarium *pl* -riums or -ria	22d
plangent	1e
plantain	4a
plasticine	4b
plasticity	25b
plasticize	25b
plateau *pl* -s or -x	4d, 22a
platelayer	27e
platypus *pl* -puses	22d
plausible	5a
plausible	28h
play	4a
playground	27e
play-off	27a
playtime	27e
plead	4b
pleasant	31
please	4b
pleasure	2b
pleasure	13

pleasure	40g
pleat	4b
plebeian	4b
plectrum or plectron *pl* -tra or -trums, or -trons	22d
Pleistocene	6b
plenary	33a
pleural (lungs)	3b
pleurisy	4e
pleurisy	34
plexus *pl* -uses or -us	22d
pliant	31
pliers	4c
plight	4c
plimsoll or plimsole	14a
plough	5c
plough	15b
plover	2c
ploy	5b
plumage	11
plumb	15
plunge	12
plural (1+)	3b
plutocracy *pl* -cies	19
plutocracy	34
plywood	8a
pneumatic	4e
pneumatic	15a
pneumonia	4e
poach	4d
poacher	40f
pocket	7
poem	4d
poem	7
poet	4d
poet	7
poetry	7
poignance	30c
poignant	5b
poignant	31
point	5b
poison	5b
poker	40b
polar	40e
polemicist	25b
police	4b
policy *pl* -cies	19
policy	34
polish	1e

Polish	1e
politician	25b
politicize	25b
politicking	25a
poll	14a
pollutant	31
pollution	1e
polony *pl* -nies	19
polyester	8a
polygamy	8a
polyglot	8a
polygon	8a
polyhedron	8a
polymer	8a
polyp	8a
polyphonic	8a
polythene	8a
pomace	2f
pommel	3b
ponchos	18b
poncy or poncey	23, 34
pontoon	4e
pony *pl* -nies	19
poodle	3b
pool	4e
poop	4e
poor	4e
poplar	40e
poppy *pl* -ppies	19
populace	2f
popular	40e
porcelain	2e
porcelain	12
porphyry	8a
porpoise	5b
porridge	11
portable	28b
portent	31
portfolios	18b
porticoes or -os	18c
portmanteau *pl* -s or -x	4d, 22a
portrait	4a
portraiture	40f
portray	4a
Poseidon	4c
positive	3d
possess	14a
possession	14b
possessor	40c

possible	28h	precipice	12
post	1a	precipitance	30c
postage	11	precipitant	31
postpone	1a	precise	7
postulant	31	predesign	4c
postural	3b	predicator	40c
posture	40f	predict	7
potable	28b	predictable	28f
potatoes	18a	predominance	30c
potential	13c	pre-echo	27b
potsherd	40e	pre-elect	27b
pouch	5c	pre-election	27b
pouf or pouffe	4e	pre-embryo	27b
poultice	4d	pre-eminence	27b
poultice	12	pre-eminent	27b
poultry	4d	pre-eminently	27b
pounce	5c	pre-empire	27b
pound	5c	pre-empt	27b
pour	4d, 9d	pre-emption	27b
pout	5c	pre-emptive	27b
powder	5c	pre-emptively	27b
power	5c	pre-emptor	27b
powwow	14	pre-emptory	27b
practice n.	12	pre-engage	27b
practice n.	34	pre-engagement	27b
practise vb.	34	pre-establish	27b
prairie	4a	pre-estimate	27b
praise	4a	pre-examination	27b
prance	30	pre-examine	27b
prattle	3b	pre-exist	27b
prawn	5a	pre-existence	27b
praxis pl -xises or -xes	22d	pre-expose	27b
pray	4a	preface	2f
preach	4b	prefecture	40f
preacher	40f	prefer	7
preassign	4c	preference	30c
pre-Augustan	27b	preferential	3b
pre-Babylonian	27b	prefix	27a
pre-British	27b	prefixion	38
pre-Byzantine	27b	pregnancy pl -cies	19
pre-Carboniferous	27b	pregnant	31
precaution	5a	prejudice	12
precautionary	33a	prelacy	34
precede	35	preliminary	33a
precedence	30c	premature	40f
preceding	35	premise	45
pre-Celtic	27b	preparatory	33c
precious	13	prepare	7
precipice	12	prepay	4a

proprietor	40c	psychos	18b
propyl	14c	psychosis	8a
propylene	8a	psychosis *pl* -oses	22d
pros	18b	ptarmigan	15a
prosaic	4a	pterodactyl	8a
prosecutor	40c	pterodactyl	14c
proselytize	8a	pterodactyl	15a
prospector	40c	pterosaur	15a
protasis *pl* -ases	22d	Ptolemy	15a
protectant	31	public-address system	27c
protector	40c	publicist	25b
protein	4b, 6a	publicity	25b
Protestant	31	publicize	25b
protocol	3b	puddle	3b
prototype	8a	puddly	46b
protuberance	30c	puerile	4e
protuberant	31	puerilely	46a
proud	5c	pugnacious	13
prove	2c	puissance	8e
provenance	30c	puissance	30c
proverb	27a	puissant	31
providence	30c	pullover n.	27e
provident	31	pulmonary	33a
providential	13c	pulse	3d
province	30d	pumice	12
provisory	33c	pummel	3b
provisos or -oes	18c	pummelled	24b
prow	5c	pummelling	24b
prowess	14a	puncher	40f
prowl	5c	punch-up n.	27a
prudent	31	punctual	13e
prurience	30c	punctuation	13e
prurient	31	puncture	40f
psalm	15a	pupil	3b
psalter	2d	puppet	7
pseudo	15a	puppy *pl* -ppies	19
pseudonym	4e	purchase	9c
pseudonym	8a	pure	4e
pseudonym	15a	purée	4e
psoriasis	15a	purgatory	33c
psychedelic	8a	purloin	5b
psychedelic	15a	purple	3b
psychiatric	8a	purply	46b
psychiatrist	8a	purpose	9c
psychiatrist	15a	purse	9c
psychical	8a	pursuant	31
psychoanalyse	8a	pursue	4e
psychoanalyse	45	pursuer	4e
psychology	8a	pursuit	4e

Q

quack	2a
quad	2a
quadrangle	2a
quadrangle	3b
quadrant	2a
quadrant	31
quadraphonic or quadrophonic	2a
quadratic	2a
quadrille	2a
quadruped	2a
quadruple	3b
quadruple	2a
quaff	2a
quaff	14a
quagmire	2a
quail	4a
quaint	4a
qualified	26
qualify	2a
quality	2a
quality pl -ties	19
quandary	33a
quangos	18b
quantify	2a
quantity	2a
quantity pl -ties	19
quantum	2a
quantum pl -ta	22d
quarantine	9a
quarrel	3b
quarrel	9a
quarrelled	24b
quarrelling	24b
quarry	9a
quarry pl -rries	19
quart	9a
quarter	9a
quarterage	9a
quarterly	9a
quarterly	8e
quartet	9a
quarto	9a
quartos	18b
quartz	9a
quash	2a
quay	4b
quay	8e
queasy	4b
queen	4b
queer	4b
quencher	40f
query pl -ries	19
question	8e
queue	4e
queue	4e
quibble	3b
quick	8e
quickie	8d
quiet	8e
quiff	8e
quiff	14a
quill	8e
quilt	8e
quince	8e
quince	30d
quintuple	3b
quintuplet	8e
quirk	8e
quit	8e
quiz	8e
quoin	5b
quoit	5b
quotation	8e
quotient	13c

R

recoilless	14b	re-endow	27b
recommend	14	re-enforce	27b
recompense	30c	re-engage	27b
reconnoitre	5b	re-enlarge	27b
reconnoitre	40d	re-enlighten	27b
reconsign	4c	re-enter	27b
record-changer	1e	re-equip	27b
recorder	7	re-erect	27b
recount	7	re-establish	27b
recoup	4e	re-evaluate	27b
recourse	4d, 9d	re-examine	27b
recover	2c	re-exhibit	27b
recover (regain)	27b	re-experience	27b
re-cover (cover again)	27b	re-export	27b
recriminator	40c	refectory	33c
recriminatory	33c	refer	7
recruit	4e	referee	4b
rectangle	3b	reference	30c
rectangular	40e	referendum pl -dums or -da	22d
rectory pl -ries	19	referent	31
rectum pl -tums or -ta	22d	referral	3b
recumbence	30c	reflection or (rare) reflexion	38
recuperator	40c	reformatory pl -ries	19
recurrence	30c	reformatory	33c
recurrent	31	refrain	4a
recusant	31	refrigerator	40c
redactor	40c	refuel	4e
redeem	4b	refugee	4b
redesign	4c	refuse vb.	7
redhead	27e	regal	3b
red-headed	27e	regard	7
redolence	30c	regime	4b
redolent	31	regiment	12
reducible	28g	region	12
redundant	31	register	12
re-echo	27b	regress	14a
reed (plant)	4b	regression	14b
re-edit	27b	regret	7
re-educate	27b	regular	40e
reef	4b	regulatory	33c
reek	4b	regulus pl -luses or -li	22d
reel	4b	rehearsal	3b
re-elect	27b	rehearse	9c
re-embark	27b	reign	4a, 6b
re-emerge	27b	reign	15a
re-emphasize	27b	rein	4a, 6b
re-employ	27b	reindeer	6b
re-enact	27b	reject	12
re-enclose	27b	rejoice	5b

rejuvenate	2c	reproducible	28g
relaxant	31	reprove	2c
relay	4a	repugnant	31
release	4b	repulse	3d
relent	7	require	8e
reliant	31	requite	8e
relief	4b	reroute	4e
relieve	4b	resalable or resaleable	28e
religion	12	rescind	15
reliquary pl -ries	19	rescue	4e
reliquary	33a	rescuer	4e
reluctant	31	researcher	40f
rely	7	resemblance	30c
remain	4a	reservoir	8e
remedy pl -dies	19	residence	30c
remembrance	30c	resident	31
remissible	28h	residential	13c
remission	14b	residue	4e
remittance	30c	resign	4c
remnant	31	resign	15a
remonstrance	30c	resilient	31
removal	3b	resistance	30c
remove	2c	resistant	31
renal	3b	resistible	28h
renew	4e	resistor	40a, 40c
renovator	40c	resonance	30c
renown	5c	resonant	31
repair	4a	respirator	40c
repay	4a	respiratory	33c
repeat	4b	resplendent	31
repel	14a	respondent	31
repellent	31	responsible	28h
repentance	30c	respray	4a
repentant	31	restaurant	31
repercussion	14b	restrain	4a
repertory	33c	restructure	1d
repetitious	13	resultant	31
replaceable	28d	resurgence	30c
reply	7	resuscitator	40c
report	7	retail	4a
repository pl -ries	19	retain	4a
repository	33c	retaliatory	33c
reprehensible	28h	retardant	31
reprehensory	33c	retch	11
repression	14b	reticence	30b
reprieve	6a	retinal	3b
reproach	4d	retoucher	40f
reproacher	40f	retraceable	28d
reprobacy	34	retractable or retractible	28h

retractor	40c	rictus *pl* -tus or -tuses	22d
retreat	4b	ridable or rideable	28e
retrocede	35	riddance	30c
retroflexion or retroflection	38	riddle	3b
reveal	4b	ridge	11
reveille	2b	riffle	3b
revel	3b	riffraff	14a
revelled	24b	rifle	3b
revelling	24b	right	4c
revelry *pl* -ries	19	rigour	40e
revenge	12	rind	1a
revenue	4e	rinsable or rinsible	28h
reverberant	31	rinse	30d
reverent	31	riot	4c
reverential	13c	ripple	3b
reversible	28h	ripply	46b
revertible	28h	risottos	18b
review	4e	rivalled	24b
revile	7	rivalling	24b
revise	45	rivalry *pl* -ries	19
revisory	33c	river	14
revolt	1a	roach	4d
revolting	1a	road	4d
revue	4e	roadie	8d
reward	9a	roadroller	27e
rhapsody	15a	roam	4d
rheo-	15a	roar	4d, 9d
rheostat	15a	roast	4d
rhesus	15a	robbery *pl* -ries	19
rhetorical	15a	robbery	33b
rheumatism	15a	rock	11
rheumatoid	5b	rocker	11
rhinal	3b	rocket	7
rhinitis	15a	rockhopper	27e
rhinoceros	15a	rodent	31
rhizo-	15a	rodeos	18b
rhododendron	15a	roe	4d
rhombus	15a	rogue	15
rhombus *pl* -buses or -bi	22d	roister	5b
rhubarb	15a	roll	1
rhyme	15a	roller	1
rhythm	8a	rollick	25b
rhythm	15a	rolling	1
rhythmicity	25b	romanticism	25b
rib-tickler	27e	romanticize	25b
rice	12	Romeos	18b
rich	11	rondeau *pl* -x	4d, 22a
rickshaw	5a	rood	4e
ricocheted or ricochetted	24b	roof	4e

roofs	17	row (quarrel)	5c
rook	2c	rowan	4d
rookie	8d	rowlock	4d
room	4e	royal	5b
roost	4e	royalty *pl* -ties	19
root	4e	-rrhoea	15a
ropable or ropeable	28e	rubbly	46b
rosary *pl* -ries	19	rubefy	7
rostrum *pl* -trums or -tra	22d	ruby	7
rotatory	33c	ruby *pl* -bies	19
rotl	3b	rudimentary	33a
rottenness	14b	rue	4e
Rottweiler	4c	rueful	4e
rouble	3b	ruer	4e
rouble	4e	ruffle	3b
rouge	4e	rule	47
rough	2c	rumble	3b
rough	15b	ruminant	31
roughage	15b	rumour	40e
roulade	4e	rumple	3b
rouleau *pl* -x or -s	22a	rumply	46b
roulette	4e	rumpus *pl* -puses	22d
round	5c	runway	4a
roundabout	27d	rupture	40f
roundel	3b	rural	3b
rouse	5c	Russian	13d
rout	5c	rusticity	25b
route	4e	rustle	3b
routine	4e	rustle	15
routine	4b	rye	4c
roux	4e	rye	8a
row (boat)	4d		

S

sab**re**	40d
sacr**al**	3b
sacrifi**ceable**	28d
sacril**egious**	7
sad**dle**	3b
safar**i**	8
safe-blower	27e
safeguard	15
saf**es**	17
saga**ci**ous	13
s**ai**d	8b, 26
s**ai**l	4a
sai**lless**	14b
s**ai**nt	4a
sala**ci**ous	13
salary *pl* -r**ies**	19
sal**eable**	28e
sal**eable**	28a
sal**low**	4d
sal**mon**	15
s**al**t	2d
saltpet**re**	40d
salut**ary**	33a
salv**age**	11
salv**os** or -**oes**	18c
sam**ple**	3b
sanatori**um** *pl* -ri**ums** or -ri**a**	22d
sand**al**	3b
sand hopper	27e
san**d**wich	15
san**gu**ine	8e
sanit**ary**	33a
sapien**ti**al	13c
sa**pp**hire	1e
sarcophag**us** *pl* -g**i** or -gus**es**	22d
sardi**ne**	4b
sardoni**cism**	25b
sar**i**	8
sarn**ie**	8d
satch**el**	3b
sat**elli**te	1e
satisfac**tory**	33c
satis**fies**	4c

satisfy	4c
Saturd**ay**	4a
sat**yr**	8a
sat**yr**ic	8a
sa**u**ce	5a
sa**u**cer	5a
sau**cy**	34
sa**u**na	5a
sa**u**nter	5a
sa**u**sage	2d
sav**able** or sav**eable**	28e
sav**age**	11
savi**our**	40e
sav**our**	40e
s**aw**	5a
s**aw**n	5a
saxo**ph**one	15a
s**ay**	4a
scabb**ard**	40e
sca**ff**old	1a
sc**al**d	2d
scalpel	3b
scand**al**	3b
scandalm**o**nger	2c
scar**ce**	12
scar**city**	12
scarec**row**	4d
scarem**o**nger	2c
scar**fs** or scar**ves**	17
s**ce**ne	12
s**ce**nery	12
scen**ery**	33b
s**ce**nt	12
s**ce**nt	15
scepti**cism**	25b
scept**re**	40d
s**ch**edule	13
s**ch**eme	15a
scherz**os** or scherzi	18b
s**ch**ist	13
schiz**os**	18b
s**ch**malz	13
s**ch**napps	13
s**ch**nozzle	13
schol**ar**	40e
s**ch**olarship	15a
s**ch**ool	4e
s**ch**ool	15a
s**ch**ooner	15a

schuss	13	seam	4b
schwa	13	sear	4b
science	6a	search	9c
scimitar	40e	searcher	40f
scintillate	12	season	4b
scissor	40c	seasonal	3b
scoff	14a	seat	4b
scold	1a	secession	14b
scoop	4e	secrecy	34
scoot	4e	secretary *pl* -ries	19
scorcher	40f	secretary	33a
score	4d	Secretary-of-State's	27e
scoundrel	3b	secure	4e
scoundrel	5c	security *pl* -ties	19
scour	5c	sedentary	33a
scout	5c	sedimentary	33a
scowl	5c	seditious	13
scrabble	3b	seducible or seduceable	28g
scramble	3b	see	4b
scrapie	8	seed	4b
scratcher	40f	seed	35
scrawl	5a	seek	4b
scrawny	5a	seem	4b
scream	4b	seen	4b
screech	4b	seep	4b
screecher	40f	seepage	11
screen	4b	seer	4b
screw	4e	seesaw	5a
scribal	3b	segregator	40c
scribble	3b	seismic	4c, 6b
scribbly	46b	seismograph	15a
scrimmage	11	seize	4b, 6a
scriptural	3b	seizure	40g
scripture	40f	selector	40c
scroll	1	self-abandonment	27d
scrotum *pl* -ta or -tums	22d	self-abasement	27d
scrounge	5c	self-abhorrence	27d
scrumptious	13	self-abnegation	27d
scruple	3b	self-absorbed	27d
scuffle	3b	self-abuse	27d
scullery *pl* -ries	19	self-accusation	27d
sculptor	40c	self-acting	27d
sculpture	40f	self-action	27d
sculpturesquely	47	self-addressed	27d
scuttle	3b	self-adhesive	27d
scythe	8a	self-adjusted	27d
sea	4b	self-administered	27d
seaborn	27f	self-admiration	27d
seal	4b	self-advertisement	27d

self-aligning	27d	**self**-effacement	27d
self-analysis	27d	**self**-elected	27d
self-appointed	27d	**self**-employed	27d
self-approval	27d	**self**-enclosed	27d
self-assertion	27d	**self**-esteem	27d
self-assurance	27d	**self**-evident	27d
self-aware	27d	**self**-examination	27d
self-catering	27d	**self**-exertion	27d
self-censored	27d	**self**-existence	27d
self-censorship	27d	**self**-expanding	27d
self-certification	27d	**self**-expression	27d
self-cleaning	27d	**self**-fertile	27d
self-closing	27d	**self**-financed	27d
self-coloured	27d	**self**-focusing	27d
self-command	27d	**self**-fulfilling	27d
self-commitment	27d	**self**-hate	27d
self-complacent	27d	**self**heal	27d
self-conceit	27d	**self**-help	27d
self-concept	27d	**self**hood	27d
self-condemnation	27d	**self**-hypnosis	27d
self-confessed	27d	**self**-image	27d
self-confidence	27d	**self**-important	27d
self-congratulation	27d	**self**-imposed	27d
self-conscious	27d	**self**-induced	27d
self-constituted	27d	**self**-indulgence	27d
self-contained	27d	**self**-inflicted	27d
self-contempt	27d	**self**-interest	27d
self-content	27d	**self**ish	27d
self-contradiction	27d	**self**-judgment	27d
self-control	27d	**self**-knowledge	27d
self-convicted	27d	**self**less	27d
self-correcting	27d	**self**-loader	27d
self-created	27d	**self**-love	27d
self-critical	27d	**self**-made	27d
self-deceit	27d	**self**-motivated	27d
self-deception	27d	**self**-murder	27d
self-defeating	27d	**self**-mutilation	27d
self-defence	27d	**self**-operating	27d
self-delusion	27d	**self**-opinionated	27d
self-denial	27d	**self**-ordained	27d
self-dependence	27d	**self**-perpetuating	27d
self-destroying	27d	**self**-pity	27d
self-determined	27d	**self**-pollination	27d
self-devotion	27d	**self**-portrait	27d
self-directed	27d	**self**-possessed	27d
self-discipline	27d	**self**-powered	27d
self-doubt	27d	**self**-praise	27d
self-drive	27d	**self**-prepared	27d
self-educated	27d	**self**-preservation	27d

self-produced	27d	sens**ory**	33c
self-promotion	27d	sent**ence**	30c
self-propelled	27d	senten**tious**	13
self-protection	27d	senti**ent**	31
self-punishment	27d	sentin**el**	3b
self-questioning	27d	sentry *pl* -r**ies**	19
self-raising	27d	septi**city**	25b
self-realization	27d	septu**ple**	3b
self-regard	27d	sepulch**re**	40d
self-regression	27d	sepul**ture**	40f
self-regulating	27d	sequ**ence**	30c
self-reliance	27d	sequen**tial**	13c
self-repeating	27d	se**qu**in	8e
self-reproach	27d	seraph *pl* -s or -**im**	22b
self-reproof	27d	serf	9c
self-respect	27d	ser**fs**	17
self-restraint	27d	serge**ant**	31
self-revealing	27d	ser**i**al	4b
self-righteous	27d	ser**mon**	9c
self-rule	27d	ser**pent**	9c
self-sacrifice	27d	ser**pent**	31
selfsame	27d	serv**able** or serv**eable**	28e
self-satisfaction	27d	serv**ant**	9c
self-sealing	27d	serv**ant**	31
self-seeking	27d	serve	9c
self-service	27d	ser**vice**	9c
self-starter	27d	ser**vice**	12
self-sufficient	27d	servi**ceable**	28d
self-tapping	27d	serviette	3a
self-taught	27d	serv**ile**	9c
self-torture	27d	servi**lely**	46a
self-trained	27d	se**ssion**	14b
self-will	27d	sett**ee**	4b
self-worth	27d	set**tle**	3b
sel**vage** or selve**dge**	11	settl**eable**	28e
sel**ves**	17	set**up**	27a
sembl**ance**	30c	seven**teen**	4b
semicircle	27d	sever**al**	3b
semicolon	27a	sever**ance**	30c
seminar**y** *pl* -r**ies**	19	**sew** (thread)	4d
semin**ary**	33a	sew**age**	11
semol**i**na	4b	sext**ant**	31
senat**e**	3a	sextu**ple**	3b
senat**or**	40c	shac**kle**	3b
seni**lely**	46a	shad**ow**	4d
seni**or**	4c	shak**able** or shak**eable**	28e
sensational	3b	shake-**up** n.	27a
se**nse**	30c	shall**ow**	4d
sensi**ble**	3b	sham**able** or sham**eable**	28e

shampoo	4e	shove	2c
shapable or shapeable	28e	shovel	2c
sharable or shareable	28e	shovel	3b
shareholder	1a	shovelled	24b
shashlik	25b	shovelling	24b
shavable or shaveable	28e	show	4d
shawl	5a	shower	5c
sheaf	4b	shrapnel	3b
shear (to clip)	4b	shrew	4e
sheath	4b	shriek	4b, 6a
sheaves	17	shrillness	14a
sheen	4b	shrinkage	11
sheep	4b	shrivel	3b
sheer (steep)	4b	shrivelled	24b
sheet	4b	shrivelling	24b
sheik or sheikh	4a, 6b	shudder	40b
shekel	3b	shuffle	3b
shellacked	25a	shuttle	3b
shell-less	27c	shyly	8c
shell-like	27c	shyness	8c
shelves	17	sibilant	31
shepherd	40e	sibyl	8a
sherd	40e	sick	11
sheriff	14a	sickle	3b
sherry pl -rries	19	sideboard	4d, 9d
shied	4c	sidle	3b
shield	4b, 6a	siege	4b, 6a
shingle	3b	sieve	2b, 6b
shingly	46b	sigh	4c
-ship	13	sight	4c
shipwreck	27d	sightseer	4b
shirk	9c	sign	3a, 4c
shirt	9c	sign	15a
shoal	4d	signal	3b
shoe	4e	signalled	24b
shoer	4e	signalling	24b
shook	2c	signatory	33c
shoot	4e	signature	3a
shopkeeper	4b	signature	40f
shopkeeper	27e	significance	30b, 30c
shopwalker	27e	silage	11
shopworker	27e	sild	1a
shore	4d	silence	30c
shortage	11	silent	31
shortie or -y	8d	silhouette	4e
short-range	1e	sillabub or syllabub	8a
should	2c	silos	18b
shoulder	4d	similar	40e
shout	5c	simile pl similies	3a, 7

smuggle	3b	solvent	31
snack	11	sombre	40d
snaffle	3b	sombreros	18b
snail	4a	some	2c
snatch	11	somebody	42
snatcher	40f	somehow	2c
sneak	4b	someone	42
sneaky	4b	somersault	5a
sneer	4b	something	27d
sneeze	4b	sometimes	2c
sniffle	3b	somewhere	2c
sniffly	46b	somnolence	30c
snitcher	40f	somnolent	31
snivel	3b	son	2c
snobbery	33b	songwriter	27e
snooker	4e	sonnet	7
snooze	4e	sonny	2c
snore	4d	soon	4e
snorkel	3b	soot	2c
snout	5c	soothsayer	4a
snow	4d	-sophy	15a
snowblower	27e	sopranos or soprani	18b
snuffle	3b	sorcerer	9c
snuggle	3b	sore	4d
soak	4d	sorrow	4d
soap	4d	sorry	9a
soar	4d, 9d	sortie	8
society	4c, 6a	sou	4e
socket	7	sough	15b
soddenness	14b	sought	15b
softie	8d	soul	4d
soil	5b	soulless	14b
solace	2f	sound	5c
solar	40e	sound mixer	27e
sold	1a	soup	4e
solder	1a	sour	5c
soldier	1a	source	4d, 9d
soldier	12	south	5c
solely	46a	southern	2c
solemnity or solemnness		souvenir	4e
or solemness	14b	sovereign	2b, 6b
solenoid	5b	sow (pig)	5c
solicitor	40c	sow (seed)	4d
solifluction or solifluxion	38	soy	5b
soliloquy *pl* -quies	19	soya	5b
solitary	33a	spacey	23
solos	18b	spacey	34
solstice	12	spaghetti	8
soluble	3b	spangle	3b

spangly	46b	spoilage	11
spaniel	3b	spoilt or spoiled	39
spare	4a	sponge	12
sparkle	3b	spoof	4e
sparrow	4d	spook	4e
spatial	13c	spool	4e
spatter	40b	spoon	4e
spawn	5a	spoor	4e
speak	4b	spot-welder	27e
spear	4b	spouse	5c
special	3b	spout	5c
speciality pl -ties	19	sprain	4a
species	6a	sprawl	5a
specificity	25b	spray	4a
specimen	12	spread	2b
specious	13	spree	4b
speckle	3b	sprinkle	3b
spectacle	3b	sprout	5c
spectacular	40e	spryly	8c
spectator	40c	spryness	8c
spectral	3b	spurt	9c
spectre	40d	sputum pl -ta	22d
spectrum pl -tra	22d	spy pl spies	19
speculum pl -la or -lums	22d	squabble	2a
speech	4b	squabble	3b
speed	4b	squabble	8e
speedway	4a	squad	2a
spelt or spelled	39	squaddie or squaddy	2a
spew	4e	squaddie or -y	8d
sphere	4b	squadron	2a
sphere	15a	squalid	2a
sphericity	25b	squall	14a
spheroid	5b	squander	2a
spheroidal	3b	square	9a
sphinx	15a	squash	2a
spicy	34	squat	2a
spillage	11	squatter	2a
spilt or spilled	39	squaw	5a
spinach	2b	squeak	4b
spinal	3b	squeal	4b
spindle	3b	squeamish	4b
spin-offs	21	squelcher	40f
spiral	3b	squib	8e
spiralled	24b	squid	8e
spiralling	24b	squiggle	3b
spittle	3b	squiggly	46b
spiv	3d	squint	8e
splendour	40e	squire	8e
spoil	5b	squirm	9c

squirm	8e	steerage	11
squirrel	3b	stein	4c
squirrel	8e	stem-winder	27e
squirt	9c	stencil	3b
stable	3b	stencilled	24b
stack	11	stencilling	24b
stadium	4b	stenography	15a
stadium pl -diums or -dia	22d	stepfather	27d
staffs or staves	17	stepmother	27d
stage	12	stereos	18b
stagnant	31	sterilely	46a
staid	4a	sternness	14b
staid adj.	8b	steroid	5b
stain	4a	stew	4e
stair	4a	stick-up n.	27a
stairway	4a	stifle	3b
stalely	46a	stilettos	18b
stallholder	1a	stillness	14a
standard	40e	stimulant	31
standoff	14a	stimulus pl -li	22d
stanza	45	stipple	3b
staple	3b	stipulatory	33c
starboard	9d	stir	9c
starcher	40f	stirrup	1e
startle	3b	stitch	11
statable or stateable	28e	stitcher	40f
stationary adj.	33a	stoat	4d
stationery n.	33b	stockpiler	27e
statistician	25b	stomach	2c
statuary	33a	stonable or stoneable	28e
statue	4e	stood	2c
statuesquely	47	stooge	4e
stature	40f	stook	4e
status pl -tuses	22d	stool	4e
statutory	33c	stoop	4e
staunch	5a	stoppage	11
stauncher	40f	storage	11
stay	4a	story pl -ries	19
stayed vb.	8b	stout	5c
steady	2b	stow	4d
steak	4a	stowage	11
steal	4b	straddle	3b
stealth	2b	straggle	3b
steam	4b	straggly	46b
steed	4b	straight	4a
steel	4b	straight	15b
steep	4b	strain	4a
steeple	3b	strange	1e
steer	4b	strangle	3b

stranglehold	1a	subsistent	31
stratum *pl* -ta or -tums	22d	substance	30c
stratus *pl* -ti	22d	subtle	3b
straw	5a	subtlety *pl* -ties	19
strawberry	5a	subtly	46b
stray	4a	subway	4a
streak	4b	succeed	4b
stream	4b	succeed	35
street	4b	success	14a
stretch	11	succour	40e
stretcher	40f	succulence	30c
strew	4e	succulent	31
stricture	40f	succumb	15
strident	31	such	11
strigil	3b	suckle	3b
stroll	1	sucre	40d
stronghold	1a	suddenness	14b
strophe	1c	sue	4e
structure	40f	suede	4a
strudel	3b	suet	4e
struggle	3b	sufferance	30c
strychnine	8a	sufficient	6a
stubble	3b	suffix	27a
stubbly	46b	suffixion	38
stubbornness	14b	sugar	13
stuccoes or -os	18c	suggestible	28h
stuck	11	suicidal	3b
student	31	suicide	12
studios	18b	suit	4e
-stuff	14a	suite	4b
stumble	3b	sullenness	14b
stupefy	7	summary	33a
stupid	7	summing-up n.	27a
sturdy	9c	Sunday	4a
sty *pl* sties	19	superlative	3d
style	8a	superrealism	14b
stylus *pl* -li or -luses	22d	superrefine	14b
subdue	4e	superreliance	14b
subheading	27a	superrespectable	14b
subject	12	superrestriction	14b
submarine	4b	superrich	14b
submersible	28h	supersede	35
submission	14b	superstitious	13
subsequent	31	supervise	45
subservient	31	supple	3b
subsidence	30c	supple	46b
subsidiary	33a	supplely	46b
subsidy *pl* -dies	19	suppliant	31
subsistence	30c	supply	46b

suppose	1e	swanherd	40e
suppository	33c	swannery	33b
suppressible	28h	swap	2a
suppression	14b	sward (grass)	9a
supremacy	34	swarm	9a
supremos	18b	swarthy	9a
sure	4e	swathable or swatheable	28e
sure	13	sway	4a
sure	13	swear	4a
surely	13	sweat	2b
sureness	13	sweep	4b
surety	13	sweet	4b
surety	13	sweetie	8d
surface	2f	swept	39
surface	9c	swerve	9c
surfboard	9d	swindle	3b
surfeit	2b, 6b	swineherd	40e
surgeon	9c	swingeing	23
surgery	9c	swinish	14d
surmise	45	swirl	9c
surname	9c	switch	11
surpass	14a	switchboard	4d
surplice	12	switcher	40f
surplus *pl* -luses	22d	swivel	3b
surprise	45	swivelled	24b
surrealism	14b	swivelling	24b
surrender	14b	swizzle	3b
surreptitious	14b	swollenness	14b
surreptitious	13	swoon	4e
surrogate	14b	swoop	4e
surround	1e	sword (weapon)	9b
surround	14b	sworn	9b
surveillance	6b	sycamore	8a
surveillance	30c	sycophant	8a
surveillant	31	sycophant	15a
survivor	9c	syllable	8a
susceptible	28h	syllabub or sillabub	8a
suspendible or suspensible	28h	syllabus	8a
suspense	30c	syllabus *pl* -buses or -bi	22d
suspensory	33c	sylph	8a
suspicious	13	sylvan	8a
sustain	4a	sylvan or silvan	8d
sustenance	30c	symbiotic	8a
suture	40f	symbol	3b
swaddle	3b	symbol	8a
swain	4a	symbolled	24b
swallow	4d	symbolling	24b
swamp	2a	symmetrical	8a
swan	2a	symmetry	8a

sympathetic	8a	synod	8a
sympathy	8a	synodal	3b
symphony	8a	synonymous	8a
symposium *pl* -siums or -sia	22d	synopsis	8a
symptom	8a	synopsis *pl* -pses	22d
synagogal	3b	synoptic	8a
synagogue	8a	syntactic	8a
synagogue	15	syntax	8a
synapse	8a	synthesis *pl* -eses	22d
synchronicity	25b	synthesize	8a
synchronize	8a	synthetic	8a
synchronous	8a	syphon or siphon	8a
syncopation	8a	syringe	8a
syncretize	8a	syrup	8a
syndicate	8a	system	8a
syndrome	8a		

T

tabernacle	3b
tablature	40f
table	1c
tableau pl -x or -s	4d, 22a
tabloid	5b
taboo or tabu	3d
tabular	40e
tachograph	15a
tackle	3b
tactician	13
tactician	25b
tail	4a
tailless	14b
tailor	4a
taint	4a
takable or takeable	28e
takeover n.	27e
take over	27g
take-up n.	27a
talent	31
talk	15
talkie	8d
tallness	14a
tallow	4d
tambourine	4b
tangent	1e
tangerine	1e
tangible	28h
tangle	3b
tangly	46b
tangos	18b
tannage	11
tansy	34
tantamount	5c
target	7
tariff	14a
tarmacked	25a
taskmaster	27e
tassel	3b
tasselled	24b
tasselling	24b
tattle	3b
taught	5a

taught	15b
taunt	5a
taut	5a
tautological	5a
tawdry	5a
tawny	5a
taxi	8
taxonomy pl -mies	19
tea	4b
teach	4b
teacher	40f
team	4b
tear (cloth)	4a
tear (drop)	4b
tear-jerker	27e
tease	4b
teasel, teazel or teazle	3b
teat	4b
technician	25b
technocracy	34
tee	4b
teem	4b
teenager	27e
teeth	4b
teetotal	4b
telegram	7
telegraph	15a
telephone	15a
telescope	7
televise	45
television	7
temperance	30c
temperature	40f
temple	3b
temporal	3b
temporary	33a
tempos or tempi	18b
tenacious	13
tenant	31
tendentious	13
tennis	1e
tense	13a
tense	30c
tensible	28h
tensilely	46a
tension	13a
tension	13a, b
tentacle	3b
tenure	40g

tepee	4b	thieve	4b
tepefy	7	thievery	33b
tepid	7	thigh	4c
term	9c	thimble	3b
terminal	3b	thinness	14b
terminate	9c	third	9c
terminus	9c	thirsty	9c
termite	9c	thirteen	4b
tern	9c	thistle	3b
terpsichore	15a	thistle	15
terrace	2f	thorough	2c
terrace	1c	thorough	15b
terrapin	1e	though	4d
terrestrial	1e	though	15b
terrible	28h	thought	15b
terrific	1e	thousand	5c
territory pl -ries	19	thread	2b
territory	33c	threat	2b
terror	1e	threw	4e
terse	9c	throat	4d
testacy	34	thrombosis pl -oses	22d
testicle	3b	throttle	3b
testis pl -tes	22d	through	4e
tetchy	11	through	15b
textural	3b	throw	4d
texture	40f	thumb	15
thatch	11	thurible	28h
thatcher	40f	Thursday	4a
thaw	5a	thwart	9a
theatre	40d	thyme	8a
thee	4b	thyroid	5b
their	4a	thyroid	8a
theocentricity	25b	ticket	7
theocracy (government)	34	tickle	3b
theocrasy (religion)	34	tickly	46b
theophany	15a	tidal	3b
theophany pl -nies	19	tie	4c
theory pl -ries	19	tiebreaker	27e
theory	33c	tied	4c
therapeutic	4e	tier	4b
therapy pl -pies	19	tight	4c
there	4a	tights	4c
thermae	22d	tillage	11
thermal	3b	timbre	40d
thesaurus pl -ri or -ruses	22d	timeserver	27e
thesis pl -eses	22, 22d	timeworker	27e
they	4a	tincture	40f
thickie or -y	8d	tingle	3b
thief	4b, 6a	tingly	46b

tinkle	3b	took	2c
tinkly	46b	tool	4e
tinsel	3b	toot	4e
tinselled	24b	tooth	4e
tinselling	24b	toothache	27d
tip-off	14a	toothbrush	27d
tipple	3b	toothpaste	27d
tissue	4e	tootle	3b
title	3b	topfull	14a
titleholder	1a	topiary	33a
to	4e	topple	3b
toad	4d	tore	4d
toast	4d	torpedoes	18a
toasty or -ie	8d	torrefy	7
tobacconist	1e	torrent	31
tobaccos or -oes	18c	torrid	7
today	4a	torsos or torsi	18b
toddle	3b	tortoise	5b
toe	4d	torture	40f
toehold	1a	totalled	24b
toffee	7	totalling	24b
tofu	3d	touch	2c
toggle	3b	toucher	40f
toil	5b	tough	2c
toilet	5b	tough	15b
toiletry pl -ries	19	tour	4e
told	1a	tousle	3b
tolerance	30a, 30c	tout	5c
tolerant	30a, 31	tow	4d
toll	1	towards	9a
tomahawk	5a	towel	3b
tomatoes	18a	towelled	24b
tomb	15	towelling	24b
tomfoolery	4e	tower	5c
tomorrow	4d	town	5c
ton	2c	towpath	4d
tonal	3b	toxicant	31
tongue	2c	toxoid	5b
tongue	15	toy	5b
tonicity	25b	traceable	28d
tonight	27a	tractor	40c
tonnage	11	tradable or tradeable	28e
tonne	2c	trade-off	14a
tonneau pl -s or -x	22a	traditional	3b
tonsil	3b	traducible	28g
tonsillitis	14d	trafficked	25a
tonsure	13	trafficker	25a
tonsure	40g	trafficking	25a
too	4e	tragedy pl -dies	19

trail	4a	treasure	13
trailer	40b	treasure	40g
train	4a	treat	4b
trait	4a	treatise	4b
traitor	4a	treatyless	8c
trajectory	12	treble	3b
trajectory	33c	treble	1c
trammel	3b	tree	4b
trammelled	24b	treehopper	27e
trammelling	24b	tremble	3b
trample	3b	tremulant	31
trampoline	4b	trench	13e
trance	12	trenchant	31
trannie or -y	8d	trencher	40f
tranquil	8e	trespass	14a
tranquillity	14d, 24b	trestle	3b
transactional	3b	trestle	15
transceiver	6a	triangle	3b
transcendence	30c	triangular	40e
transcendent	31	tribal	3b
transference	30c	tribunal	3b
transfixion	38	trickle	3b
transgression	14b	tricycle	3b
transhumant	31	trident	31
transient	31	tried	4c
transistor	40c	trifle	3b
transitional	3b	trilby pl -bies	19
transitory	33c	trimestral	3b
transmissible	28h	trio	4b
transmission	14b	triple	3b
transmit	14b	triple	1c
transparent	31	triumph	15a
transship or tranship	14b	triumphal	3b
trapezium pl -ziums or -zia	22d	troll	1
trauma	5a	troop	4e
travel	3b	trophy pl -phies	19
travelled	24b	trouble	3b
travelling	24b	trouble	2c
travelogue	15	trough	15b
trawl	5a	trounce	5c
tray	4a	troupe	4e
treachery	33b	trousers	5c
treacle	3b	trousseau pl -x or -s	4d, 22a
treacle	4b	trout	5c
treacly	46b	trowel	3b
tread	2b	trowel	5c
treadle	3b	trowelled	24b
treason	4b	trowelling	24b
treasure	2b	troy	5b

truant	31	turn-up n.	27a
truculence	30c	turpentine	9c
truculent	31	turquoise	5b
trudge	11	turret	7
true	47	turtle	3b
true	4e	tussle	3b
truffle	3b	tutelage	11
truly	47	tutu	3d
trumpet	7	tuxedos	18b
trundle	3b	twaddle	3b
trustee	4b	tweak	4b
try pl tries	19	tweed	4b
tubal	3b	tweet	4b
tubercular	40e	tweezers	4b
tubular	40e	twice	12
Tuesday	4a	twiddle	3b
Tuesday	4e	twinkle	3b
tulip	13e	twitch	11
tumble	3b	twitcher	40f
tumbler	40b	two	15
tumefy	7	twofold	1a
tumid	7	tycoon	8a
tummy pl -mmies	19	tying	26
tumour	40e	tympanum pl -nums or -na	22d
tumulus pl -li	22d	tympany	8a
tunable or tuneable	28e	typecaster	27e
tunnel	3b	typesetter	27e
tunnelled	24b	typewriter	27e
tunnelling	24b	typhoid	5b
turban	9c	typhoid	8a
turbine	9c	typhoon	8a
turbulence	30c	typhus	8a
turbulent	31	typos	18b
-ture	13e	tyrannical	1e
turfs or turves	17	tyranny	8a
turmoil	5b	tyranny pl -nnies	19
turn	9c	tyrant	8a
turnip	9c	tyrant	31
turnover n.	27e	tyre	4c
turn over	27g	tyre	8a
turntable	27d	tyros	18b

U

unregenerate	48b
unreplaceable	28d
unruly	47
unsaleable	28e
unsatisfactory	33c
unsaturation	48b
unscrupulosity	48b
unseen	4b
unshakable or unshakeable	28e
unsolvable	48c
unsophistication	48b
unsubstantiality or insubstantiality	48b
unsure	4e
unsuscebtible	48b
unthinkability	48b
until	3b
untold	1a
untoward	9a
unusual	4e
unwise	45
unwrap	15
up	27a

uphold	1a
upkeep	4b
upper	24a
upright	4c
uproar	4d, 9d
ups-and-downs	21
upsetting	24b
upside-down	27f
upstairs	27h
upstream	27h
uptown	27h
upwind	27h
urge	9c
urgent	9c
urinal	3b
usable or useable	28e
usage	11
usual	4e
utensil	3b
uterus pl -ri	22d
uvula	2c
uvular	40e

V

vacancy *pl* -cies	19
vaccination	1e
vacuum *pl* -cuums or -cua	22d
vaginal	3b
vagrant	31
vague	15
vaguely	47
vain	4a
valance	30c
valiant	31
valleys	19
valour	40e
valuable	3h
value	4e
valuer	4e
valve	3d
vandal	3b
vanilla	1e
vanish	14d
vanity or vainness	14b
vanquish	8e
vantage	11
vapour	40e
variance	30c
variant	31
vascular	40e
vase	4a
vault	2d, 5a
vaunt	5a
veal	4b
vegetable	7
veggie	8d
vehement	31
vehicle	3b
veil	4a, 6b
veiling	24
veilless	14b
vein	4a, 6b
velvet	7
venal	3b
vendor	40a
veneer	4b
vengeance	30c

ventilator	40c
ventricle	3b
ventriloquist	8e
venture	40f
veracious (honest)	13
verb	9c
verbal	3b
verdant	31
verdict	9c
verdure	40g
verge	9c
verger	9c
verified	26
vermin	9c
vernal	3b
versatilely	46a
verse	9c
vertebral	3b
vertex *pl* -texes or -tices	22d
vertical	9c
vertigoes or vertigines	18a
vessel	3b
vesture	40f
vetoer	4d
vexatious	13
viaduct	4c
vibrant	31
vicar	40e
vicarage	11
viceroy	5b
vicinity	12
vicious	13
victory *pl* -ries	19
victory	33c
victualled	24b
victualling	24b
videos	18b
view	4e
viewfinder	27e
viewpoint	27d
vigil	3b
vigilant	31
vigour	40e
vilely	46a
village	11
villain	1e
vincible	28h
vinery	33b
viniculture	40f

vint**age**	11	vo**gue**	15
vin**yl**	8a, 14c	vo**gue**ing	23
vi**o**la	4c	v**oi**ce	5b
vi**o**late	4c	voice-over n.	27e
vio**lence**	30c, 31	v**oi**d	5b
vio**lent**	31	volcan**oes** or **-os**	18c
vi**o**linist	24b	v**ol**t	1a
vira**goes** or **-os**	18c	v**ol**tage	1a
vir**al**	3b	vol**tage**	11
vir**g**in	9c	volu**ble**	3b
vir**g**inal	3b	volunt**ary**	33a
vir**t**ual	9c	volun**teer**	4b
vir**t**ual	13e	vomit**us** pl -tus**es**	22d
vir**tue**	4e	v**oo**d**oo**	4e
vir**tue**	9c	vora**ci**ous (greedy)	13
virtuos**os** or virtuosi	18b	vort**ex** pl -tex**es** or -ti**ces**	22d
virul**ent**	31	vou**cher**	5c
vir**us** pl -rus**es**	22d	vou**cher**	40f
vi**s**count	15	v**ow**	5c
visc**us** pl visc**era**	22d	vow**el**	3b
vis**ible**	28h	vow**el**	5c
visit**or**	40c	vo**y**age	5b
viticul**ture**	40f	vulner**able**	28b
viva**ci**ous	13	vul**ture**	40f
vocabul**ary**	33a	v**ying**	26
vocation**al**	3b		

W

wad	2a
wadding	2a
waddle	3b
waddle	2a
waddly	46b
wadi	2a
waffle	2a
waffle	3b
waffly	46b
waft	2a
wag	2a
wage	12
waggle	2a
waggle	3b
waggly	46b
wagon or waggon	2a
waif	4a
wail	4a
waist	4a
waistcoat	27d
wait	4a
waitress	4a
waive	4a
walk	15
walkie-talkie	8
walkie-talkie	27d
walkover n.	27e
wallaby pl -bies	19
wallah	2a
wallet	2a
wall-less	27c
wall-like	27c
wallop	2a
wallow	2a
wallow	4d
wally	2a
walrus pl -ruses or -rus	22d
waltz	2d
waltz	2a
wan	2a
wand	2a
wander	2a
wangle	2a

wangle	3b
wanness	14b
want	2a
wanton	2a
wantonness	14b
warble	9a
ward	9a
warden	9a
warder	9a
wardrobe	9a
warehouse	27d
wares	9a
warfare	9a
warhead	9a
warlock	9a
warlord	9a
warm	9a
warmonger	2c
warning	9a
warp	9a
warrant	9d
warrant	31
warren	9a
warrior	9a
wart	9a
was	2a
wash	2a
washery	33b
washing-up n.	27a
wasp	2a
wastage	11
waste	1c
wastrel	3b
watch	2a
watch	11
watcher	40f
water	9a
watt	2a
wattle	3b
wattle	2a
wax	2a
way	4a
waylay	4a
weak	4b
wealth	2b
wean	4b
weapon	2b
wear	4a
weary	4b

weasel	3b	wheyey	23
weather	2b	which	11
weave	4b	whiffle	3b
wedge	11	while	15
Wednesday	4a	whimper	15
weed	4b	whine	15
weedkiller	27e	whinny *pl* -nnies	19
week	4b	whip	15
weekend	27d	whirl	15
weep	4b	whisk	15
weevil	4b	whisker	15
weigh	4a	whisper	15
weigh	15b	whistle	3b
weight	4a, 6b	whistle	15
weight	15b	whittle	3b
weir	4b, 6a	who	15
weird	4b	whoever	15
weird	6a	whole	15
welcher	40f	whole	46a
welcome	14a	wholly	1
welder	40b	wholly	46a
welfare	14a	whoop	4e
well-aimed	27f	whooping-cough	15
well-bred	27f	whose	15
well-liked	27c	why	15
well-loved	27c	wicket	7
well-off	14a	widget	11
wencher	40f	widow	4d
whack	2a	wield	4b, 6a
whale	15	wiggle	3b
wham	2a	wiggly	46b
wharf	9a	wild	1a
wharves or wharfs	17	wilful	14a
what	2a	willie	8d
whatever	15	willow	4d
wheat	4b	wimple	3b
wheedle	3b	wince	30d
wheedle	4b	wincey	34
wheel	4b	wincher	40f
wheelbarrow	4d	wind (breeze)	1a
wheelie	8d	wind (coil)	1a
wheelwright	4c	windfall	14a
wheeze	4b	winding-up n.	27a
when	15	window	4d
whenever	15	winery	33b
where	15	winkle	3b
wherever	15	winnow	4d
whether	15	wise	45
whey	4a	wiseacre	40d

witch	11	worshipped	24b
witchery	33b	worshipper	24b
withdrawnness	14b	worshipping	24b
withhold	1a	wort	9b
witness	14a	worth	9b
wives	17	worthy	9b
wizard	40e	would	2c
woad	4d	wound (coiled)	5c
wobble	3b	wound (hurt)	4e
wobbly	46b	wow	5c
woe	4d	wrack	15
woggle	3b	wraith	15
wold	1a	wrangle	3b
woman	2c	wrap	15
womb	1	wrapover n.	27e
womb	4e	wrath	15
womb	15	wreak	4b
women	2b	wreak	15
won	2c	wreath	4b
wonder	2c	wreath	15
wonderful	2c	wren	15
wondrous	41	wrest	15
wont	1	wrestle	3b
won't	1	wrestle	15
woo	4e	wretch	11
wood	2c	wretch	15
woodcarver	27e	wriggle	3b
woodcutter	24b	wriggly	46b
woodcutter	27e	wright	4c
wooden	39a	wring	15
woodenness	14b	wrinkle	3b
woodworker	27e	wrinkle	15
woolgrower	27e	wrist	15
woollen	24a	writ	15
woolly	24a	write	15
word	9b	write-up n.	27a
work	9c	writhe	15
work	9b	wrong	15
world	9b	wrought	15b
worm	9b	wrought	15
wormery	33b	wrung	15
worn	9b	wryly	8c
worry	9b	wryness	8c
worse	9b	wych-elm	8a
worship	9b		

PART TWO

Rules of
English Spelling

VOWELS

Rule I

<u>A vowel followed by two consonants</u>

- **A stressed single vowel followed by two consonants (or followed by one consonant at the end of a word)** (for *f*, *s*, *z* and *l*, cf. rule 14a) **is usually short** (i.e. says its sound):
  e.g. *adder, admiral, flotsam, hammock, pilgrim; abet.*

Singular exceptions: *camellia, comb, folk, gross, indict, loth, ninth, only, patrol, pint, womb, wont, won't, yolk.*

+ a number of words with the syllable *-oll-* and their cognates:
controller, droll, extolling, knoll, patroller, roll, roller, scroll, stroll, toll, troll, wholly.

General Exceptions:

Ia — **The vowel is always long in monosyllabic words and their compounds which contain the combinations *-old-*, *-olt-* and *-ind-*.**

-old-	behold	marigold	toehold
	blindfold	old	told
	bold	olden	twofold
	cold	scold	unfold
	enfold	shareholder	untold
	fold	sold	uphold
	foretold	stallholder	withhold
	gold	stranglehold	wold
	hold	stronghold	
	household	titleholder	

also long in *scaffold, solder* and *soldier*

-olt-	bolt	jolt	voltage
	colt	smolt	
	dolt	volt	

also long in *coltsfoot, molten, revolt* and *revolting*

-ind-	behind	find	minder
	bind	grind	rind
	bindweed	hind	wind* (coil)
	blind	kind	
	blinder	mind	

*short /i/ if *wind* means strong breeze

– The combinations -*ild*- and -*ost*-, when used in monosyllabic words and their compounds, can either have a long or short vowel.

	long	short		long	short
-ild-	child mild wild	build children guild sild	**-ost-**	almost ghost host most post postpone	accost cost frost lost

1b – Where the vowel is followed by *r*, *w* or *y* it combines with these consonants to form a different vowel sound.
e.g. *cord*, *newt*, *daylight*.

1c – When a vowel is followed by the consonant digraphs -*ch*-, -*ph*- and -*th*- and most two-letter blends, they are considered to be one consonant:
e.g. *ache; strophe; bathe; acre, appropriate, disciple, febrile, nitrate, table, waste* (but note *both, bother, treble, triple*).

However, this does not normally apply to three-consonant blends, e.g. *lustre*, but there are exceptions, e.g. *pastry* and cf. 1d.

1d – Prefixes (or words) which end in a long, stressed vowel sound when placed at the start of compound words often have a long vowel sound before two or three consonants:
e.g. *descramble, destabilize, preshrink, restructure* and *skyscraper*.

1e – The combination -*ange*- is more often pronounced with a long /a/ as in the following list.

-ange-	angel arrange change danger deranged endanger estrange	exchange grange interchange mange manger moneychanger outrange	range ranger rearrange record-changer short-range strange unchangeable

However, the following words have a short /a/.

-ange-	anger banger clanger flange	hanger mangetout melange phalange	plangent tangent tangerine

Note: the *g* is not soft in *anger, banger, clanger* and *hanger*.
Note *orange* with a short /i/ sound and *blancmange* with a short /o/ sound.

Special Note

A stressed vowel followed by *one* consonant in the middle of a word may be long or short. This often causes spelling difficulties. A short vowel is often followed by two consonants so we may come to expect it in every case (cf. rule 14d).

– This expectation is reinforced by the rule that we all learnt as young children that we double the consonant after a short vowel, to keep it short, when adding an ending beginning with a vowel, e.g. *hat—hatter*. We must remember that this only applies to monosyllabic words. Other words do not always double the consonant (cf. rule 24a).

Whether to double the consonant or not is a notorious difficulty in English spelling. The following are a few of the words that can cause problems:

assassin	café	mattress	suppose
atom	canonical	mechanical	surround
aver	desert (sand; leave)	moccasin	tennis
banister	desiccated	operation	terrace
barrier	dessert (sweet)	paraffin	terrapin
battalion	dominant	parrot	terrestrial
berry	ebb	polish	terrific
bilious	errand	Polish	terror
billiards	finish	pollution	tobacconist
blossom	Finnish	privy	tyrannical
Britain	harass	professor	umbrella
Briton	kilogram	raffia	vaccination
Brittany	kilometre	sapphire	vanilla
buccaneer	lily	satellite	villain
bulrush	linoleum	stirrup	

Rule 2

Tricky short vowel sounds

2a

– *-a-*

– *-a-* after *-qu-, w-* or *wh-* often sounds */o/*.

-qua-

quad	quaff	squaddie
quadrangle	qualify	or squaddy
quadrant	quality	squadron
quadraphonic	quantify	squalid
or quadrophonic	quantity	squander
quadratic	quantum	squash
quadrille	quash	squat
quadruped	squabble	squatter
quadruple	squad	

-wa- or -wha-	swamp	wallah	want
	swan	wallet	wanton
	swap	wallop	was
	wad	wallow	wash
	wadding	wally	wasp
	waddle	waltz	watch
	wadi	wan	watt
	waffle	wand	wattle
	waft	wander	what

Exceptions: *quack, quagmire, wag, waggle, wagon* (or *waggon*), *wangle, wax, whack* and *wham*. (For examples of quar-, war- and whar-, see rule 9a.)

2b — -*ea*- and -*ei*-

— -*ea*- sometimes sounds like a short /e/.

-ea-	ahead	health	ready
	bread	heather	realm
	broadth	heaven	spread
	breakfast	heavy	steady
	breast	instead	stealth
	breath	jealous	sweat
	cleanser	lead n.	thread
	dead	leant	threat
	deaf	leapt	tread
	dealt	leather	treasure
	death	meadow	unhealthy
	displeasure	meant	unpleasant
	dread	measure	wealth
	dreadful	pheasant	weapon
	feather	pleasure	weather
	head	read (past tense)	

Note also the short /e/ sound in *again, against, ate, bury, friend, jeopardize, jeopardy, leopard* and *many*.

— -*ei*- sometimes sounds like a short /a/, /e/ or /i/.

It is a short /a/ in *reveille*, a short /e/ in *heifer* and *leisure* and a short /i/ in *calceiform, counterfeit, cuneiform, foreign, forfeit, sovereign* and *surfeit*.

There is also a short /i/ in *breeches, busy, lettuce, minute* (as in time), *palate, pretty, sieve, spinach* and two in *women*.

– *-o-* (especially followed by *n*), *-oo-* and *-ou-* sometimes sound like a **short /u/.** For the purposes of these rules the phonetic sound /ʌ/ (*but*) is counted with the sound /u/ (*put*) as a short /u/ (cf. Introduction and rule 5).

-o-	accompany	fishmonger	scaremonger
	accomplice	honey	smother
	accomplish	ironmonger	some
	among	Monday	somehow
	another	monetary	sometimes
	become	money	somewhere
	bosom	mongrel	son
	brother	monk	sonny
	come	monkey	stomach
	comfortable	monkfish	thorough
	comforter	month	ton
	comfrey	mother	tongue
	company	none	tonne
	compass	nothing	uncomfortable
	conjure	once	warmonger
	costermonger	one	woman
	does	onion	won
	done	other	wonder
	dozen	scandalmonger	wonderful

-oo-	blood	forsook	rook
	book	good	shook
	brook	hood	soot
	cook	hook	stood
	crook	hooky	took
	flood	look	wood
	foot	nook	

-ou-	could	should	trouble
	cousin	southern	would
	enough	touch	young
	rough	tough	

The stressed combination -uv- in English words is always pronounced with a long /u/, e.g. *duvet, juvenile, rejuvenate* and *uvula*.

– **A short /u/ sound followed by v is always written -ov- except in the informal *guv* or *guv'nor*.**

-ov-	above	dove	recover
	beloved	glove	shove
	covenant	govern	shovel
	cover	love	slovenly
	covet	oven	
	discover	plover	

Note the long /u/ sound in *approve, disprove, immovable, improve, move, prove, remove, reprove*, but the long /o/ in *cloven, covert, drove, over*, and the short /o/ in *hover*.

2d – -au- and -al-

– *au* sounds like a short /o/ in *austere, Australia, Austria, cauliflower, hydraulic* and *sausage*.

– **The a in -al- in the following words and the -au- in *fault, vault* are pronounced as a short /o/ in many places where English is spoken. In Received Pronunciation in England, they are pronounced as /aw/.**

-al-	altar	exalt	paltry
	alter	false	psalter
	alteration	falter	salt
	altercation	halt	scald
	alternate	halter	smalt
	balsa	malt	waltz
	cobalt	palsy	

2e – Unstressed -ai-

– **-ai- in the ending -ain sounds like a short /i/ in *bargain, captain, chamberlain, fountain, mountain* and *porcelain*.**
Note that the stressed -ai- in *again* sounds like a short /e/.

2f – Unstressed -ace

– **The unstressed ending -ace usually sounds like /iss/.**

-ace	furnace	pinnace	solace
	menace	pomace	surface
	palace	preface	

Note that -ace sounds like an indeterminate sound /əs/ in *populace* and *terrace*.

Four reasons for a silent *e*

3a – A silent *e* is put after a single consonant (or consonant digraph or blend) to make the previous vowel long:
e.g. *baste, capsule, concrete, hope.*

Note that a long /e/, especially at the end of a word, can be written with *i* followed by a consonant and silent *e*, e.g. *machine* (cf. rule 4b).

However, the ending *-ine* can be pronounced with a short /i/ (*famine, heroine*) or a long /i/ (*asinine*) or a long /e/ (*magazine*) (cf. rule 4b).

There are many words where there seems no necessity for a silent *e*:
e.g. *are, axe, bade, caste, doctrine, examine, gone, granite, heroine, hurricane, live* (vb.), *medicine, pirate, private, programme, senate, serviette* and all the diminutive nouns ending in *-ette*.

There are some words where the *e* is sounded, e.g. as a long /e/ in *anemone* and a short /i/ in *simile* (plural *similies*).

Note: a silent *g* has the effect of making the previous vowel long, e.g. *sign* but *signature*.

3b – No English word ends in a consonant plus *-l*, if we except the words in which that *l* is preceded by *r, w* or *y*.
Note also *kohl* and *rotl*.

In the endings *-ble, -cle, -dle, -fle, -gle, -kle, -ple, -sle, -tle* and *-zle*, the silent *e* introduces the indeterminate sound schwa between the consonant and the *l*. Rare and specialized words have been omitted here (but note that *gunwale* is pronounced /gunnəl/). The sounds /bəl/, /kəl/ and /səl/, which cause special difficulty, are treated first.

– **The sound /bəl/**

Rule 28 deals with the words ending in *-able* and *-ible*.

The words ending in *-bal* and *-bel* are given with the lists of *-al* and *-el* endings on pp. 133–135.

The endings *-bil, -bol* and *-bul* are rare and occur only in *gerbil, gambol* (skip) and *symbol*. The *i* in *gerbil* should have the full pronunciation.

There are only a few other words which end with the sound /bəl/:

-ble	bauble	mumble	stable
	bramble	nimble	stumble
	cable	noble	thimble
	capable	parable	treble
	chasuble	ramble	tremble
	double	rouble	trouble
	fable	rumble	tumble
	grumble	scramble	valuable
	humble	sensible	voluble
	jumble	soluble	

-bble	babble	gabble	rabble
	bobble	gobble	scrabble
	bubble	hobble	scribble
	cobble	nibble	squabble
	dabble	nobble	stubble
	dibble	pebble	wobble
	dribble	quibble	

– **The sound /kəl/**

The sound /kəl/ at the end of a word can be confusing because it can be written -cal, -cle or -kle (and in one or two other ways, too).

There are no words ending in -ccle or -kkle.

The endings -cel and -cil belong with the sound /səl/ and therefore with the ending -sle (see below).

The only word ending in -kal is *jackal* and the only words ending with -kel are *nickel, shekel, snorkel* and *yokel*.

The endings -col and -kol are rare indeed, producing only *protocol* and *skol*.

– **The endings -cal, -cle and -kle**

If the word is an adjective, it is nearly always written -cal; note especially the ending ical. The list of -al endings on pp. 133–134 shows that this is a common adjectival suffix.

If the word is a noun, it is written with the ending -cle except for *ankle, buckle, cockle, fickle, freckle, hackle, honeysuckle, knuckle, ramshuckle, sickle* and verb forms ending in -kle which can stand as nouns too.

-cle	article	cycle	receptacle
	bicycle	follicle	spectacle
	canticle	icicle	tabernacle
	carbuncle	manacle	tentacle
	cenacle	miracle	testicle
	chronicle	monocle	treacle
	circle	muscle	tricycle
	clavicle	obstacle	uncle
	corpuscle	oracle	vehicle
	cubicle	particle	ventricle
	cuticle	pinnacle	

If the word is a verb, it is almost always written with the ending *-kle*.
Note that *circle* and *cycle* may be verbs as well as nouns.

-kle			
	cackle	rankle	tickle
	chuckle	shackle	tinkle
	crackle	sparkle	trickle
	crinkle	speckle	twinkle
	heckle	sprinkle	winkle
	pickle	suckle	wrinkle
	prickle	tackle	

– **The sound /səl/**

The sound /səl/ at the end of a word takes different forms:

e.g. *hassle*
 tousle
 tussle

 cancel
 chancel
 parcel

 council
 pencil
 stencil

Codicil and *excel* should prove no problem because the last vowel in each is given its full pronunciation.

Note that the *s* in *aisle, isle* and *lisle* is silent.

The largest group of words ending in the /səl/ sound are words with a silent *t* (see rule 15).

-stle			
	apostle	gristle	thistle
	bristle	hustle	trestle
	bustle	jostle	whistle
	castle	pestle	wrestle
	epistle	rustle	

-dle	addle	fuddle	poodle
	boodle	girdle	puddle
	bridle	griddle	riddle
	brindle	handle	saddle
	bundle	huddle	sidle
	candle	hurdle	spindle
	cradle	idle	straddle
	cuddle	kindle	swaddle
	curdle	ladle	swindle
	dandle	meddle	toddle
	dawdle	middle	treadle
	diddle	muddle	trundle
	doddle	needle	twaddle
	doodle	noodle	twiddle
	dwindle	paddle	waddle
	fiddle	peddle	wheedle
	fondle	piddle	

-fle	battle	ruffle	snuffle
	muffle	scuffle	stifle
	piffle	shuffle	trifle
	raffle	skiffle	truffle
	riffle	snaffle	waffle
	rifle	sniffle	whiffle

-gle	angle	ingle	snuggle
	bangle	jangle	spangle
	beagle	jiggle	squiggle
	boggle	jingle	straggle
	bugle	juggle	strangle
	bungle	jungle	struggle
	burgle	mangle	tangle
	dangle	mingle	tingle
	dingle	niggle	toggle
	eagle	octangle	triangle
	gaggle	ogle	waggle
	gargle	quadrangle	wangle
	giggle	rectangle	wiggle
	goggle	shingle	woggle
	gurgle	single	wrangle
	haggle	smuggle	wriggle

-ple			
	ample	nipple	septuple
	apple	participle	sextuple
	couple	people	simple
	crimple	pimple	staple
	cripple	pineapple	steeple
	crumple	principle (rule)	stipple
	dapple	purple	supple
	dimple	quadruple	temple
	disciple	quintuple	tipple
	example	ripple	topple
	grapple	rumple	trample
	maple	sample	triple
	multiple	scruple	wimple

-tle			
	battle	little	skittle
	beetle	mantle	spittle
	bluebottle	mettle	startle
	bottle	mottle	subtle
	brittle	myrtle	tattle
	cattle	nestle	throttle
	chortle	nettle	title
	entitle	prattle	tootle
	fettle	rattle	turtle
	gentle	scuttle	wattle
	hurtle	settle	whittle
	kettle	shuttle	

-zle			
	bamboozle	frazzle	nuzzle
	dazzle	grizzle	puzzle
	drizzle	guzzle	sizzle
	embezzle	muzzle	swizzle
	fizzle	nozzle	teazle*

*an alternative to *teasel* and *teazel*

There are few words associated with the endings *-il, -ol* and *-ul*. The first set ends in the sound /əl/ and so can be confused with the words ending in *-le*. The words in the second set should be pronounced with a full vowel sound for the last vowel and, if pronounced correctly, should cause no confusion.

/əl/ ending:

basil	gambol	pistol	utensil
carol	idol	pupil	
consul	mongol	symbol	
fossil	petrol	tonsil	

full vowel sound ending:

benzol	instil	mogul	until
distil	daffodil	pistil	vigil
extol	lentil	strigil	

Special Note

The sound /əl/ after (in particular) the letters *m, n, qu-, r, v, w* or *x* is usually written with *-al* or *-el*, e.g. *animal, squirrel*.
The ending *-le* does not occur after these letters, except for *axle* and a few rare words ending in *-rle*. Since *-al* and *-el* can be confused when the ending is not stressed, lists follow.

-al

abdominal	cataclysmal	doctrinal
abnormal	catarrhal	electoral
abortional	cathedral	emotional
abysmal	central	encephal-
additional	cerebral	ephemeral
adenoidal	choral	epochal
admiral	chordal	equal
adrenal	communal	eternal
amoral	conditional	exceptional
anal	confessional	external
anecdotal	confraternal	extramural
animal	confrontational	feral
annal	congregational	feudal
annual	conjectural	fictional
antiphonal	conjugal	final
apocryphal	constitutional	floral
arsenal	conventional	formal
astral	conversational	frugal
atonal	coral	funeral
aural	corporal	fungal
autumnal	creedal or credal	fungicidal
banal	criminal	general
baptismal	cultural	germicidal
behavioural	cymbal	germinal
betrothal	decimal	global
bilateral	dermal	guttural
binal	devotional	herbal
bridal	diagonal	herbicidal
cannibal	diphthongal	hexagonal
capital	dismal	hierarchical
cardinal	diurnal	homicidal
carnal	doctoral	hormonal

continued

hospital
hymnal
illegal
immoral
impersonal
inaugural
infanticidal
infernal
infinitesimal
informal
insecticidal
institutional
integral
intentional
interdenominational
internal
international
intestinal
irrational
jackal
journal
larvicidal
lateral
legal
lethal
liberal
literal
lustral
madrigal
magistral
mammal
marginal
maternal
matronal
maximal
mayoral
medicinal
mineral
minimal
mistral
monarchal
moral
municipal
mural
national
natural
Neanderthal
neural

neutral
nocturnal
nominal
nonconstitutional
nonlethal
normal
notional
numeral
nymphal
occasional
occupational
offal
opal
operational
optimal
optional
oral
ordinal
original
oval
paranormal
parasiticidal
paschal
pastoral
paternal
patriarchal
patricidal
patronal
pectoral
pedal
penal
peripheral
personal
pleural (lungs)
plural (1+)
postural
primal
principal
principal (person)
prismoidal
procedural
prodigal
professional
promotional
proportional
pyramidal
rational
referral

regal
rehearsal
removal
renal
retinal
rhinal
rural
sacral
sandal
scandal
scribal
scriptural
seasonal
sensational
several
signal
spectral
spheroidal
spinal
spiral
suicidal
synagogal
synodal
temporal
terminal
textural
thermal
tidal
tonal
traditional
transactional
transitional
tribal
tribunal
trimestral
triumphal
tubal
urinal
vaginal
vandal
venal
verbal
vernal
vertebral
viral
virginal
vocational

angel	fuel	pastel
ariel	funnel	petrel
bagel or beigel	gavel	pixel
barrel	ginnel	pommel
bevel	gospel	pretzel
bezel	grapnel	pummel
bowel	gravel	quarrel
brothel	grovel	rebel
bushel	gruel	revel
cancel	gunnel*	roundel
caramel	hazel	satchel
caravel	hostel	scalpel
carousel	hotel	scoundrel
carrel	hovel	sentinel
cartel	infidel	shekel
chancel	jewel	shovel
channel	kennel	shrapnel
chapel	kernel	shrivel
chattel	kestrel	snivel
chisel	label	snorkel
citadel	laurel	spaniel
cockerel	level	squirrel
cruel	libel	strudel
cudgel	lintel	swivel
damsel	mackerel	tassel
darnel	mantel	tinsel
decibel	marvel	towel
diesel	minstrel	trammel
dishevel	model	travel
doggerel	mongrel	trowel
dowel	morsel	tunnel
drivel	mussel	vessel
duel	navel	vowel
duffel	nickel	wastrel
easel	novel	weasel
enamel	panel	yodel
fennel	parallel	yokel
flannel	parcel	

*an alternative to *gunwale*
Note *carol* and *petrol*.

The sound /shəl/ at the end of a word is usually written *-cial* or *-tial*:
e.g. *special, preferential*.

3c – A silent *e* is put after *c* and *g* to make them sound respectively /s/ and /j/: e.g. *once, fringe* (cf. rule 12).

3d – A silent *e* is normally used after a full word ending with *v*, or a consonant and *u* (*avenue, clue*), or a consonant and *-uls* (*convulse, dulse, impulse, pulse, repulse*).

-ve	adjective	eve	superlative
	have	imperative	valve
	comparative	narrative	
	diminutive	positive	

The only English words ending in *v* are *grav, Slav* and the slang words *chiv, guv* and *spiv*. Note p*arev*.

The only words ending in a consonant and *u* are:
cornu, coypu, ecru, emu, genu, gnu, guru, Hindu, jujitsu, menu, tabu (an alternative to *taboo*), *tofu, tutu* + other words of more obviously foreign origin.

Rule 4   <u>Vowel digraphs which sound like long vowels</u>

– A long vowel is often written as a vowel digraph, e.g. *-ai-*. **As a general rule if *r* is added to the vowel digraph the pronunciation is usually that of the (long) vowel plus *-re*.**

Note the 'r' becomes the indeterminate schwa sound (/ə/as in *China*) when it occurs at the end of a word as in *pair*. When a vowel is added, the *r* is pronounced as in *pairing*. This rule refers mainly to stressed syllables.

4a – Long /a/ sound

– A long /a/ is usually *-ai-*, *-ay-* or *-ei-*.

-ai-		
abstain	bait	cocaine
acclaim	bewail	complain
acquaint	blackmail	complaint
afraid	braid	constrain
aid	Braille	contain
ail	brain	curtail
aim	braise	daily
ascertain	bridesmaid	dais
assail	campaign	daisy
attain	chain	declaim
avail	chilblain	detail
await	cinquain	detain
bail	claim	disclaim

continued

-ai-

disdain	maintain	retain
drain	maize	sail
entertain	migraine	saint
exclaim	nail	slain
explain	obtain	snail
fail	ordain	sprain
failure	paid	staid
faint	pail	stain
faith	pailing	straight
faithful	pain	strain
flail	paint	strait
frail	plaice	sustain
gaily	plain	swain
gain	plantain	tail
gainsay	portrait	tailor
gait	praise	taint
grain	proclaim	trail
hail	quail	train
jail	quaint	trait
laid	raid	traitor
lain	rail	vain
liaise	railway	waif
maid	rain	wail
maiden	raisin	waist
mail	refrain	wait
maim	remain	waitress
main	restrain	waive
mainstay	retail	

In the ending -*aic* the long /a/ is followed by a short /i/ sound:
e.g. *Aramaic, archaic, Hebraic, mosaic, Pharisaic, prosaic.*

-ay-	allay	gateway	portray
	anyway	gay	pray
	array	halfway	prepay
	assay	hay	railway
	astray	headway	ray
	away	hearsay	relay
	bay	heyday	repay
	bayonet	highway	respray
	betray	holiday	runway
	bray	hooray	say
	clay	inlay	slay
	crayfish	interplay	slipway
	crayon	lay	soothsayer
	day	layer	speedway
	decay	mainstay	spray
	defray	may	stairway
	delay	midday	stay
	dismay	mislay	stray
	display	noway	subway
	dray	outstay	sway
	essay	overlay	today
	fray	overstay	tray
	freeway	pathway	way
	gainsay	pay	waylay
	gangway	play	

Note that *Sunday, Monday, Tuesday, Wednesday, Thursday, Friday* and *Saturday* all end with a short /i/ sound.

-ei-	abseil	neigh	skein
	beige	neighbour	sleigh
	ceilidh	obeisance	veil
	feign	reign	vein
	feint	rein	weigh
	inveigh	sheik	weight

Note the long /a/ and soft *g* in *gaol*.

-ey (at the end of a word) and **-ea-** with the long /a/ sound occur rarely and in the following words:
grey, obey, prey, they, whey and *break, great, steak.*

Some words that we have taken from French sound *e* like a long /a/:
e.g. *ballet, beret, bouquet, buffet, crepe, croquet, fete, parquet, suede.*

Note the long /a/ in *gauge* and the short /a/ in *plaid* and *plait.*

Combinations with *r* follow the general rule (cf. rule 4: they sound like the -*are* in *bare, spare*) and, at the end of a word, *r* becomes the indeterminate sound schwa after the long /a/.

-air-	affair	fairy	pair
	air	flair	prairie
	airy	hair	repair
	chair	hairy	stair
	dairy	lair	stairway
	fair	laird	unfair
	fairly	millionaire	

-*eir* and -*ear* (also sounding like the -*are* in *bare*) occur rarely and in the following words: *heir, their* and *bear, pear, swear, tear* (cloth), *wear*.

Note the word *there* with the same sound. Note that *heart* and *hearth* sound /ar/ and that *vase* has this /ar/ sound too.

4b – Long /e/ sound

– A long /e/ is usually -*ee*-, -*ea*-, -*ie*- or -*ei*- (or *i*).

-ee-	agree	eel	green
	asleep	eighteen	greet
	bee	exceed	heed
	beech (tree)	fee	heel
	beef	feeble	indeed
	been	feed	indiscreet
	beet (vegetable)	feel	interviewee
	beetle	feet	jeep
	between	fifteen	keel
	bleed	filigree	keen
	bleep	flee (run)	keep
	breed	fleece	kneel
	breeze	fleet	lee
	cheek	fourteen	leek
	cheese	free	leeway
	creed	freedom	licensee
	creek	freehold	meek
	creep	freestyle	meet
	decree	freeway	need
	deed	freeze	nineteen
	deem	geese	patentee
	deep	genteel	payee
	degree	ghee	pedigree
	disagree	glee	peek
	discreet	greed	peel

continued

-ee-

peen	settee	tee
peep	seventeen	teem
peevish	sheen	teeth
peewee	sheep	teetotal
peewit	sheet	tepee
proceed	shopkeeper	thee
queen	sixteen	thirteen
redeem	sleek	tree
reed (plant)	sleep	trustee
reef	sleet	tweed
reek	sleeve	tweet
reel	sneeze	tweezers
referee	speech	umpteenth
refugee	speed	unseen
screech	spree	upkeep
screen	steed	weed
see	steel	week
seed	steep	weep
seek	street	weevil
seem	succeed	wheedle
seen	sweep	wheel
seep	sweet	wheeze

-ea-

anneal	cheat	east
appeal	clean	Easter
appease	cleat	easy
beach (sea)	cleave	eat
beacon	conceal	eaves
bead	congeal	eavesdrop
beak	creak	entreat
beaker	cream	feast
beam	crease	feat
bean	creature	feature
beast	deal	flea (insect)
beat (hit)	dean	freak
beneath	decrease	gleam
bereaved	defeat	glean
bleach	demeanour	grease
bleak	disease	heal
bleat	dream	heap
breach	each	heat
bream	eager	heath
breathe	eagle	heathen
cease	easel	heave
cheap	easily	ideal

continued

-ea-

increase	peat	squeal
jeans	plead	squeamish
knead	please	steal
leach	pleat	steam
lead vb.	preach	streak
leaf	queasy	stream
leak	reach	tea
lean	read (present tense)	teach
leap	ream	team
lease	reap	tease
leash	reason	teat
least	release	treacle
leave	repeat	treason
mead	retreat	treat
meagre	reveal	treatise
meal	scream	tweak
mean	sea	underneath
measles	seal	uneasy
meat	seam	unleash
misdemeanour	season	veal
neat	seat	weak
ordeal	sheaf	wean
outreach	sheath	weave
pea	sleazy	wheat
peace	sneak	wreak
peach	sneaky	wreath
peak	speak	zeal
peal	squeak	

-ie-	achieve	grief	shriek
	aggrieve	grieve	siege
	believe	handkerchief	skied
	brief	niece	thief
	chief	piece	thieve
	diesel	priest	wield
	field	relief	yield
	fiend	relieve	
	frieze	shield	

(See rule 6a for other words in which the -ie- sounds /e/.)

-ei-	caffeine	conceive	plebeian
	casein	deceit	protein
	ceiling	deceive	receipt
	codeine	heinous	receive
	conceit	perceive	seize

Key and *quay* both have the long /e/ sound.

Long /e/ can also be written with an *i* (if stressed).

antique	marine	routine	tambourine
aubergine	plasticine	sardine	trampoline
ballerina	police	semolina	trio
kiosk	ravine	submarine	
machinery	regime	suite	

Note that in words like *cafeteria, editorial, idiom, medial, pedestrian, piano, serial* and *stadium* the *i* is not stressed and is consequently pronouned as a short /i/.

Note *area, idea, meteor* and *people*.

Combinations of long /e/ with *r* follow the general rule (cf. rule 4: they sound like the *-ere* in *interfere, sincere, sphere*) and, at the end of a word, *r* becomes the indeterminate sound schwa after the long /e/.

-eer-	beer	engineer	racketeer
	career	jeer	seer
	cheer	leer	sheer (steep)
	cheerful	peer	sightseer
	cheerio	peerage	sneer
	deer	pioneer	steer
	domineer	profiteer	veneer
	electioneer	queer	volunteer

-ear-		
appear	endear	sear
arrears	fear	shear (to clip)
beard	footgear	smear
bleary	gear	spear
clear	hear	tear (drop)
dear	near	weary
dreary	nearly	year
ear	rear	

-ier-		
bier	clavier	skier
cashier	fierce	tier
cavalier	pier	
chandelier	pierce	

-eir- occurs rarely and in *weir* and *weird*.

The word *eyrie* sounds like the *-ere* in *interfere* with a long /e/ sound at the end.

For *-ue-* and *-ve-* see rule 10.

4c   –   **Long /i/ sound**

–   **A long /i/ is usually *-igh-*, *-ig* (with *n*) or *-ei-*.**

-igh-		
alight	foresight	outright
alright	forthright	plight
aright	fortnight	right
blight	fright	sigh
bright	frightful	sight
cartwright	headlight	slight
copyright	high	thigh
daylight	knight	tight
delight	light	tights
downright	midnight	upright
enlighten	might	wheelwright
fight	mighty	wright
flight	nigh	
floodlight	night	

-ign-		
align	design	realign
assign	ensign	reassign
benign	malign	reconsign
condign	misalign	redesign
consign	preassign	resign
countersign	predesign	sign

-ei-	eiderdown	height	Rottweiler
	either	heist	seismic
	Fahrenheit	leitmotiv	stein
	Geiger counter	neither	
	gneiss	Poseidon	

-ie- is often pronounced with a schwa following the *i*, which indicates the spelling, e.g. *society*. It has a long /i/ sound (with no schwa) in *tied, dried, fried, shied, tried,* verbs ending in *-fy* which changes to *-fies*, e.g. *satisfy—satisfies,* and at the end of a monosyllabic word, e.g. *tie*.

-ye occurs rarely and in *aye, bye, dye, eye, goodbye, lye* and *rye*.

The *i* in *-io-* and *-ia-* usually has a long, stressed /i/ sound at the beginning of a word and a short, unstressed /i/ sound at the end of a word.

For instances of *i* with a long /e/ sound, cf. rule 4b.

long stressed /i/ sound at beginning:

bio-	diary	pioneer	viaduct
dial	liable	pious	viola
diamond	lion	riot	violate

Note: *di-* also has a long /i/ sound, e.g. *diurnal*, and *bionic* has a long /i/ sound followed by a short /o/ sound at the beginning.

short, unstressed /i/ sound at end:

caviar	junior	period	senior
genial	medial	pinion	zodiac
jovial	menial	radial	

Note the long /i/ in *choir*.

Combinations of long /i/ with *r* follow the general rule (cf. rule 4: they sound like the *-ire* in *fire*) and, at the end of a word, *r* becomes the indeterminate sound schwa after the long /i/ sound, e.g. *admire, ire*.

eir- and *-yre* occur rarely and in *eirenic* (a variant of *irenic*) and *byre, lyre, pyre, tyre*.

-ier- occurs in *brier, crier, drier, fiery, flier, hieroglyphics, pliers* and in other verbs ending in *-y* which add the *-er* of the agent, e.g. *occupy—occupier*.

4d – Long /o/ sound

– A long /o/ is usually *-oa-*, *-ow-*, *-ou-* or *-oe-* (or *-eau* at the end of a word).

-oa-		
afloat	gloat	oath
approach	goad	poach
bemoan	goal	reproach
bloat	goat	roach
boast	groan	road
boat	groat	roam
cloak	load	roast
coach	loaf	shoal
coal	loam	soak
coast	loan	soap
coat	loath	stoat
cocoa	loaves	throat
croak	moan	toad
encroach	moat	toast
float	oaf	unload
foal	oak	woad
foam	oat	

-ow-		
aglow	grow	scarecrow
arrow	growth	shadow
barrow	hallow	shallow
bellow	harrow	show
below	hollow	slow
bestow	know	snow
billow	landowner	sorrow
blow	low	sow (seed)
borrow	lower	sparrow
bow (arrow)	lowly	stow
bowdlerize	mallow	swallow
bowl	mellow	tallow
bowling	minnow	throw
bungalow	morrow	tomorrow
burrow	mow	tow
callow	narrow	towpath
crow	owe	undertow
elbow	own	wallow
fallow	pillow	wheelbarrow
flow	rainbow	widow
flown	row (boat)	willow
follow	rowan	window
furrow	rowlock	winnow
glow	sallow	yellow

-ou-	boulder	poultice	soul
	dough	poultry	though
	mould	shoulder	
	moult	smoulder	

-oe-	aloes	oboe	toe
	doe	poem	woe
	foe	poet	
	hoe	roe	

-eau	beau	nouveau	tableau
	bureau	plateau	trousseau
	chateau	portmanteau	
	gateau	rondeau	

There is a long /o/ in *brooch; chauffeur, mauve; sew* (thread)*; comb;* and *yeoman.*

-ore does not produce a long /o/:
e.g. *ashore, implore, score, shore, snore, sore, tore.*
These endings produce the 'sympathy' sound /aw/ (rule 5a).

Combinations with *-oa-* plus *r* follow the general rule (cf. rule 4: they sound like the *-ore* in *tore*), always having the 'sympathy' sound /aw/, and, at the end of the word, *r* becomes the indeterminate sound schwa after this 'sympathy' sound.

-oar-	boar	hoarse	sideboard
	board	hoary	soar
	coarse	keyboard	switchboard
	hoar	oar	uproar
	hoard	roar	

Note: combinations with *-our-* occur rarely and in *course, court, four, mourn, pour, recourse, source* and *your* (producing the 'sympathy' sound).

However, the ending *-oer* does produce a long /o/ followed by the indeterminate sound schwa and occurs rarely and in *goer, hoer, vetoer.*

– A long /u/ is usually *-oo-*, *-ou-*, *-eu-*, *-ew-*, or *-ue* at the end of a word.

It can also sometimes be *-ui-*:
e.g. *bruise, cruise, cruiser, fruit, juice, nuisance, pursuit, recruit, sluice, suit.*

-oo-			
balloon	hoof	root
bamboo	hoop	school
bassoon	hoot	scoop
bloom	loo	scoot
booby	loom	shampoo
boom	loon	shoot
boon	loony	sloop
boost	loop	smooch
boot	loopy	smooth
booth	loose	snooker
booty	loot	snooze
booze	maroon	soon
brood	monsoon	spoof
broom	moo	spook
cartoon	mooch	spool
cheroot	mood	spoon
choose	moody	stooge
coo	moon	stook
cool	moose	stool
coop	moot	stoop
coot	mushroom	swoon
croon	noon	swoop
cuckoo	noose	tomfoolery
doom	ooze	too
drool	papoose	tool
droop	phooey	toot
food	pontoon	tooth
fool	pool	troop
foolish	poop	voodoo
gloom	proof	whoop
gooey	racoon	woo
goon	rood	zoo
goose	roof	zoom
groom	room	
groove	roost	

-ou-	boudoir	group	routine
	bougainvillea	louvre	roux
	bouquet	pirouette	silhouette
	boutique	pouf or pouffe	sou
	burnouse	ragout	soup
	coup	recoup	souvenir
	coupon	reroute	through
	croup	rouble	troupe
	crouton	rouge	uncouth
	douche	roulade	wound (hurt)
	ghoul	roulette	you
	gourmand	route	youth

-eu-	eucalyptus	euphoria	Pentateuch
	Eucharist	Europe	pharmaceutical
	eugenic	feud	pneumatic
	eulogy	feudal	pneumonia
	eunuch	leukaemia	pseudonym
	euphemism	neutral	queue
	euphony	neutron	therapeutic

Note the /y/ sound in *lieu*.

-ew-	anew	few	preview
	askew	flew	renew
	bedew	grew	review
	bejewel	Hebrew	screw
	blew	hew	shrew
	brew	interview	sinew
	cashew	Jew	skew
	chew	jewel	slew
	clerihew	knew	spew
	crew	lewd	stew
	curfew	mildew	strew
	dew	nephew	threw
	drew	new	view
	ewe	pew	yew
	ewer	pewter	

Note: the combination *-ew-* sometimes introduces a /y/ sound before the long /u/, e.g. *stew*.

-ue-	argue	hue	rue
	blue	imbue	rueful
	clue	influence	statue
	cruel	issue	subdue
	cruet	muesli	sue
	cue	overdue	suet
	due	pursue	tissue
	duel	queue	true
	duet	refuel	Tuesday
	flue	rescue	undue
	fluent	residue	value
	fuel	revenue	virtue
	glue	revue	

The *e* in *-ue-* becomes a schwa sound when followed by a consonant, e.g. *fuel*, an /i/ in *cruet*, *suet*, and an /e/ in *duet*. The *u* often begins with a /y/ sound.

-oe- occurs rarely and in *shoe* and *canoe*.

Note the long /u/ in *do, to* and *womb*.

In many words with a long /u/ sound, a /y/ sound is introduced before the /u/ sound:
e.g. *duty, endure, unicorn, uniform, union, unusual, usual.*

The consonant *y* never appears before a long /u/ sound in English except for *bayou, yoo-hoo, you* and *youth*. In all other words the sound /yoo/ is written with a simple *u, -ue-* or a vowel digraph only, without a *y*.

Combinations of long /u/ with *r* follow the general rule (cf. rule 4: they sound like the *-ure* in *cure*) with **-eur, -uer** and **-ure** and usually introduce a /y/ sound before the *u*. At the end of a word, *r* becomes the indeterminate sound schwa after the long /u/, e.g. *valuer*.

-eur-	entrepreneurial	neurology	pleurisy
	neural	neurosis	
	neuritis	neurotic	

-uer-	arguer	issuer	ruer
	construer	puerile	valuer
	continuer	pursuer	
	gluer	rescuer	

-ure-	assure	lure	secure
	cure	manure	sure
	endure	mature	unsure
	impure	pure	
	insure	purée	

Combinations with *-oor* and *-our* also sound like the *-ure* in *cure* but without the /y/ sound. There are few examples: *moor, poor, spoor* and *bourgeois, detour, dour, gourd, tour*. Note *doer, lassoer, shoer*.

Rule 5   The other three vowel digraph sounds

For the purposes of these spelling rules, we have roughly classified the vowel sounds of English into long (vowel with silent *e*), short (vowel without silent *e*) and indeterminate schwa /ə/and a combination of these sounds, e.g. the long /o/ and short /i/ in *going*. To complete the classification we need to mention three sounds, produced by a combination of vowels, that cannot be broken up into the vowel sounds mentioned above.

5a   –   The 'sympathy' sound produced by *-au-* and *-aw-*
(See rule 2d for *-al-* producing /awl/ in Received Pronunciation in England and rule 4d for the 'sympathy' sound in *-ore, -oar-* and some words with *-our-*.)

-au-		
aeronautical	cause	launch
applaud	caustic	laundry
astronaut	cauterize	marauder
auburn	caution	maul
auction	clause	mausoleum
audacious	claustrophobia	naught
audible	cosmonaut	naughty
audience	daub	nausea
audio-	daughter	nautical
auditorium	daunt	pauper
aught	dinosaur	pause
augment	exhaust	plausible
augur	faun	precaution
August	flaunt	raucous
aural	fraud	raunchy
aurora	fraught	sauce
auspices	gaudy	saucer
auspicious	gaunt	sauna
austere	gauntlet	saunter
author	gauze	slaughter
authority	glaucoma	somersault
auto-	haughty	staunch
automatic	haul	taught
autopsy	haulage	taunt
auxiliary	haunch	taut
baulk	haunt	tautological
Caucasian	hypocaust	trauma
caught	inaudible	undaunted
caul	jaunt	vault
cauldron	juggernaut	vaunt
caulk	laud	

-aw-	awe	flaw	sawn
	awesome	gawky	scrawl
	awful	gnaw	scrawny
	awkward	hawk	seesaw
	awl	hawthorn	shawl
	awning	jackdaw	spawn
	bawdy	jaw	sprawl
	bawl	jigsaw	squaw
	brawny	law	straw
	caw	lawn	strawberry
	claw	outlaw	tawdry
	crawfish	overdrawn	tawny
	crawl	paw	thaw
	dawdle	pawl	tomahawk
	dawn	pawn	trawl
	draw	pawnbroker	yaw
	drawer	prawn	yawl
	drawl	raw	yawn
	drawn	rickshaw	
	fawn	saw	

Note the 'sympathy' sound in *abroad, broad* and *broadcast*.

5b – The 'calling' sound produced by *-oi-* and *-oy-*

-oi-	adenoid	despoil	joint
	adjoin	devoid	joist
	adroit	disappoint	loin
	alkaloid	disjointed	loiter
	android	ellipsoid	lymphoid
	aneroid	embroider	mastoid
	anoint	embroil	moist
	anthropoid	enjoin	noise
	appoint	exploit	oil
	asteroid	fibroid	ointment
	avoid	foil	ovoid
	boil	foist	paranoia
	boisterous	fungoid	paranoid
	broil	globoid	poignant
	celluloid	goitre	point
	choice	groin	poison
	cloister	haemorrhoids	porpoise
	coil	hoist	prismoidal
	coin	invoice	purloin
	cystoid	join	quoin

continued

-oi-	quoit	solenoid	tortoise
	recoil	spheroid	toxoid
	reconnoitre	spoil	turmoil
	rejoice	steroid	turquoise
	rheumatoid	tabloid	typhoid
	roister	thyroid	unavoidable
	sirloin	toil	voice
	soil	toilet	void

Note: in *chamois* (leather) *-ois* is pronounced as a short /i/.

-oy-	ahoy	coy	joyful
	alloy	coyote	joystick
	annoy	decoy	loyal
	boy	deploy	oyster
	boycott	destroy	ploy
	buoy	disloyal	royal
	buoyant	employ	soy
	clairvoyant	enjoy	soya
	cloy	envoy	toy
	convoy	flamboyant	troy
	corduroy	gargoyle	viceroy
	cowboy	joy	voyage

5c   –   The 'pain' sound produced by *-ou-* and *-ow-*

-ou-	abound	compound	douse
	about	confound	drought
	account	couch	espouse
	accountant	council	expound
	aground	counsel	flounce
	aloud	count	flour
	amount	countenance	flout
	announce	counteract	foldout
	around	counterfeit	foul
	arouse	counterfoil	found
	background	countless	foundry
	blouse	county	fount
	bough	crouch	fountain
	bounce	denounce	gouge
	bound	devour	gout
	bout	devout	grouch
	carouse	discount	ground
	cloud	doubt	grouse
	clout	doughty	grout

continued

-ou-

hidebound	outgoings	scour
hound	outlandish	scout
hour	outlaw	scrounge
house	outlet	shout
impound	outlook	slouch
joust	outpatient	slough
loud	outrage	snout
lounge	outset	sound
louse	outside	sour
lout	outsize	south
mound	outstanding	spouse
mount	outward	spout
mouse	outwit	sprout
mouth	plough	stout
noun	pouch	tantamount
ounce	pounce	thousand
our	pound	tout
ourselves	pout	trounce
out	profound	trousers
outclass	proud	trout
outdated	round	voucher
outer	rouse	wound (coiled)
outfall	rout	
outfit	scoundrel	

-ow-

allow	downfall	owl
anyhow	download	powder
blowzy	downright	power
bow	downy	prow
bowel	dowry	prowl
brow	drown	renown
brown	drowsy	row (quarrel)
clown	eiderdown	scowl
cow	endow	shower
coward	fowl	sow (pig)
cower	frown	tower
cowl	gown	town
cowslip	growl	trowel
crowd	how	vow
crown	howl	vowel
dowdy	jowl	wow
dowel	meltdown	yowl
down	now	

Rule 6 — The rules for -*ie*- and -*ei*-

6a — Provided the letters sound long /e/,
i before *e* except after *c*.

-ie-	achieve	fiend	pierce
	aggrieve	fierce	piezoelectricity
	believe	grief	priest
	besiege	grievous	reprieve
	brief	handkerchief	shield
	chandelier	hygiene	shriek
	chief	liege	siege
	coterie	mischief	thief
	field	piece	wield

(See rule 4b for other words in which the -*ie*- sounds /e/.)

Exceptions to this rule are words with a vowel sound with variable pronunciations, e.g. *either, neither,* the words *seize, weir, weird* and some chemical words like *caffeine, casein, codeine* and *protein*.

The *c* exception covers the following and their derivatives:

-cei-	ceiling	deceive	receive
	conceit	inconceivable	transceiver
	conceive	perceive	
	deceit	receipt	

Words with -*ie*- after *c* that do not sound like long /e/ (and therefore not falling under this rule) are not numerous. They are:

i) *coefficient, concierge, deficient, efficient, glacier, prima-facie, proficient, science, society, species, sufficient* and their derivatives;

ii) words ending in -*cy* that add suffixes beginning with *e*, e.g. *fancy—fancied, fancier;*

iii) words ending with the suffix -*facient* (making), e.g. *liquefacient*.

6b — With sounds long /a/ or /i/,
Write *e* and then the *i*.

-ei-	beige	gneiss	Pleistocene
	ceilidh	height	reign
	deign	heinous	rein
	eiderdown	heir	reindeer
	eight	heist	seismic
	eighteen	inveigh	sheik or sheikh
	eighty	inveigle	skein
	eisteddfod	kaleidoscope	sleigh
	Fahrenheit	leitmotiv	surveillance
	feign	neigh	veil
	feint	neighbour	vein
	freight	neither	weight
	geisha	obeisance	

Some -*ei*- words have the long /e/ sound. They are the same as the exceptions to rule 6a given after the first list.

Note that the above rules, 6a and 6b, cover the three long vowel sounds, /e/, /a/ and /i/. The short vowel sounds /e/ and /i/ can be written with -*ie*- or -*ei*-. The few words falling into this category are *calceiform, counterfeit, cuneiform, foreign, forfeit, friend, heifer, leisure, sieve, sovereign* and *surfeit*.

Rule 7   <u>When an _e_ sounds like a short /i/</u>

— An unaccented _e_ often sounds like a short /i/, especially at the beginning of a word, e.g. _destroy._

-e-			
	banquet	excuse	recorder
	basket	explosion	recount
	billet	ferret	refer
	blanket	forest	refuse vb.
	bonnet	honestly	regard
	bracket	jacket	regret
	bucket	jagged	relent
	bullet	mallet	rely
	bulletin	market	reply
	carpet	naked	report
	casket	neglect	revile
	chicken	packet	rocket
	college	pellet	simile
	cornet	pocket	skeleton
	cricket	poem	socket
	eclipse	poet	sonnet
	effect	poetry	target
	electric	precise	telegram
	electrician	predict	telescope
	electricity	prefer	television
	eleven	prepare	ticket
	enormous	present vb.	trumpet
	enthusiasm	preserve	turret
	equipment	pretend	vegetable
	especially	privilege	velvet
	event	puppet	wicket
	eventuality	racket	

Note the two short /i/s in _sacrilegious._

Many of the occurrences of this rule are with the prefixes *be-* and *de-*.

be-			
	because	begun	beloved
	become	behalf	bemoan
	bedeck	behave	bemuse
	bedevil	behaviour	beneath
	bedew	behead	bequeath
	bedraggle	beheld	beside
	befit	behest	bestow
	before	behind	betray
	befriend	behold	betroth
	began	behove	between
	beget	bejewel	betwixt
	begin	belabour	beware
	begonia	belated	bewildered
	begrudge	believe	bewitched
	beguile	belong	beyond

de-			
	debar	defence	demean
	debase	defend	demeanour
	debate	defer	demented
	debauch	defiant	demise
	deceit	deficient	demolish
	deceive	defile	demure
	decide	define	denial
	deciduous	deflate	denomination
	decipher	deflect	denote
	decision	deform	denude
	decisive	defraud	denunciate
	declare	defray	deny
	declension	defy	depart
	decline	degenerative	department
	declivity	degrade	departure
	decrease	degree	depend
	decree	dejected	depict
	decrepit	delay	deplete
	decry	delete	depletion
	decumbent	deliberate	deplorable
	deduce	delicious	deplore
	deduct	delight	deponent
	deface	delineate	deport
	defame	delirious	deposit
	default	deliver	depository
	defeat	delude	depraved
	defect	demand	depress

continued

de-			
deprive	despatch	deter
deranged	despicable	detergent
deride	despise	deteriorate
derisible	despite	determine
derisory	despoil	detest
derive	despond	detract
describe	destroy	develop
description	destruct	device
deserve	detach	devise
design	detain	devoid
desire	detect	devote
desist	detective	devour
despair	detention	devout

Note particularly *liquid, liquefy; putrid, putrefy; rarefy; ruby, rubefy; stupid, stupefy; tepid, tepefy; torrid, torrefy* and *tumid, tumefy*.
The vowel difference in these words occurs in the change from verb to noun or adjective. The verbs use the vowel of the Latin infinitive ending, whereas the nouns and adjectives use the vowel of the Latin past participle ending.

The ending *-meter* is pronounced with a short /i/ when unstressed, e.g. *diameter, parameter*.

There is a short /i/ at the end of the words *chocolate, coffee, toffee*, with an alternative indeterminate sound schwa at the end of *chocolate*.

Rule 8   <u>When *i* (or *-ie*) and *y* can be confused, and also *u* and *w*</u>

–   **Long and short /i/ sounds are usually written with a letter *i* at the beginning and in the middle of a word and nearly always with the letter *y* at the end of a word,** e.g. *icily, ignominy*.
     Note *dryable, dryly* (or *drily*), *dryness* and *drier* (or *dryer*), *driest* (or *dryest*).
     The word *colliery* sounds the *i* as a /y/.

–   **When a word ending in a vowel and *y* adds a suffix, it retains the *y*:**
     e.g. *enjoyment, joyless, keyed*.
     For exceptions see section 8b.

–   **When a word ending in a consonant and *y* adds a suffix, the *y* usually changes to *i*,** e.g. *merriment*.
     For the exceptions, e.g. *dryness*, see section 8c.
     Note: some words have a sound like a short /i/ followed by a /y/ sound (as in *year*), e.g. *carrying, million, onion, radio*, but these sounds are always written with a single *i* or *y* because, except for *biyearly*, the combination *-iy-* never occurs in English.

Sections 8a–8d give the exceptions which have *y* at the beginning and in the middle of a word and *-ie* at the end of a word with an /i/ sound, e.g. *movie*.
The following are also exceptions:
broccoli, coterie, cowrie, menagerie, pixie, safari, sari, scrapie, sortie, spaghetti, taxi and *walkie-talkie*.

Exceptions:

8a – **Words of Greek origin** like *cycle* and *psychology* **have y at the beginning or in the middle of the word**.
Nearly all the following words are of Greek origin.

-y-

acronym	cylinder	hydrant
analysis	cymbal	hydrated
anodyne	cynic	hydraulic
anonymity	cynical	hydro-
anonymous	cypher*	hydroelectric
anticyclone	cypress	hydrogen
antitype	cyst	hydrometer
antonym	cystitis	hygiene
apocalypse	cytoplasm	hymn
apocalyptic	dialyse	hype
apocryphal	dryad	hyper-
archetype	dynamic	hypersensitive
asphyxiate	dynamite	hyperspace
asymmetric	dynamo	hyphen
asymmetry	dynasty	hypnosis
barysphere	dysentery	hypnotize
bathysphere	dyspepsia	hypocaust
beryl	embryo	hypocrisy
bicycle	encyclopedia or	hypocrite
breathalyse	encyclopaedia	hypotenuse
buoyancy	enzyme	hypothesis
byre	eponymous	hysterectomy
byte	etymology	hysterical
Byzantine	eucalyptus	idyll
calypso	eurhythmic	labyrinth
canyon	glycerin	laryngitis
cataclysm	gryphon	lych gate*
catalyst	gymkhana	lynch
catalytic	gymnasium	lynx
chlorophyll	gymnast	lyre
chrysalis	gynaecology	lyric
chrysanthemum	gypsum	martyr
coccyx	(Gypsy) gypsy*	mayor
cotyledon	gyro-	metaphysics
crypt	halcyon	methylated
crystal	hieroglyphics	metonym
cyan	homonym	misogyny
cybernetic	hyacinth	monogynous
cyclone	hybrid	myopic
cygnet	hydrangea	myriad

continued

mysterious	psychedelic	sympathy
mystery	psychiatric	symphony
mystic	psychiatrist	symptom
myth	psychical	synagogue
mythical	psychoanalyse	synapse
mythology	psychology	synchronize
nylon	psychosis	synchronous
nymph	pterodactyl	syncopation
oxygen	pygmy (Pygmy)*	syncretize
panegyric	pyjamas	syndicate
papyrus	pylon	syndrome
paralyse	pyramid	synod
paralysis	pyre	synonymous
paroxysm	pyromaniac	synopsis
pharynx	pyrotechnic	synoptic
physical	python	syntactic
physician	rhythm	syntax
physics	rye	synthesize
physiognomy	satyr	synthetic
physiology	satyrica*	syphon*
physique	scythe	syringe
plywood	sibyl	syrup
polyester	slyly	system
polygamy	strychnine	thyme
polyglot	style	thyroid
polygon	sycamore	tycoon
polyhedron	sycophant	tympany
polymer	syllable	typhoid
polyp	syllabub*	typhoon
polyphonic	syllabus	typhus
polythene	sylph	tyranny
porphyry	sylvan*	tyrant
presbyter	symbiotic	tyre
propylene	symbol	vinyl
proselytize	symmetrical	wych-elm
prototype	symmetry	xylophone
pseudonym	sympathetic	zephyr

* These words can take *i* or *y*, the more common spelling being given here: *cipher, (Gypsy) gypsy, lich gate, pygmy (Pygmy), siphon, syllabub and sylvan.*

8b – Some words ending in a vowel and *y* and followed by a suffix change the *y* to an *i*:
e.g. *laid, paid, said.*
Note the difference between *stayed* (vb.) and *staid* (adj.).

8c – A few words ending in a consonant and *y* and followed by a suffix beginning with a consonant keep the *y*, e.g. *flyless,* and composite words, e.g. *flyleaf.*

-y-	bellyful	shyly	spryness
	busyness (being busy)	shyness	treatyless
	dryly	slyly	wryly
	dryness	slyness	wryness
	flyless	spryly	

8d – Most diminutives and colloquial and slang words ending with a short / i/ sound are spelt *-ie* (with occasionally an alternative ending in *-y*), or *-y* (*-ie*).

-ie or -y	alky or -ie	dinkie	nooky or -ie
	auntie or -y	druggie	oldie
	Aussie	ducky or -ie	pressie or
	baddie or -y	floozy or -ie	prezzie
	birdie	or floosie	quickie
	bogie or -y	folkie or -y	roadie
	bolshie or -y	foodie or -y	rookie
	boogie	footsie	sarnie
	bookie	freebie	shortie or -y
	bootie	girlie	smarty or -ie
	brassie	goalie	smoothie or -y
	brickie	goolie or -y	softie
	brownie	granny or -ie	squaddie or -y
	budgie	groupie	sweetie
	caddie or -y	hanky or -ie	talkie
	cardie or -y	hippie or -y	thickie or -y
	chappie	jacksie or -y	toasty or -ie
	charlie	junky or -ie	trannie or -y
	chippy or -ie	kiddy or -ie	veggie
	clippie	lassie	wheelie
	collie	mammy or -ie	willie
	commie or -y	mashie or -y	yorkie
	conchie or -y	meanie	yuppie or -y
	cutie	movie	zombie or -y
	deary or -ie	nightie or -y	

– **When _u_ sounds like /w/.**

Q never occurs on its own but always in the combination -_qu_-.

When -_qu_- is at the beginning or in the middle of a word the _u_ sounds like a /w/ to produce the sound /kw/ except for _quay_ and _mannequin_.

-qu-			
	inquiry	quarterly	require
	inquisition	question	requite
	inquisitive	quick	sequin
	liquid	quiet	squabble
	liquidate	quiff	squib
	liquidity	quill	squid
	liquidize	quilt	squint
	obliquitous	quince	squire
	obsequious	quintuplet	squirm
	palanquin	quirk	squirrel
	perquisite	quit	tranquil
	prerequisite	quiz	vanquish
	propinquity	quotation	ventriloquist

When this -_qu_- occurs at the end of a word, it always has a silent _e_ and sounds like /k/, e.g. _antique_.

If a word that ends with _k_ unites with a word that begins with _w_, it does not produce a true /kw/ sound because the words are usually sounded as separate syllables, e.g. _backward_. Apart from this, the only occurrence of the letter combination -_kw_- in a word is _awkward_.

Note the /w/ sound in _puissance_ and _reservoir_.

Similarly, sometimes when _g_ is followed by a _u_, the _u_ is pronounced as a /w/, as in the following examples:

-gu-			
	anguish	guano	penguin
	bilingual	language	sanguine
	distinguish	languid	unguent
	extinguish	linguist	

Rule 9   <u>An *r* after vowels</u>

An *r* following a vowel usually prolongs the sound of the vowel:
e.g. *car, cur.*

Some vowel combinations with *r* cause trouble. These are given in rules 9a–9d.

9a — After *-qu-, w* or *wh-, -ar-* **has the sound which is written *-or-*,** usually the 'sympathy' sound /aw/ as in *corn* (cf. rule 5a).
(In a few words, e.g. *quarantine, quarrel, quarry, warrant, warren* and *warrior, -ar-* has the sound /o/ as in *sorry*.)

-quar-	headquarters quarantine quarrel quarry	quart quarter quarterage quarterly	quartet quarto quartz

-war- **and** **whar-**	athwart award dwart forewarn legwarmer lukewarm reward sward (grass) swarm swarthy	thwart towards untoward warble ward warden warder wardrobe warfare warhead	warlock warlord warm warning warp warrant warren warrior wart wharf

Exceptions: *antiquarian, antiquary, aquarium, square* and *wares.*
Note the sound /aw/ in *water* and the /ar/ sound in *clerk.*

9b — *-or-* after *w* sounds /er/.

wor-	word work worm	worth worship world	worse wort worthy

Exceptions: *sword* (weapon), *sworn* and *worn* (/aw/ sound) and *worry* (/-ʌr-/ sound).

9c — The indeterminate sound schwa can be written, when stressed, *-ear-, -er-, -ir-, -ur-, -or-, -our-*:
e.g. *learn; perfect; bird; fur; work; courtesy,*
and, when unstressed, *-er-, -or-, -re-, -ar-* and *-our-* (cf. rule 40):
e.g. *baker; actor; acre; beggar; harbour.*

The stressed schwa causes most difficulty. Compare the following lists. In most words the schwa sound is stressed.

-ear-	early	heard	rehearse
	earn	hearse	search
	earnest	learn	yearn
	earthy	pearl	

-er-	berth	mercantile	serpent
	certain	mercenary	servant
	certify	merchant	serve
	certitude	mercury	service
	fern	mercy	servile
	fertile	merge	sorcerer
	fervent	mermaid	swerve
	fervour	nerve	term
	gerbil	percolate	terminate
	germ	perfect	terminus
	her	perk	termite
	herb	permanent	tern
	herbicide	permeate	terse
	herd	permit n.	verb
	hermit	perquisite	verdict
	jerk	persecute	verge
	jerkin	person	verger
	jersey	pert	vermin
	kerb	pertinent	verse
	kernel	serf	vertical
	lantern	sermon	

-ir-	birch	first	squirm
	bird	gird	squirt
	birth	girl	stir
	circle	girth	swirl
	circuit	kirk	third
	dirk	mirth	thirsty
	dirt	shirk	virgin
	fir	shirt	virtual
	firm	skirt	virtue

-ur-	blur	hurt	surgery
	blurb	lurch	surname
	burst	lurk	survivor
	churn	murmur	turban
	curl	occur	turbine
	curtain	purchase	turn
	curvaceous	purpose	turnip
	curve	purse	turpentine
	discursive	spurt	urge
	excursion	sturdy	urgent
	furry	surface	
	further	surgeon	

-our-	courtesy	journal	journey
	favourite	journalist	

Note that *courage* and *nourish* have a short /u/.

9d — The sound /or/ (the 'sympathy' sound /aw/) **can be written, when stressed,** -or , oar :
e.g. *north, boar,*
and -our-:
e.g. *course, court, four, mourn, pour, recourse, source, your* (cf. rule 4d).

-oar-	aboard	hoard	sideboard
	boar	hoarse	skateboard
	board	hoary	skirtingboard
	cardboard	keyboard	soar
	clapperboard	motherboard	starboard
	coarse	oar	surfboard
	dashboard	outboard	uproar
	hoar	roar	

Note *floor* and *door*.

Rule 10   _-ae-_ and _-oe-_

- **The combinations -_ae_- and -_oe-_[1] are both pronounced as a long /e/ when stressed**, except _manoeuvre,_ so are often confused:
  e.g. _archaeology, Caesar, paediatrics; diarrhoea._

-ae-	aesthetic	encyclopedia	orthopaedic
	anaesthetize	or encyclopaedia	paediatrician
	archaeology	faeces	paedophile
	or archeology	gynaecology	palaeolithic
	athenaeum	haemoglobin	palaeontology
	defecate	haemophilia	
	or defaecate	haemorrhage	
	dieresis	haemorrhoids	
	or dieraesis	leukaemia	

-oe-	cenobite	fetus	manoeuvre
	or coenobite	or foetus	onomatopoeia
	coeliac	homeopathy	penology
	diarrhoea	or homoeopathy	

In many words, the spelling has been reduced to the letter _e_:
e.g. _ecumenical, medieval, pedagogy, pederast, penology_ and _phenomenon._

Note that words ending in _-rrhage_ and _-rrhoea_ (which mean a discharge or flow) have a double _r_ and an _h._

---

[1] In American English, nearly all of these words, except _coeliac_ and _onomatopoeia,_ are spelt with an _e_ in place of -_ae_- or -_oe-_, as the following examples show:
anesthetize, archaeology or _archeology, athenaeum_ or _atheneum, defecate, dieresis, encyclopedia, feces, gynecology, hemoglobin, hemophilia, hemorrhage, hemorrhoids, leukemia, medieval, orthopedic, paleolithic, paleontology, pederast, pediatrician, pedophilia; cenobite, diarrhea, fetus, homeopathy, maneuver, penology._

CONSONANTS

Rule 11   <u>*-ck-*, *-dge-* and *-tch-* after short vowels and the ending *-age* when
unstressed</u>

–   When a stressed short vowel (one that says its sound) is followed by a
/k/, /j/ or /ch/ sound, these sounds are written respectively *-ck-*, *-dge-* (cf.
rule 36) and *-tch-*.

-ck-	deck	rack	smack
	flock	rock	smock
	kick	rocker	snack
	luck	sick	stack
	o'clock	slack	stuck

-dge-	abridge	dodge	lodge
	acknowledge*	dredge	lodger
	acknowledgment or	drudge	midget
	acknowledgement*	edge	nudge
	badge	fidget	porridge
	badger	fledgling or	ridge
	bludgeon	fledgeling	selvage or
	bridge	fridge	selvedge*
	budgerigar	fudge	sledge
	budget	gadget	sludge
	budgie	grudge	smudge
	cadge	hedge	trudge
	cartridge	hodgepodge	wedge
	cudgel	knowledge*	widget
	didgeridoo	ledge	

* Note: unstressed *-edge* sounds /idge/ in these words.

-tch-	batch	ditch	ketch
	bitch	escutcheon	kitchen
	blotch	etching	latch
	butcher	fetch	match
	catch	glitch	notch
	catchment	hatch	pitch
	catchword	hatchet	ratchet
	clutch	hitch	retch
	crotchet	hotchpotch	sketch
	crutch	hutch	snatch
	dispatch	itch	stitch

continued

-tch-	stretch	thatch	witch
	switch	twitch	wretch
	tetchy	watch	

Exceptions: *attach, detach, machete, macho, much, rich, such* and *which*.

– An unstressed *-age* sounds like /idge/.

-age	acreage	frontage	plumage
	adage	garage	postage
	advantage	garbage	presage
	anchorage	haemorrhage	ravage
	appendage	haulage	salvage
	average	heritage	savage
	baggage	hermitage	scrimmage
	bandage	homage	seepage
	beverage	hostage	sewage
	bondage	image	shortage
	breakage	imagery	shrinkage
	cabbage	language	silage
	carnage	leakage	slippage
	carriage	leverage	spillage
	cartilage	linkage	spoilage
	cleavage	luggage	steerage
	cooperage	manage	stoppage
	corkage	marriage	storage
	cottage	message	stowage
	courage	mileage or milage	tannage
	coverage	mortgage	tillage
	damage	package	tonnage
	discourage	parentage	tutelage
	dosage	passage	usage
	dotage	pasturage	vantage
	drainage	patronage	vicarage
	encourage	peerage	village
	foliage	personage	vintage
	footage	pilgrimage	voltage
	forage	pillage	wastage

Rule 12   <u>Soft _g_ and _c_</u>

- _g_ sounds /j/ when followed by _e, i_ or _y_:
  e.g. _gent, giant, Gypsy_.
  But there are many exceptions to this rule.

-g-	agent	genre	(Gipsy) gipsy
	agility	gent	giraffe
	barge	genteel	gist
	bulge	gentile	gorgeous
	cage	gentle	(Gypsy) gypsy
	camouflage	genuflect	hinge
	challenge	genuine	huge
	charge	genus	imagine
	dangerous	geo-	ingenious
	dingy	geography	large
	dungeon	geology	manger
	engine	geranium	mirage
	exaggerate	gerbil	oblige
	gelatin or gelatine	geriatric	pageant
	gelignite	germ	passenger
	gem	german	pigeon
	gender	German	plunge
	gene	germane	rage
	genealogy	gerund	regiment
	general	gestation	region
	generate	gesticulate	register
	generous	gesture	religion
	genesis	giant	revenge
	genial	gigantic	sponge
	genie	gill (measure)	stage
	genital	gin	wage
	genitive	ginger	
	genocide	ginseng	

Exceptions:

- In words beginning with _gi-_ the exceptions outnumber the occurrences of the rule:
  e.g. _giddy, gift, gigabyte, giggle, gill_ (fish), _gilt, gimel, gimlet, gimmick, gingham, girl, girt, girth, gismo, give_.

- **When making a second word by adding an ending beginning with _e_ or _i_ to a first word, the pronunciation of _g_ is the same as in the first word,**
  e.g. _cringer, singer; bringing, cringing_.
  Note _singeing_ to differentiate from _singing_.

- Other exceptions are the hard _g_ in _begin, finger, gear, Geiger, geisha, get,_ and the soft _g_ in _margarine_.
  Note the /j/ sound in _soldier_.

No English word ends in -j, -je or -jen (*hajj* is a foreign word), so this sound at the end of a word is always written -ge.

The combination -jy- does not occur in English. It is always written -gy-.

The combinations -je- and -ji- are not numerous so they are given in full.

Since je- begins a number of frequently used words, some may be tempted to write je- at the beginning of a word in place of ge-.

-je-		
abject	jeer	jetty
adjective	jejune	Jew
conjecture	jelly	jewel
dejected	jeopardize	majesty
eject	jerk	object
inject	jerry	project
interject	jersey	reject
jealous	jester	subject
jeans	jet	trajectory
jeep	jetsam	

-ji-		
jib	jingle	jive
jibe	jink	jujitsu
jiffy	jinks	or jujutsu
jig	jinn	or jiujutsu
jigsaw	jinx	
jilt	jitter	

– *c* sounds /s/ when followed by *e*, *i* or *y*:
   e.g. *cell; excite; cycle.*

-c-		
ace	decision	priceless
acid	embrace	race
brace	exciting	recent
bracelet	exercise	recite
braces	face	rice
celery	fascinate	scarce
cement	fence	scarcity
centigrade	genocide	scene
centimetre	introduce	scenery
centipede	iridescent	scent
cereal	lance	scintillate
ceremony	necessary	specimen
certificate	necklace	suicide
cigar	pence	trance
cigarette	place	twice
cinders	porcelain	vicinity
citizen	precipice	

Note: for words ending in *c* adding an ending beginning with *e* or *i*, see rule 25.

s is hardly ever written immediately after *x*, when the *x* plus /s/ sound is followed by a vowel, perhaps because there is an /s/ sound in *x*.

For an /s/ sound after *x* use *c* with *e* or *i*.

-xc-	exceed	except	excise
	excel	excess	excite

The only exceptions to this rule are the following unusual words and their derivatives:
axseed, exsanguine, exscind, exsect, exsert and *exsiccate*.

Note: the ending *-ice* sounds /iss/ when it is not accented.

-ice	accomplice	dentifrice	notice
	apprentice	edifice	novice
	artifice	hospice	office
	avarice	in-service	orifice
	benefice	injustice	poultice
	bodice	jaundice	practice n.
	caddice	justice	precipice
	chalice	lattice	prejudice
	coppice	liquorice	pumice
	cornice	malice	service
	cowardice	malpractice	solstice
	crevice	mortice	surplice

Rule 13 <u>The /sh/ sound</u>

–   **To begin the first syllable, use *sh-*** except for *sugar, sure, sureness, surely* and *schedule, schist, schmalz, schnapps, schnozzle, schuss, schwa.*

–   **To begin any other syllable, use *-ci-*, *-si-* or *-ti-*** except for *cushion, fashion,* the ending *-ship* and the following words using *-sur-*.

-sur-	assure	exposure	pressure
	censure	fissure	sure
	composure	insurance	surely
	embrasure	insure	surety
	enclosure	leisure	tonsure
	ensure	measure	treasure
	erasure	pleasure	

Note that when *-sur-* is preceded by a vowel, the /sh/ sound is voiced, as in the /ʒ/ or /zh/ sound in *measure*. *Collage* also has this sound.

There are not many words using -ci- (see also rule 25b).

-ci-	ancient	efficient	pertinacious
	appreciate	fascia or facia	precious
	associate	ferocious	pugnacious
	atrocious	inauspicious	rapacious
	audacious	injudicious	sagacious
	beautician	loquacious	salacious
	capacious	luscious	specious
	capricious	mathematician	suspicious
	coercion	mendacious	tactician
	conscience	meretricious	tenacious
	conscious	noviciate or	veracious (honest)
	commercially	novitiate	vicious
	conscientious	obstetrician	vivacious
	contumacious	officious	voracious (greedy)
	deficient	pernicious	
	efficacious	perspicacious	

The entries using the common endings -sion and -tion, e.g. tension, nation, are too numerous to give.

The main words ending in -tious are:

-tious	abstentious	flirtatious	repetitious
	ambitious	fractious	scrumptious
	bumptious	incautious	seditious
	cautious	infectious	sententious
	conscientious	licentious	superstitious
	expeditious	nutritious	surreptitious
	facetious	ostentatious	tendentious
	factious	pretentious	unpretentious
	fictitious	propitious	vexatious

13a – *-si-* is used where the syllable before it ends in s or the word that it is derived from ends in *-s(e)*:
e.g. *mission, tense—tension.*

13b – If the sound /shən/ uses *-si-,* it usually needs a consonant plus *-sion* or *-ssion,* e.g. *tension, mission,* as *-si-* following a vowel sound usually says the sound /zh/, e.g. *television.*

13c – **Some words ending in -ce have derivatives in -ti-:**
e.g. *existence—existential, palace—palatial, penitence—penitential.*

Some of the following words which end in *-tial* fall into this category.

-ti-	circumstantial	martial	propitiate
	existential	noviciate or novitiate	providential
	experiential	nuptial	quotient
	impartial	palatial	residential
	impatient	patient	reverential
	initial	penitential	sapiential
	initiate	pestilential	sequential
	insatiable	potential	spatial

13d – **The sound /shən/ can be the endings *-cian* (cf. rule 25b), *-sian* (nearly all indicating nationalities, with some examples below) and *ocean*.**

For *-ection* or *-exion* see rule 38.

-sian	Asian	Elysian	Persian
	Cartesian	Frisian	Russian
	Carthusian	Indonesian	
	Dionysian	Malaysian	

Hessian and *Parisian* keep the /s/ and /z/ sounds.

Anxious, noxious and *crucifixion* have a /sh/ sound.

13e – **Some words of French origin use *-ch-* to make the /sh/ and /ch/ sounds, as in most of the following examples.**

-ch-	avalanche	chateau	machine
	branch	chef	moustache
	chaise	clench	parachute
	chalet	cliche	ranch
	chassis	inch	trench

Note: the /ch/ sound occurs frequently in *-ture* (see rule 40f) and in other *-tu-* combinations.

| **-tu-** | fortunate | punctual | tulip |
| | fortune | punctuation | virtual |

Rule 14   <u>Double consonants</u>

- *j, q, v, x* and *y* are never doubled in English words, except for some informal words using double *v* like *civvy, navvy*:
  e.g. *boxer, liver, river*.

- *h, k* and *w* are doubled only in compound words, e.g. *powwow*.

- All the other consonants, viz. *b, c, d, f, g, l, m, n, p, r, s, t* and *z*, may be doubled.

Whether or not to double a consonant is one of the most frequently encountered problems in English spelling. The following words can cause difficulties.

cassette	disappear	hurry	omelette
chaffinch	excellent	innocent	palette
colossal	gorilla	instalment	recommend
confetti	happen	irritable	
corridor	happiness	irritate	
dilemma	hiccup	lollipop	

14a

- **At the end of a word** (or the first part of a compound word), *f, s* and *z* are often doubled and *l* is sometimes doubled:
  e.g. *cuff; ass; press; jazz; idyll*.

These are mostly one-syllable words, some two-syllable words and their derivatives, and words with the suffix *-ness*.

Note also *egg* and *add*.

-ff			
	bailiff	off	skiff
	chiffchaff	quaff	standoff
	cuff	quiff	-stuff
	gruff	riffraff	tariff
	liftoff	scoff	tip-off
	mastiff	sheriff	trade-off
	midriff	skewwhiff	well-off

-ss			
	abbess	amiss	brass
	abscess	ass	business
	abyss	assess	buttress
	access	bass	canvass vb.
	across	bless	carcass
	address	bliss	or carcase
	albatross	blunderbuss	caress
	amass	boss	chess

continued

-ss			
	class	duress	largess
	compass	edelweiss	or largesse
	compress	egress	-less
	concuss	embarrass	moss
	confess	emboss	-ness
	congress	engross	percuss
	crass	-ess	possess
	cress	excess	press
	criss-cross	express	princess
	cross	floss	process
	cuss	fortress	profess
	cutlass	fuss	progress
	cypress	glass	prowess
	depress	gloss	regress
	digress	grass	success
	discuss	harass	surpass
	dismiss	harness	trespass
	distress	heiress	unless
	doss	impress	witness
	dress	ingress	
	dross	jackass	

-l			
	annul	distil	impel
	appal	enrol	instil
	brimful	enthral	rebel
	or brimfull	excel	repel
	carrel	extol	
	or carrell	fulfil	

-ll			
	atoll	holdall	plimsoll
	chlorophyll	idyll	or plimsole
	deskill	install	poll
	droll	or instal	squall
	gill	mall	windfall

Words ending in double *l* when used as a prefix or suffix lose an *l*.[2]

-l-			
	almost	belfry	handful
	already	careful	skilful
	altogether	chilblain	ungrateful
	always	disgraceful	welcome
	bashful	fulfil	welfare
	beautiful	fulsome	wilful

---

[2] In American English *skillful* and *willful*

Exceptions: *fullback, full face* (adj.), *fullface* (advb.).

Also, words ending in double *l* lose an *l* before suffixes beginning with a consonant (*skilful*)**, except for *-ness*.**

-llness	chillness	fullness	smallness
	drollness	illness	stillness
	dullness or dulness	shrillness	tallness

In seeming exceptions to this rule, it will be found that the word ending in double *l* is used as the root word:
e.g. *fibrefill, landfill, overfill; overspill; pitfall; brimfull, chock-full, choke-full, chuck-full, cram-full, half-full, overfull, topfull.*

14b   –   **As prefixes and suffixes are written in full,** adding them often results in a double consonant.

For exceptions, see rule 14a above.

comm-	comma	commercial	commonness
	command	commiserate	communicate
	commeasure	commission	communion
	commemorate	commissionaire	communiqué
	commence	commitment	communism
	commend	committee	
	commensurate	commodity	

diss-	dissatisfy	disservice	dissoluble
	dissect	dissident	dissolute
	dissemble	dissimilar	dissolution
	disseminate	dissimulate	dissolve
	dissent	dissipate	dissonant
	dissertation	dissociate	

ill-	illegal	illicit	illogical
	illegible	illimitable	illuminate
	illegitimate	illiquid	illusion
	illiberal	illiterate	illusory

interr-	interracial	interrelate	interrupt
	interregional	interreligious	
	interregnum	interrogate	

imm-		
immaculate	immigrant	immolate
immanent	immigrate	immoral
immaterial	imminent	immortal
immature	immiscible	immovable
immeasurable	immitigable	immune
immediate	immobile	immunization
immemorial	immobilize	immure
immense	immoderate	
immerse	immodest	

miss-		
misshapen	misspend	misstate
misspell		

superr-		
superrealism	superreliance	superrestriction
superrefine	superrespectable	superrich

surr-		
surrealism	surreptitious	surround
surrender	surrogate	

unn-		
unnamed	unneeded	unnerve
unnatural	unnegotiable	unnoticed
unnecessary	unneighbourly	

-nness		
barrenness	hiddenness	stubbornness
brazenness	humanity	suddenness
brownness	or humanness	sullenness
cleanness	keenness	swollenness
commonness	leanness	thinness
cravenness	meanness	unbrokenness
crimsonness	misshapenness	uncleanness
drunkenness	mistakenness	uncommonness
evenness	modernity	unevenness
foreignness	or modernness	unknownness
forlornness	openness	vanity
forsakenness	plainness	or vainness
forswornness	rottenness	wanness
frozenness	soddenness	wantonness
goldenness	solemnity	withdrawnness
greenness	or solemnness	woodenness
heartbrokenness	or solemness	
heathenness	sternness	

The Latin prefix *ad-* (meaning moving towards, changing into or intensifying) causes a lot of double consonants because before *c, f, g, l, n, p, r, s* and *t* the *d* of *ad-* is dropped and the following consonant is doubled, e.g. *accelerator*.

Ad- before *-qu-* drops the *d* and produces *-cqu-*, because we cannot have a double *q*.

Similarly the Latin prefix *ob-* (meaning towards, against or in the way of) produces a double consonant when used before *c, f* and *p*.

Before *m*, the *b* of *ob-* disappears, without doubling the *m* to give *omit* and *omission*. Similarly the *d* of *ad-* disappears before *-sc-*, *-sp-* and *-st-*: e.g. *ascribe, aspire, astern*.

These double consonants originated in Latin but we inherited them and the words still usually carry, in some way, the meanings of the Latin prefixes.

Not all the double consonants given below originate from *ad-* or *ob-* but most of them do.

acc-	accede	acclivity	account
	accelerator	accolade	accredit
	accent	accommodate	accrue
	acceptant	accompany	accumulate
	access	accomplished	accurate
	accident	accord	accursed
	acclaim	accordion	accuse
	acclimatize	accost	accustom

acqu-	acquaintance	acquire	acquit
	acquiesce	acquisition	acquittal

add-	add	addition	address
	addendum	additive	adduce
	adder	addle	
	addict	add-on	

aff-	affable	affirm	affranchise
	affair	affix	affray
	affect	afflatus	affricative
	afferent	afflict	affright
	affidavit	affluent	affront
	affiliate	afford	
	affinity	afforestation	

agg-	agglomeration	aggravate	aggrieved
	aggradation	aggregate	aggro
	aggrandizement	aggressive	

all-	allay	alleviate	allude
	allegation	alley	allure
	allege	alliance	allusion
	allegiance	alligator	alluvial
	allegorical	alliteration	ally
	alleluia	allocution	
	allergic	allow	

ann-	annal	anniversary	annual
	anneal	annotate	annuity
	annex	announce	annul
	annihilate	annoy	annunciation

app-	appalling	appendix	appraise
	apparatus	appertain	appreciate
	apparel	appetite	apprehend
	apparent	applaud	apprehensible
	apparently	applause	apprehensive
	apparitor	apple	apprentice
	appeal	appliance	apprise
	appearance	applicant	approach
	appease	apply	approbation
	appellant	appoint	appropriate
	appendage	apportion	approve
	appendicitis	apposite	approximate

arr-	arraign	arrears	arrogate
	arrange	arrest	arrow
	arrant	arrive	
	array	arrogant	

ass-	assailant	assess	assizes
	assassin	assessor	associate
	assault	asset	assonance
	assayer	assiduous	assortment
	assemble	assign	assuage
	assent	assimilate	assume
	assert	assistance	assure

179

att-	attach	attenuate	attract
	attack	attest	attribute
	attain	attic	attrition
	attempt	attire	attune
	attend	attitude	
	attention	attorney	

occ-	occasion	occult	occur
	occidental	occupation	occurrence
	occlude	occupy	

off-	offal	offensive	official
	offence	offer	officiate
	offend	office	officious

opp-	oppilate	oppose	opprobrium
	opponent	opposite	oppugn
	opportunity	oppress	

Words ending in *t* that add the suffix *-sion* change the *t* to *s*:
e.g. *admit—admission, commit—commission.*

Some examples of this occur in the following list of words ending in *-ssion*.

-ssion	accession	dispossession	procession
	admission	emission	profession
	aggression	expression	recession
	cession	fission	regression
	commission	impression	remission
	compassion	intermission	repercussion
	compression	mission	repression
	concession	obsession	secession
	concussion	omission	session
	confession	oppression	submission
	decommission	passion	suppression
	decompression	percussion	transgression
	depression	permission	transmission
	discussion	possession	

Headmistressship is the only word with three *s*'s and *transship* has an
alternative *tranship*.

Words ending in *l* which add *-like* use a hyphen, except for *mammallike*.

Words ending in *l* or double *l* add the suffix *-less* with a hyphen, except for *goalless, heelless, jailless, mealless, railless, recoilless, sailless, soulless, tailless, veilless. Skilless* is an alternative to *skill-less*.

14c – **Some wrongly expect a double *l* after a single vowel, when the final syllable is accented** (*annul, appal, enrol*), because monosyllabic words ending in a single vowel and *l* almost invariably have double *l*. See the examples towards the end of rule 14a.

Note that many scientific words end in *-yl*:
e.g. *butyl, ethyl, phenyl, propyl, pterodactyl* and *vinyl*.
But note *chlorophyll*.

14d – **A stressed vowel followed by one consonant is often short,** especially when the consonant is followed by *i*:
e.g. *finish, vanish* but *swinish*.

This is true of endings like *-iferous, -ilia, -iliate, ility, -iterate,* and *-licily.*

Because a stressed vowel followed by two consonants is usually short, we often expect a stressed vowel followed by one consonant to be long. Note *tranquillity* and *tonsillitis*.

A knowledge of word derivation is useful; *inoculate* has one *n* but *innocuous*, because it means 'not nocuous', has two. *Battalion* is from the same source as *battle. Bilious* is from the word *bile. Committee* is from the Latin *com* plus *mittere. Desiccated* is from the Latin *de* plus *siccare*.

Rule 15   The silent consonants *b, c, d, g, -gh-, h, k, l, m, n, p, s, t* and *w,* and the silent vowel *u*

Examples of all the silent letters (except *e*) are given below.

-b-	aplomb	doubtful	numb
	bomb	dumb	plumb
	catacomb	honeycomb	succumb
	climb	jamb	thumb
	comb	lamb	tomb
	crumb	limb	womb

-c-	ascend	indict	rescind
	crescent	miscellaneous	scent

-d-	grandchild	grandmother	sandwich
	granddaughter	grandson	
	grandfather	handsome	

-h-	dinghy everywhere gherkin whale whatever when whenever	where wherever whether while whimper whine whip	whirl whisk whisker whisper why

-k-	acknowledge knack knapweed knave knead knee kneel knell	knew knickers knick-knack knife knight knit knob knock	knocker knot know knowledge knuckle knur or knurr knurl

-l-	almond balk caulk chalk	colonel folk halve palm	salmon talk walk

m-	mnemonic		

-n	autumn	column	condemn

-s-	aisle corps	island isle	viscount

-t-	apostle bristle bustle castle chasten christen epistle fasten	forecastle glisten gristle hasten hustle jostle listen mistletoe	moisten nestle often* pestle rustle thistle trestle whistle

* A variant pronunciation sounds the *t*.

-u-	ague	guardian	languorous
	analogue	guerilla	league
	biscuit	guess	meringue
	brogue	guest	misguided
	built	guidance	monologue
	buy	guide	morgue
	catalogue	guild	pedagogue
	colleague	guile	plague
	demagogue	guilt	prologue
	dialogue	guinea	rogue
	disguise	guise	safeguard
	drogue	guitar	synagogue
	epilogue	harangue	tongue
	fatigue	intrigue	travelogue
	fugue	intriguing	vague
	guard	languor	vogue

-w-	answer	wraith	wring
	two	wrap	wrinkle
	unwrap	wrath	wrist
	who	wreak	writ
	whoever	wreath	write
	whole	wren	writhe
	whooping-cough	wrest	wrong
	whose	wrestle	wrought
	wrack	wretch	wrung

15a – *-ch-* (sounds /k/), *-ph-* (sounds /f/), *-pn-* (sounds /n/),
-ps- (sounds /s/), *-pt-* (sounds /t/), *-rh-* (sounds /r/) **and often
-gn- (sounds /n/) point to the Greek origin of a word.**

-ch-	chaos	enchiridion	school
	chiropodist	lichen	schooner
	chiropody	orchestra	terpsichore
	Christian	scheme	
	Christmas	scholarship	

-ph-

agoraphobia
alphabet
amorphous
amphibious
amphitheatre
amphora
anthropomorphic
antiphon
aphid
aphorism
aphrodisiac
apocrypha
apostrophe
asphalt
asphyxiate
atmosphere
atrophy
autobiography
autograph
bibliophile
blaspheme
cardiograph
catastrophe
-cephalic
choreograph
cinematography
cipher
claustrophobia
colophon
Dictaphone
digraph
diphthong
dolphin
earphone
ectomorph
emphasis

emphatic
endomorph
ephemeral
Epiphany
epitaph
euphemism
euphoria
geomorphic
gramophone
-graph
grapheme
haemophilia
haemophiliac
headphones
homophobia
homophone
hyphen
lithograph
lymph
mesomorph
metaphoric
microphone
monograph
-morph
morpheme
morphine
morphology
nymph
oesophagus
ophthalmic
paedophile
paragraph
payphone
peripheral
phantom
-phany

pharaoh
pharmaceutical
pharmacy
pheasant
philately
-phile
Philip
Philippines
philosophy
phlegm
phlegmatic
-phobia
phone
-phone
phoneme
phonetic
phoney
phonograph
photograph
phrase
phylactery
prophet
saxophone
seismograph
siphon
-sophy
sphere
sphinx
stenography
sycophant
tachograph
telegraph
telephone
theophany
triumph
xylophone

pn-

pneumatic

ps-

psalm
pseudo

pseudonym
psoriasis

psychedelic
psychiatrist

pt-

ptarmigan
pterodactyl

pterosaur
Ptolemy

receipt

-rh-	antirrhinum	rheo-	rhododendron
	catarrh	rheostat	rhombus
	cirrhosis	rhesus	rhubarb
	eurhythmic	rhetorical	rhyme
	haemorrhage	rheumatism	rhythm
	haemorrhoids	rhinitis	-rrhoea (e.g.
	myrrh	rhinoceros	diarrhoea)
	rhapsody	rhizo-	

-gn-	arraign	ensign	gnosis
	assign	feign	gnostic
	benign	foreign	gnu
	campaign	gnarl	impugn
	condign	gnat	malign
	consign	gnaw	reign
	deign	gneiss	resign
	design	gnome	sign

15b – The silent -*gh*-

This produces different sounds:

i) **after *i* it lengthens the vowel,** e.g. *sigh* (see examples in rule 4c above).

ii) **after -*ei*- it usually produces a long /a/:**
   e.g. *eight, freight, inveigh, neigh, neighbour, sleigh, weigh, weight.*

   Exceptions: in two words it produces a long /i/, *height* and *sleight* (of hand).

iii) **after -*ai*- it produces a long /a/ in one word,** *straight.*

iv) **after -*au*- it usually produces /aw/:**
   e.g. *caught, daughter, distraught, fraught, haughty, naught, naughty, onslaught, slaughter, taught.*

   Exceptions: it produces /af/ in *draught* and *laugh.*

v) **after -*ou*- it usually produces /aw/**
   e.g. *bought, brought, fought, nought, ought, sought, thought, wrought.*

Exceptions:

/ow/ in *bough, doughty, drought, plough, slough* and *sough*
/ew/ in *through*
/of/ in *cough* and *trough*
/uf/ in *enough, rough, roughage* and *tough*
long /o/ in *although, dough, furlough* and *though*

Note: *borough* and *thorough* end with the sound /ə/

PLURALS

Rule 16   <u>Hissing endings</u>

— **Words which end in a sound like a hiss (the sibilants *-ch*, *-sh*, *-s*, *-ss*, *-x* and *-z*) add *-es* to make a plural:**
e.g. *churches; bushes; buses; crosses; boxes; buzzes.*

The same rule applies to verbs with sibilant endings that add an *s*:
e.g. *catches, pushes.*

Note that some words with an ending in *-is* change it to *-es* (*basis—bases*) and endings in *-us* usually change to *-i* (cf. rule 22d (ii) and (v)).

Rule 17   <u>Words which end in *-f* and *-fe*</u>

— **Words with and ending in one *f* (or *-fe*) change it to *v* and add *-es* to make a plural:**
e.g. *beef—beeves.*

-ves	beeves	leaves	sheaves
	calves	lives	shelves
	elves	loaves	wives
	knives	selves	

Exceptions: *beliefs, chefs, chiefs, griefs* (OED), *proofs, roofs, safes* and *serfs.*
Note *dwarfs* or *dwarves, hooves* or *hoofs, scarfs* or *scarves, turfs* or *turves* and *wharves* or *wharfs.*

Words ending in double *f* just add *s*, but note *staffs* or *staves.*

Rule 18   <u>Words which end in *-o*</u>

— **Monosyllables and more common words form their plurals in *-oes*; longer, abbreviated and less common words form their plurals in *-os*.**

This general rule does have some exceptions.

18a – Plurals in -*oes*

   i) **monosyllables** like *goes*

   ii) **words used as much in the plural as in the singular, often the names of animals and plants,** e.g. *buffalo—buffaloes*

-oes	buffaloes	heroes	torpedoes
	dingoes	jingoes	vertigoes
	dominoes	lingoes	or vertigines
	echoes	potatoes	
	embargoes	tomatoes	

18b – Plurals in -*os*

   i) **long words** like *archipelagos* (or *archipelagoes*), *armadillos*

   ii) **abbreviated words** like *photos, pros*

   iii) **words seldom used in the plural and technical words** like *crescendos, infernos.*

   iv) **when the *o* comes after a vowel sound** as in *cameos, embryos, folios*

   v) **strange words** like *centos, matzos*

   vi) **proper names** like *Lotharios, Neros, Romeos*

-os	adagios	credos	jumbos
	albinos	demos	kimonos
	antipastos	diminuendos	largos
	avocados	discos	libidos
	bambinos	dynamos	librettos
	Biros	egos	or libretti
	bistros	Eskimos	lidos
	boleros	fandangos	limbos
	bordellos	flamencos	logos
	calypsos	gigolos	maestri
	cantos	giros	or maestros
	capos	gismos	magnetos
	casinos	guanos	matzos
	cellos	hippos	memos
	chinos	impresarios	merinos
	concertos	infernos	metros
	contraltos	intermezzos	micros

continued

-os		
morellos	radios	studios
mustachios	risottos	supremos
octavos	rodeos	tangos
oratorios	scherzos	tempos
pantos	or scherzi	or tempi
patios	schizos	torsos
pesos	silos	or torsi
pimentos	solos	tuxedos
ponchos	sombreros	typos
portfolios	sopranos	tyros
psychos	or soprani	videos
quangos	stereos	virtuosos
quartos	stilettos	or virtuosi

It will be clear from the above that more words form a plural in -*os* but many are less used words. Hence the common assumption that most words have a plural in -*oes* apart from a few exceptions.

18c   –   **Plurals in either -*os* or -*oes***

-os or -oes		
archipelagos or -oes	flamingos or -oes	mosquitoes or -os
banjos or -oes	frescoes or -os	peccadillos or -oes
bimbos or -oes	gazebos or -oes	placebos or -oes
bingos or -oes	ghettos or -oes	porticoes or -os
bravadoes or -os	grottoes or -os	provisos or -oes
calicoes or -os	haloes or -os	salvos or -oes
cargoes or -os	hoboes or -os	stuccoes or -os
dadoes or -os	indigos or -oes	tobaccos or -oes
dodos or -oes	innuendos or -oes	viragoes or -os
farragos or -oes	mangoes or -os	volcanoes or -os
fiascos or -oes	manifestoes or -os	

Rule 19 <u>Words which end in -*y*</u>

– **Words which end in a consonant plus *y* change the *y* to *i* and add -*es* to make a plural,** except proper names like *Germanys, Marys*:
  e.g. *babies, cities, copies.*

– **Words ending in a vowel plus *y* simply add *s*** (cf. rule 8):
  e.g. *alleys, bays, boys, jarveys, jockeys, joeys, monkeys, valleys.*

-ies		
	ability *pl* -ties	body *pl* -dies
	academy *pl* -mies	boundary *pl* -ries
	actuary *pl* -ries	brandy *pl* -dies
	adversary *pl* -ries	brewery *pl* -ries
	adversity *pl* -ties	brolly *pl* -llies
	agency *pl* -cies	buggy *pl* -ggies
	agony *pl* -nies	burglary *pl* -ries
	allegory *pl* -ries	bursary *pl* -ries
	allergy *pl* -gies	busby *pl* -bies
	amenity *pl* -ties	cabby *pl* -bies
	amnesty *pl* -ties	caddy *pl* -dies
	anchovy *pl* -vies	calamity *pl* -ties
	anniversary *pl* -ries	canary *pl* -ries
	annuity *pl* -ties	candy *pl* -dies
	anthology *pl* -gies	cannery *pl* -ries
	antipathy *pl* -thies	canopy *pl* -pies
	antiquary *pl* -ries	capillary *pl* -ries
	antiquity *pl* -ties	casualty *pl* -ties
	anxiety *pl* -ties	category *pl* -ries
	apathy *pl* -thies	cavity *pl* -ties
	apostasy *pl* -sies	centenary *pl* -ries
	apothecary *pl* -ries	century *pl* -ries
	armoury *pl* -ries	certainty *pl* -ties
	army *pl* -mies	city *pl* cities
	artery *pl* -ries	colloquy *pl* -quies
	aunty *pl* -ties	colony *pl* -nies
	austerity *pl* -ties	comedy *pl* -dies
	autopsy *pl* -sies	company *pl* -nies
	aviary *pl* -ries	conspiracy *pl* -cies
	baby *pl* -bies	constituency *pl* -cies
	bakery *pl* -ries	consultancy *pl* -cies
	balcony *pl* -nies	contingency *pl* -cies
	baptistry *pl* -ries	copy *pl* -pies
	battery *pl* -ries	country *pl* -ries
	belly *pl* -llies	county *pl* -ties
	beneficiary *pl* -ries	cry *pl* cries
	bibliography *pl* -phies	currency *pl* -cies

continued

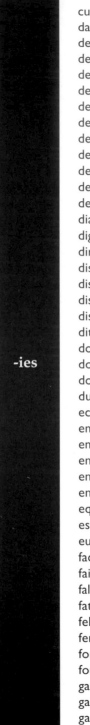

-ies

curry *pl* -rries
dairy *pl* -ries
deanery *pl* -ries
deficiency *pl* -cies
delicacy *pl* -cies
delivery *pl* -ries
democracy *pl* -cies
dependency *pl* -cies
depositary *pl* -ries
depository *pl* -ries
deputy *pl* -ties
destiny *pl* -nies
devilry *pl* -ries
diary *pl* -ries
dignity *pl* -ties
directory *pl* -ries
discovery *pl* -ries
discrepancy *pl* -cies
dispensary *pl* -ries
distillery *pl* -ries
ditty *pl* -tties
dolly *pl* -llies
dowry *pl* -ries
doxology *pl* -gies
duty *pl* -ties
ecology *pl* -gies
embassy *pl* -ssies
emergency *pl* -cies
energy *pl* -gies
enquiry *pl* -ries
entry *pl* -ries
equity *pl* -ties
estuary *pl* -ries
eulogy *pl* -gies
faculty *pl* -ties
fairy *pl* -ries
fallacy *pl* -cies
fatality *pl* -ties
felony *pl* -nies
ferry *pl* -rries
formulary *pl* -ries
foundry *pl* -ries
galaxy *pl* -xies
gallery *pl* -ries
gantry *pl* -tries

glossary *pl* -ries
granary *pl* -ries
gravy *pl* -vies
grocery *pl* -ries
guppy *pl* -ppies
hanky *pl* -kies
harmony *pl* -nies
heresy *pl* -sies
hierarchy *pl* -chies
hippy* *pl* -ppies
history *pl* -ries
hobby *pl* -bbies
ignominy *pl* -nies
industry *pl* -ries
infirmary *pl* -ries
iniquity *pl* -ties
injury *pl* -ries
inquiry *pl* -ries
inventory *pl* -ries
ivory *pl* -ries
ivy *pl* -vies
jury *pl* -ries
laboratory *pl* -ries
lady *pl* -dies
larceny *pl* -nies
laundry *pl* -ries
lavatory *pl* -ries
lectionary *pl* -ries
legacy *pl* -cies
liability *pl* -ties
library *pl* -ries
livery *pl* -ries
lobby *pl* -bbies
lorry *pl* -rries
lottery *pl* -ries
loyalty *pl* -ties
luxury *pl* -ries
malady *pl* -dies
mercenary *pl* -ries
ministry *pl* -ries
miscellany *pl* -nies
misery *pl* -ries
mockery *pl* -ries
monarchy *pl* -chies
monastery *pl* -ries

continued

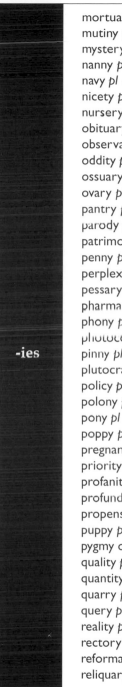

-ies

mortuary *pl* -ries
mutiny *pl* -nies
mystery *pl* -ries
nanny *pl* -nnies
navy *pl* -vies
nicety *pl* -ties
nursery *pl* -ries
obituary *pl* -ries
observatory *pl* -ries
oddity *pl* -ties
ossuary *pl* -ries
ovary *pl* -ries
pantry *pl* -ries
parody *pl* -dies
patrimony *pl* -nies
penny *pl* -nnies
perplexity *pl* -ties
pessary *pl* -ries
pharmacy *pl* -cies
phony *pl* -nies
photocopy *pl* -pies
pinny *pl* -nnies
plutocracy *pl* -cies
policy *pl* -cies
polony *pl* -nies
pony *pl* -nies
poppy *pl* -ppies
pregnancy *pl* -cies
priority *pl* -ties
profanity *pl* -ties
profundity *pl* -ties
propensity *pl* -ties
puppy *pl* -ppies
pygmy or pigmy *pl* -mies
quality *pl* -ties
quantity *pl* -ties
quarry *pl* -rries
query *pl* -ries
reality *pl* -ties
rectory *pl* -ries
reformatory *pl* -ries
reliquary *pl* -ries

remedy *pl* -dies
repository *pl* -ries
revelry *pl* -ries
rivalry *pl* -ries
robbery *pl* -ries
rosary *pl* -ries
royalty *pl* -ties
ruby *pl* -bies
salary *pl* -ries
scullery *pl* -ries
secretary *pl* -ries
security *pl* -ties
seminary *pl* -ries
sentry *pl* -ries
sherry *pl* -rries
sky *pl* skies
soliloquy *pl* -quies
speciality *pl* -ties
spy *pl* spies
story *pl* -ries
sty *pl* sties
subsidy *pl* -dies
subtlety *pl* -ties
taxonomy *pl* -mies
territory *pl* -ries
theophany *pl* -nies
theory *pl* -ries
therapy *pl* -pies
toiletry *pl* -ries
tragedy *pl* -dies
trilby *pl* -bies
trophy *pl* -phies
try *pl* tries
tummy *pl* -mmies
tyranny *pl* -nnies
uncertainty *pl* -ties
vacancy *pl* -cies
victory *pl* -ries
wallaby *pl* -bies
whinny *pl* -nnies
yuppy* *pl* -ppies

*alternatives to *hippie* and *yuppie*

Rule 20   <u>Endings in *-s* are not always followed by a plural verb</u>

 20a   –   **Some words which end in 's' can be both singular and plural,** e.g. *innings*.

20b   –   **Names of diseases and sciences are singular:**
e.g. *measles; acoustics.*

20c   –   **Names of behaviour are plural** e.g. *antics.*

Note: proper names follow the normal rule (cf. rule 16), the plural adding *-es*: e.g. *Evanses, Joneses.*

Rule 21   <u>Compound words</u>

–   **Compound words usually make the first word plural** (*mothers-in-law*) **but some are treated as single words** (*court-martials*) **especially if they are from verbs** (*knock-outs, spin-offs*) **or end in *-ful*** (*handfuls*).

Some make both parts plural, like compounds with *man* or *woman* (*menservants*) **and usually words with *and*** (*ins-and-outs, ups-and-downs*).

Note: in phrases with *Lord*, if *Lord* is an adjective, it does not become plural (*Lord Mayors*) but if it is a noun, it alone becomes plural (*Lords of Appeal*).

Rule 22   <u>Foreign words</u>

–   **With foreign words, where there is a choice, there is a tendency to use the English plural** (*formulas, indexes*) **but some words have only a foreign form** (*bases, theses*).

 22a   –   **Some French words ending in *-eau* add *x* in the plural.**

-eau	
bandeau *pl* -x	plateau *pl* -s or -x
beau *pl* -s or -x	portmanteau *pl* -s or -x
bureau *pl* -s or -x	rondeau *pl* -x
chateau *pl* -x or -s	rouleau *pl* -x or -s
flambeau *pl* -x or -s	tableau *pl* -x or -s
gateau *pl* -x	tonneau *pl* -s or -x
morceau *pl* -x	trousseau *pl* -x or -s
nouveau *pl* -x	

22b — The plural of Hebrew words sometimes ends in -im:
e.g. *cherubs, cherubim; seraphs, seraphim.*

22c The plural of some Italian words sometimes ends in -*i* but most of the *o* words add *s*, e.g. *bambinos* or *bambini* (cf. rule 18b).

22d — Latin and Greek words give the most difficulty:
    i)   endings in -*a* generally change to -*ae*, e.g. *dramatis personae.*

-a	
alga *pl* -ae	formula *pl* -as or -ae
alumna *pl* -ae	larva *pl* -ae
amoeba *pl* -ae or -as	minutiae
amphora *pl* -ae or -as	nebula *pl* -ae or -as
aqua *pl* -ae or -as	thermae

    ii)   nearly all endings in -*is* change to -*es*.

-is	
analysis *pl* -yses	hypothesis *pl* -eses
antithesis *pl* -eses	metamorphosis *pl* -oses
apodosis *pl* -oses	morphosis *pl* -oses
axis *pl* -xes	neurosis *pl* -oses
basis *pl* -ases	oasis *pl* -ases
catalysis *pl* -yses	parenthesis *pl* -eses
chassis *pl* chassis	periphrasis *pl* -ases
chrysalis *pl* -ises or -ides	praxis *pl* -xises or -xes
crisis *pl* -ises	protasis *pl* -ases
diaeresis or dieresis *pl* -eses	psychosis *pl* -oses
dialysis *pl* -yses	synopsis *pl* -pses
eisegesis *pl* -eses	synthesis *pl* -eses
ellipsis *pl* -pses	testis *pl* -tes
emphasis *pl* -ases	thesis *pl* -eses
exegesis *pl* -eses	thrombosis *pl* -oses
genesis *pl* -eses	

    iii)   endings in -*ex* and -*ix* generally change to -*ices*.

-ex or -ix	
appendix *pl* -dixes or -dices	helix *pl* -lices or -lixes
calix *pl* -lices	index *pl* -dexes or -dices
cervix *pl* -vixes or -vices	matrix *pl* -trices or -trixes
codex *pl* -dices	vertex *pl* -texes or -tices
cortex *pl* -tices	vortex *pl* -texes or -tices

iv) **endings in -*on* and -*um* change to -*a* (or add *s* or change to -*a*).**

-on	automaton *pl* -tons or -ta	ganglion *pl* -glia or -glions
	criterion *pl* -ria or -rions	phenomenon *pl* -na or -nons

-um	antependium *pl* -dia	maximum *pl* -mums or -ma
	antrum *pl* -tra	medium *pl* -dia or -diums
	aquarium *pl* -riums or -ria	memorandum *pl* -dums
	arboretum *pl* -ta or -tums	or -da
	atrium *pl* -tria	millennium *pl* -niums
	auditorium *pl* -riums or ria	or -nia
	bacterium *pl* -ria	minimum *pl* -mums or -ma
	candelabrum or -bra *pl* -bra	momentum *pl* -ta or -tums
	cerebrum *pl* -brums or -bra	moratorium *pl* -ria
	ciborium *pl* -ria	or -riums
	condominium *pl* -niums	optimum *pl* -ma or -mums
	consortium *pl* -tia	ovum *pl* -va
	continuum *pl* -nua or -nuums	planetarium *pl* -riums
	corrigendum *pl* -da	or -ria
	cranium *pl* -niums or -nia	plectrum or plectron *pl*
	crematorium *pl* -riums	-tra or -trums, or -trons
	or -ria	quantum *pl* -ta
	curriculum *pl* -la or -lums	rectum *pl* -tums or -ta
	datum *pl* -ta	referendum *pl* -dums
	delirium *pl* -riums or -ria	or -da
	delphinium *pl* -niums or -nia	rostrum *pl* -trums or -tra
	dictum *pl* -tums or -ta	sanatorium *pl* -riums
	effluvium *pl* -via or -viums	or -ria
	emporium *pl* -riums or -ria	scrotum *pl* -ta or -tums
	equilibrium *pl* -riums or -ria	spectrum *pl* -tra
	erratum *pl* -ta	speculum *pl* -la or -lums
	exemplum *pl* -pla	sputum *pl* -ta
	exordium *pl* -diums or -dia	stadium *pl* -diums or -dia
	forum *pl* -rums or -ra	stratum *pl* -ta or -tums
	fulcrum *pl* -crums or -cra	symposium *pl* -siums
	gymnasium *pl* -siums or -sia	or -sia
	honorarium *pl* -riums or -ria	trapezium *pl* -ziums or -zia
	horologium *pl* -gia	tympanum *pl* -nums or -na
	leprosarium *pl* -ria	vacuum *pl* -cuums or -cua
	mausoleum *pl* -leums or -lea	

v) **Latin endings in** *-us* **generally change to** *-i* **or** *-uses* (or do either) (*alumni; caucuses; discuses* or *disci*) **but sometimes become** *-era* **or** *ora* (*genera; córpora*).
Rarely the *-us* **remains in the plural** (*rictus*).

<table>
<tr><td rowspan="45">-us</td><td>abacus pl -ci or -cuses</td><td>meniscus pl -sci or -scuses</td></tr>
<tr><td>alumnus pl -ni</td><td>metacarpus pl -pi</td></tr>
<tr><td>apparatus pl -tus or -tuses</td><td>metatarsus pl -si</td></tr>
<tr><td>bacillus pl -li</td><td>micrococcus pl -ci</td></tr>
<tr><td>bronchus pl -chi</td><td>narcissus pl -suses or -si</td></tr>
<tr><td>cactus pl -tuses or -ti</td><td>nautilus pl -luses or -li</td></tr>
<tr><td>calculus pl -luses</td><td>nexus pl -us</td></tr>
<tr><td>callus pl -luses</td><td>nimbus pl -bi or -buses</td></tr>
<tr><td>campus pl -puses</td><td>nucellus pl -li</td></tr>
<tr><td>cantus pl -tus</td><td>nucleus pl -clei or -cleuses</td></tr>
<tr><td>carolus pl -luses or -li</td><td>octopus pl -puses</td></tr>
<tr><td>caucus pl -cuses</td><td>oesophagus pl -gi</td></tr>
<tr><td>census pl -suses</td><td>omnibus pl -buses</td></tr>
<tr><td>chorus pl -ruses</td><td>onus pl onuses</td></tr>
<tr><td>circus pl -cuses</td><td>opus pl opuses or opera</td></tr>
<tr><td>coccus pl -ci</td><td>palp pl -ps, or palpus pl -pi</td></tr>
<tr><td>corpus pl -pora</td><td>papyrus pl -ri or -ruses</td></tr>
<tr><td>crocus pl -cuses</td><td>phallus pl -li or -luses</td></tr>
<tr><td>cumulus pl -li</td><td>platypus pl -puses</td></tr>
<tr><td>denarius pl -narii</td><td>plexus pl -uses or -us</td></tr>
<tr><td>dianthus pl -thuses</td><td>radius pl -dii or -diuses</td></tr>
<tr><td>discus pl -scuses or -sci</td><td>regulus pl -luses or -li</td></tr>
<tr><td>eucalyptus or eucalypt
   pl -ptuses, -pti or -pts</td><td>rhombus pl -buses or -bi</td></tr>
<tr><td>excursus pl -suses or -sus</td><td>rictus pl -tus or -tuses</td></tr>
<tr><td>fetus or foetus pl -tuses</td><td>rumpus pl -puses</td></tr>
<tr><td>focus pl -cuses or -ci</td><td>sarcophagus pl -gi or -guses</td></tr>
<tr><td>fungus pl -gi or -guses</td><td>sinus pl sinuses</td></tr>
<tr><td>genius pl -niuses or -nii</td><td>status pl -tuses</td></tr>
<tr><td>genus pl -nera or -nuses</td><td>stimulus pl -li</td></tr>
<tr><td>gladiolus pl -lus, -li or -luses</td><td>stratus pl -ti</td></tr>
<tr><td>habitus pl -tus</td><td>stylus pl -li or -luses</td></tr>
<tr><td>hiatus pl -tuses or -tus</td><td>surplus pl -luses</td></tr>
<tr><td>hibiscus pl -scuses</td><td>syllabus pl -buses or -bi</td></tr>
<tr><td>humerus pl -ri</td><td>thesaurus pl -ri or -ruses</td></tr>
<tr><td>ictus pl -tuses or -tus</td><td>tumulus pl -li</td></tr>
<tr><td>impetus pl -tuses</td><td>umbilicus pl -ci</td></tr>
<tr><td>incubus pl -bi or -buses</td><td>uterus pl -ri</td></tr>
<tr><td>lapsus pl -psus</td><td>virus pl -ruses</td></tr>
<tr><td>linctus pl -tuses</td><td>viscus pl viscera</td></tr>
<tr><td>locus pl -ci</td><td>vomitus pl -tuses</td></tr>
<tr><td>magus pl -gi</td><td>walrus pl -ruses or -rus</td></tr>
</table>

ADDING ENDINGS THAT BEGIN WITH A VOWEL

Rule 23   <u>When a silent *e* is dropped</u>

    – **A silent *e* is generally dropped before an ending beginning with a vowel, unless it is needed to keep a *c* or *g* soft or to distinguish a word from another with the same spelling:**
       e.g. *gluing* but *dyeing, singeing, swingeing*.
       Note 'a bolt of *lightning*' but 'the dark was *lightening*'.

Exceptions: *acreage, lineage, mileage* or *milage, rateable,* and *ageing, cueing, vogueing*.

    – **Verbs with an ending in -*ate* generally drop the -*ate* before -*able*** (*appreciable, demonstrable*) **except for most two-syllable words:**
       e.g. *debate, debatable; inflate, inflatable*.

    – **Most words drop the *e* when adding the adjectival ending *y* because** y **stands for** i (cf. rule 8), **which in the following examples keeps the *c* soft.**
       e.g. *bouncy, cadency, icy, racy*.

The following words may drop or keep the *e*:
chancy or *chancey, cliquey* or *cliquy, horsy* or *horsey, pacey* or *pacy, plaguy* or *plaguey, poncy* or *poncey, pricey* or *pricy*.

Exceptions: original words ending in -*ue* (*bluey, gluey*) or -*y* (*clayey, wheyey*). *Hole* becomes *holey* (in accordance with rule 23) to distinguish it from *holy* (saint). *Dicey* and *spacey* are exceptions, too, and note *fiery*.

Rule 24   <u>When consonants are doubled</u>

General Rule

    – **Double the last consonant to keep the vowel short only if the accent falls on it in the lengthened word,** e.g. *hat—hatter*. **However,** l **is almost always doubled except when adding the suffix -*ity*.**

The difficulty of whether to double a consonant or leave it single, when adding an ending beginning with a vowel, only arises when the original word ends in a short vowel and a single consonant (except *w, x* and *y*) that is stressed. The problem is how to keep the vowel short.

Words that end with a simple long vowel or vowel digraph sound or two consonants, e.g. *accused, adopted, mealy, veiling,* are not considered because this difficulty does not arise.
Note *ideally* and *really*.

24a – With monosyllabic words, double the consonant after a short vowel (to keep it short), e.g *upper*.

Do not double the consonant after a long vowel (there is no need).

Exceptions: *cruelly, woollen, woolly*.

24b – With words of more than one syllable, if the accent in the lengthened word is on the syllable before the ending, double the last consonant: e.g. *beginning* (be *gin* ning), *forbidden, forgotten, occurrence, upsetting*.

If the accent is not on that syllable leave the consonant single: e.g. *filleted, galloper*.

– *l* is almost always doubled:[3]
e.g. *gradually, marvellous, occasionally* (except *paralleled, paralleling, parallelogram, railing*, and note *doweling* or *dowelling*),
except when adding the ending -ity:
e.g. *cordiality* (except *tranquillity*).

Exceptions: *outfit, outrun, woodcut and worship*[4], which double the last consonant (*outfitter, outrunner, woodcutter, worshipper, worshipped, worshipping*), and *violinist* and *manikin* (or *mannikin*), which do not.
Note the verb *biases* or *biasses, biasing* or *biassing, biased* or *biassed*.

Note *chagrined, richocheted* or *richochetted* and *crocheted*. These French words are not strictly exceptions because the preceding vowel is long.

It would make an exceptionally long list to give all the doubled consonants, so just the endings **-lled** and **-lling**, which sometimes cause difficulty, are given.

-lled	appalled	cudgelled	gravelled
	apparelled	devilled	grovelled
	barrelled	dialled	jewelled
	bevelled	dishevelled	kennelled
	bowelled	dowelled	labelled
	cancelled	drivelled	laurelled
	carolled	duelled	libelled
	cavilled	enamelled	marshalled
	channelled	enthralled	marvelled
	chiselled	equalled	medalled
	compelled	fuelled	metalled
	controlled	funnelled	modelled
	counselled	gambolled	panelled

continued

[3]In American English, these words are spelt with one *l* except for *appalled, appalling, compelled, compelling* and *enthralled, enthralling*, with *appall* and *enthrall*. Also when *y* is added, the *l* is usually doubled (e.g. *gradually*). *Marvelous* retains its single *l*.
[4]In American English, *worshiping, worshiped*.

-lled	parcelled	rivalled	tinselled
	pedalled	shovelled	totalled
	pencilled	shrivelled	towelled
	perilled	signalled	trammelled
	pistolled	spiralled	travelled
	pummelled	stencilled	trowelled
	quarrelled	swivelled	tunnelled
	ravelled	symbolled	victualled
	revelled	tasselled	

-lling	appalling	fuelling	pummelling
	barrelling	funnelling	quarrelling
	bevelling	gambolling	ravelling
	bowelling	gravelling	revelling
	cancelling	grovelling	rivalling
	carolling	gruelling	shovelling
	cavilling	jewelling	shrivelling
	channelling	kennelling	signalling
	chiselling	labelling	spiralling
	compelling	laurelling	stencilling
	controlling	libelling	swivelling
	counselling	marshalling	symbolling
	cudgelling	marvelling	tasselling
	devilling	medalling	tinselling
	dialling	metalling	totalling
	dishevelling	modelling	towelling
	dowelling	panelling	trammelling
	drivelling	parcelling	travelling
	duelling	pedalling	trowelling
	enamelling	pencilling	tunnelling
	enthralling	perilling	victualling
	equalling	pistolling	

Rule 25 — <u>Words ending in -c when adding an ending beginning with *e* or *i*</u>

- When a word ending in -c adds an ending beginning with *e* or *i*, there are two possibilities:

 25a — Add *k* before the common endings **-ed** (*bivouacked, mimicked, shellacked, tarmacked, trafficked*), **-er** (*havocker, mimicker, trafficker*), **-ing** (*havocking, mimicking, politicking, trafficking*) **and -y** (*garlicky, gimmicky, panicky, physicky, smart-alecky, zincky*).

25b — Add nothing before less common endings **-ian, -ism, -ist, -ity** and **-ize** (or **-ise**).

-cian		
academician	mathematician	politician
arithmetician	musician	statistician
clinician	obstetrician	tactician
cosmetician	optician	technician
electrician	paediatrician	
magician	physician	

-cism		
academicism	ecclesiasticism	laicism
aestheticism	eclecticism	lyricism
agnosticism	empiricism	monasticism
asceticism	eroticism	mysticism
athleticism	esotericism	neuroticism
Catholicism	exoticism	romanticism
classicism	fanaticism	sardonicism
cynicism	historicism	scepticism

-cist		
Celticist	eugenicist	physicist
classicist	geneticist	polemicist
cyberneticist	historicist	publicist
empiricist	lyricist	
ethicist	mosaicist	

-city		
alcoholicity	eccentricity	rusticity
aromaticity	egocentricity	septicity
authenticity	elasticity	specificity
catholicity	endemicity	sphericity
causticity	ethnicity	synchronicity
chromaticity	historicity	theocentricity
chronicity	plasticity	tonicity
concentricity	publicity	
domesticity	rhythmicity	

-cize	catholicize	Gallicize	metaphysicize
	classicize	Gnosticize	mythicize
	criticize	Gothicize	plasticize
	elasticize	Hispanicize	politicize
	ethicize	italicize	publicize
	fanaticize	laicize	romanticize

Note the similar words: *beautician, dietician, mortician; Anglicism, ecumenicism* (which is an alternative to *ecumenism*); *biblicist, mythicist, pharmacist; anglicize, exorcize, Graecize, ostracize.*

Note that the sound /ik/ in the endings of root words of more than one syllable is always written *-ic*, e.g. *arithmetic* and never *-ick* or *-ik* except in *beatnik, gimmick, limerick, maverick* and *rollick* and some rare words: *dornick, killick, luderick, maffick, shashlik* and *skerrick.*

Rule 26   <u>Verbs ending in -*y*</u>

– **When adding an ending beginning with a vowel, verbs ending in -*y* keep the *y* if it is preceded by a vowel, otherwise the *y* changes to *i*** (cf. rule 19):
e.g. *allayed, assayed, belayed, delayed, essayed* and *applied, dried, occupied, qualified, verified.*

Exceptions: *laid, paid* and *said* and their compounds and before the ending -*ing* (to avoid double *i*):
e.g. *applying, drying.*

When adding -*ing* to words ending in -*ie*, the first *i* changes to *y* to avoid a double *i*, which hardly ever occurs in English:
e.g. *dying, lying, tying, vying.*
Note *dying* but *dyeing.*

HYPHENS

Rule 27   <u>Hyphens and compound words</u>

Note that the grammatical use of hyphens to indicate sense, e.g. *a little, used machine* and *a little-used machine*, is beyond the remit of this book (cf. Introduction).

Hyphens used to separate prefixes and suffixes from words

Hyphens are mostly used to unite words but they do have some use as separators. Generally prefixes and suffixes are written without a hyphen, even when this results in a double letter (cf. rule 14b). Adverbs and prepositions used in compound words are a special case, so they will be treated first.

27a – **When an adverb or a preposition is used as a *prefix*, it is usually joined without a hyphen.**

Note *offshore* and *offstage*, and *on* and *under* in the following examples, which are used like prefixes.

nobody	nowhere	pronoun	suffix
nonchronological	onset	proverb	tonight
nonfiction	prefix	semicolon	undergrowth
nonsense	preposition	subheading	underwear

There are exceptions, e.g. *off-centre, off-load, off-peak* and *off-street*.

– **When an adverb or preposition is used as a *suffix* for a *noun*, it is likewise often joined without a hyphen,** except for *-up*, e.g. *countdown*.

With the corresponding **verbs** (including verbs with *up*), the adverb or preposition is written **as a separate word,** e.g. *count down*.

With **adjectives,** the adverb or preposition is often **hyphenated** (cf. rule 27f).

The following list gives some nouns of this class and the corresponding verbs.

breakdown n.	blast off vb.	comedown n.	cut out vb.
break down vb.	burnout n.	come down vb.	dropout n.
blackout n.	burn out vb.	countdown n.	drop out vb.
black out vb.	clampdown n.	count down vb.	
blastoff n.	clamp down vb.	cutout n.	

The exceptions are words ending in *-up* (see below) and words with a more restricted or technical sense, e.g. *jump-off, mid-off, play-off; break-out* and *fade-out*.

– Nouns ending in the suffix *-up* are usually hyphenated.

-up			
	blow-up n.	flare-up n.	pin-up n.
	booze-up n.	frame-up n.	press-up n.
	break-up n.	freeze-up n.	punch-up n.
	brush-up n.	high-up n.	shake-up n.
	build-up n.	hold-up n.	sit-up n.
	burn-up n.	knock-up n.	smash-up n.
	bust-up n.	lash-up n.	stick-up n.
	call-up n.	line-up n.	summing-up n.
	carve-up n.	make-up n.	take-up n.
	clear-up n.	mark-up n.	turn-up n.
	close-up n.	mix-up n.	washing-up n.
	cover-up n.	mock-up n.	winding-up n.
	dust-up n.	paste-up n.	write-up n.
	fill-up n.	pick-up n.	

The exceptions are these short, frequently used words:
backup, checkup, cleanup, crackup, linkup, lockup, setup.

27b – **With prefixes, a hyphen is used in various situations:**

i) **to separate two identical vowels and in the case of *non-n-*.**
However, *co-* does not need a hyphen before another *o.*

anti-icer	non-native	pre-emptor
anti-imperialism	non-natural	pre-emptory
anti-imperialist	non-naturalism	pre-engage
anti-inflammatory	non-navigable	pre-engagement
anti-inflationary	non-negotiable	pre-establish
cooperate	non-nervous	pre-estimate
or co-operate	non-nuclear	pre-examination
coopt or co-opt	no-one or no one	pre-examine
coordinal	pre-echo	pre-exist
or co-ordinal	pre-elect	pre-existence
coordinate	pre-election	pre-expose
or co-ordinate	pre-embryo	re-echo
de-emphasize	pre-eminence	re-edit
de-energization	pre-eminent	re-educate
de-energize	pre-eminently	re-elect
de-escalate	pre-empire	re-embark
de-escalation	pre-empt	re-emerge
fore-edge	pre-emption	re-emphasize
neo-orthodox	pre-emptive	re-employ
non-national	pre-emptively	re-enact

continued

re-enclose	re-enlighten	re-evaluate
re-endow	re-enter	re-examine
re-enforce	re-equip	re-exhibit
re-engage	re-erect	re-experience
re-enlarge	re-establish	re-export

ii) **to separate letters which otherwise might suggest a wrong combination for pronunciation:**
e.g. *co-worker, de-ice.*

iii) **to separate a prefix from a capital letter:**
e.g. *pre-Augustan, pre-Babylonian, pre-British, pre-Byzantine, pre-Carboniferous, pre-Celtic.*

iv) **to distinguish a word with an English prefix** from the same word with the same prefix but taken from another language, with a different meaning:
e.g. *re-cover* and *recover.*

v) **when the prefix applies to more than one word:**
e.g. *pre-twentieth century.*

27c – **A hyphen is normally used with suffixes in two situations:**

i) **to separate three identical consonants.**

The following cases occur with the endings *-less* and *-like.*

| **-ll-less** | gill-less | shell-less | wall-less |
| | hull-less | skill-less | |

| **-ll-like** | cell-like | gull-like | wall-like |
| | gill-like | shell-like | |

In rule 14a we noted that the letters doubled at the end of a word are f, l, s and z.

There are no words with a sequence of three f's or z's.

The other words with a sequence of three l's are *full-length, well-liked* and *well-loved.*

The words with a sequence of three s's are:
cross-sectional, cross-slide, cross-stitch, Inverness-shire, Kinross-shire, process-server and *public-address system.*
Headmistressship is the only undivided word with a sequence of three s's.
Note *cross section* and *moss stitch.*

ii) **to add -*like* to some words of more than one syllable:**
   e.g. *chameleon-like, cherry-like, cylinder-like, daughter-like.*

Exceptions: words that are frequently used, e.g. *businesslike.*

Note: -*like* is joined to a one-syllable word without a hyphen:
e.g. *birdlike, boxlike, catlike, childlike, creamlike, cuplike.*

Exceptions: words that end in *l* (cf. rule 14b).

No hyphen is needed to join -*less* and -*worthy* to words, e.g. *reckless, noteworthy,* except where three *l*'s occur with -*less* as noted above.

27d – **Hyphens used to join words**

If two separate words are used so frequently together that they acquire a special meaning, they are either joined with a hyphen or written as one word.

Words that are already joined with a hyphen, because of frequent or specialized usage, may, by very frequent usage, come to be written as one word.

This process is accelerated if the words are short and the first is accented more than the second.

It is difficult to know whether to write them as one word or as two words with a hyphen. It would be impossible to give all these compound words in a short work such as this. However, it is possible to formulate some general rules and give examples.

Some General Rules

   Indications that the words should be joined as one word are:
   ● **very frequent usage**
   ● **short words**
   ● **the first word is stressed more than the second.**

corkscrew	semicircle	toothache	waistcoat
headache	shipwreck	toothbrush	warehouse
highjack	something	toothpaste	weekend
passport	stepfather	turntable	
roundabout	stepmother	viewpoint	

Indications that the words should be joined with a hyphen are:

- frequent or specialized usage, e.g. *walkie-talkie*;
- the juxtaposition of two letters that suggest a wrong pronunciation, e.g. *do-gooder*;
- the first word is *half* or *self*.

half-			
	half-a-crown	half-crazy	half-informed
	half-a-dollar	half-crown	half-instinctive
	half-afraid	half-day	half-intoxicated
	half-alive	half-dazed	half-jack
	half-and-half	half-dead	half-joking
	half-anglicized	half-deaf	half-knowledge
	half-ashamed	half-demented	half-learned
	half-asleep	half-deserted	half-leather
	half-awake	half-developed	half-length
	half-baked	half-digested	half-lie
	half-ball	half-dollar	half-life
	half-barrel	half-done	half-light
	half-begging	half-dozen	half-mad
	half-begun	half-dressed	half-marathon
	half-bent	half-dried	half-mast
	half-blind	half-drowned	half-mile
	half-blood	half-drunk	half-minute
	half-blue	half-eaten	half-monthly
	half-boot	half-educated	half-moon
	half-bottle	half-empty	half-mourning
	half-bound	half-English	half-naked
	half-breed	half-expectant	half-nelson
	half-brother	half-famished	half-note
	half-buried	half-filled	half-open
	half-butt	half-forgotten	half-pagan
	half-castle	half-formed	half-pay
	half-century	half-forward	half-pedalling
	half-circle	half-frozen	half-petrified
	half-civilized	half-fulfilled	half-pie
	half-civilly	half-full	half-plate
	half-clad	half-grown	half-playfully
	half-clothed	half-hardy	half-pleased
	half-cock	half-heard	half-price
	half-completed	half-hearted	half-protesting
	half-concealed	half-hitch	half-proved
	half-conscious	half-hoping	half-questioning
	half-consumed	half-hour	half-raw
	half-convinced	half-human	half-reluctant
	half-cooked	half-inch	half-remembered
	half-covered	half-inclined	half-repentant

continued

half-	half-rhyme	half-sister	half-track
	half-right	half-size	half-trained
	half-rotten	half-slip	half-true
	half-round	half-smile	half-truth
	half-savage	half-sole	half-understood
	half-second	half-starved	half-used
	half-section	half-stated	half-verified
	half-seen	half-step	half-wild
	half-sensed	half-submerged	half-wrong
	half-serious	half-tide	half-year
	half-shut	half-timber	half-yearly
	half-silvered	half-title	

Exceptions: *halfback, halfbeak, halfpenny, halftone, halfway, halfwitted* and *half board, half eagle, half frame, half gainer, half holiday, half landing, half measure, half volley.*

self-	self-abandonment	self-closing	self-denial
	self-abasement	self-coloured	self-dependence
	self-abhorrence	self-command	self-destroying
	self-abnegation	self-commitment	self-determined
	self-absorbed	self-complacent	self-devotion
	self-abuse	self-conceit	self-directed
	self-accusation	self-concept	self-discipline
	self-acting	self-condemnation	self-doubt
	self-action	self-confessed	self-drive
	self-addressed	self-confidence	self-educated
	self-adhesive	self-congratulation	self-effacement
	self-adjusted	self-conscious	self-elected
	self-administered	self-constituted	self-employed
	self-admiration	self-contained	self-enclosed
	self-advertisement	self-contempt	self-esteem
	self-aligning	self-content	self-evident
	self-analysis	self-contradiction	self-examination
	self-appointed	self-control	self-exertion
	self-approval	self-convicted	self-existence
	self-assertion	self-correcting	self-expanding
	self-assurance	self-created	self-expression
	self-aware	self-critical	self-fertile
	self-catering	self-deceit	self-financed
	self-censored	self-deception	self-focusing
	self-censorship	self-defeating	self-fulfilling
	self-certification	self-defence	self-hate
	self-cleaning	self-delusion	self-help

continued

self-	self-hypnosis	self-pollination	self-reproof
	self-image	self-portrait	self-respect
	self-important	self-possessed	self-restraint
	self-imposed	self-powered	self-revealing
	self-induced	self-praise	self-righteous
	self-indulgence	self-prepared	self-rule
	self-inflicted	self-preservation	self-sacrifice
	self-interest	self-produced	self-satisfaction
	self-judgment	self-promotion	self-sealing
	self-knowledge	self-propelled	self-seeking
	self-loader	self-protection	self-service
	self-love	self-punishment	self-starter
	self-made	self-questioning	self-sufficient
	self-motivated	self-raising	self-tapping
	self-murder	self-realization	self-taught
	self-mutilation	self-regard	self-torture
	self-operating	self-regression	self-trained
	self-opinionated	self-regulating	self-will
	self-ordained	self-reliance	self-worth
	self-perpetuating	self-repeating	
	self-pity	self-reproach	

Exceptions: *selfheal, selfhood, selfish, selfless, selfsame,* and their derivatives.

i) **Where two words are joined and the second ends in -er and the first is the object of the verb, they are more often written as one word, especially if the resulting word is a well-known job.**

backpacker	icebreaker	pawnbroker	tiebreaker
ballplayer	ironmaster	peacemaker	timeserver
billposter	ironworker	peashooter	timeworker
bondholder	jawbreaker	pigsticker	treehopper
boneshaker	lawbreaker	pipefiller	typecaster
bookbinder	matchmaker	platelayer	typesetter
bootlegger	minehunter	printmaker	typewriter
caseworker	moneymaker	roadroller	viewfinder
copyholder	newscaster	rockhopper	weedkiller
doorkeeper	newsmonger	shopkeeper	woodcarver
dressmaker	newsreader	shopwalker	woodcutter
fishmonger	noisemaker	shopworker	woodworker
flycatcher	nutcracker	snowblower	woolgrower
gamekeeper	painkiller	songwriter	
gatekeeper	pallbearer	stockpiler	
gunfighter	pathfinder	taskmaster	

baby-minder	eye-catcher	land-holder	safe-blower
baby-sitter	glass-maker	leaf-hopper	spot-welder
bell-ringer	gold-digger	lotus-eater	stem-winder
book-keeper	head-banger	mind-reader	tear-jerker
dog-catcher	head-hunter	page-turner	
(but dog	honey-eater	rat-catcher	
handler)	lady-killer	rib-tickler	

Note: *heat seeker, lime burner, sand hopper* and *sound mixer.*

ii) **Adjectives plus noun in which the attribute refers to the whole thing are usually written as one word,** e.g. *redhead.*

egghead	paperback	paperknife	playground
everything	(but soft cover)	paperweight	playtime
fathead	paperboy	paperwork	teenager
hothead	paperclip	petticoat	

Note that the addition of -ed may hyphenate these compound nouns as well as hyphenate separate words:
e.g. *redhead—red-headed, club foot—club-footed.*

iii) **Compounds in which the adjective follows the noun are written as separate words** (*court martial, heir apparent*) **unless they are well used combinations** (*mother-in-law*) **or used as a verb or in the possessive case** (he was *court-martialled*, the *Secretary-of-State's* case).

iv) **Some nouns from verb plus adverb combinations are becoming written as one word** because of greater frequency.

changeover n.	handover n.	pullover n.	walkover n.
crossover n.	hangover n.	pushover n.	wrapover n.
flashover n.	layout n.	takeover n.	
flyover n.	leftover n.	turnover n.	

Note: *going-over* n., *once-over* n., *voice-over* n.

27f – Compound adjectives

i) **Generally use a *hyphen* for *compound adjectives*.**

These composite adjectives may be an adjective or noun qualifying an adjective or participle:
e.g. *air-cooled, bright-red, card-carrying, easy-going, sky-high*, but note *seaborne*.

They may also be verb and adverb combinations, e.g. *made-up*, or whole phrases used as adjectives, e.g. *door-to-door*.
Note *upside-down*.

Exception: when the first word is an adverb, they are written separately (cf. (ii) below) or, if the first word is a preposition, they are written without a hyphen:
e.g. *overhead, underground*.

ii) **Where an adverb is used *before* a non-verbal adjective, it is usually written separately,** e.g. a doubly unfortunate remark, **unless the adverb might be mistaken for an adjective,** e.g. *extra-curricular*.

If an adverb is joined before or after a participle (see the final note after rule 27h) **or *after* an adjective, a hyphen is usually used:**
e.g. *high-handed, well-aimed, well-bred; all-over, broken-down, low-down*.

27g – Compound verbs

i) **Compound nouns used as verbs do not change the way they are written unless an adverb or preposition is used as a suffix, in which case the adverb or preposition is written separately** (cf. rule 27a):
e.g. *overflow, overtake, overturn* but *flow over, take over, turn over*.

ii) **When a noun phrase is used as a verb, it is usually hyphenated:**
e.g. *court martial* n., *court-martial* vb.
This extends to participial use, e.g. *court-martialled*, and fits the rule for compound adjectives above in rule 27f.

27h – Compound adverbs

i) **A preposition joined to a noun without the article is usually written as one word.**

betweentimes	downtown	overhead	upwind
betweenwhiles	downwind	upstairs	
downstage	overarm	upstream	
downstairs	overboard	uptown	

Note *on foot, on horseback* and *in-house*.

ii) **Adverbs formed from hyphenated, compound adjectives are also hyphenated,** e.g. *absent-mindedly.*

A final note
Hyphens can often be avoided by changing attributive use (an ill-mannered boy) to predicative use (the boy was ill mannered) or by using a preposition, e.g. five-minute intervals, intervals of five minutes.

BEGINNINGS
AND ENDINGS

Rule 28   *-able* or *-ible*

As with *-er* and *-or* (cf. rules 40b and 40c), the difficulty arises because both suffixes have the same meaning and usually the same pronunciation.

– *-able*

28a – **Nouns take -able:**
e.g. *clubbable* or *clubable, saleable.*

28b – **Full words take -able unless you can add -ion to them.**

In the vast majority of cases *-able* is added to a full word but there are some *parts* of words that take *-able* such as:

-able	affable	indomitable	memorable
	arable	ineffable	palpable
	cognizable	inevitable	portable
	dubitable	inexorable	potable
	equitable	inscrutable	probable
	formidable	insuperable	unconscionable
	habitable	malleable	vulnerable

28c – **Words or parts of words ending in -at or -ate take -able:**
e.g. *accelerable, conciliable, disintegrable, eliminable.*

Compatible is the only word ending in *-atible.*

Note that adjectives formed from verbs with an ending in *-ate* generally drop the *-ate*:
e.g. *appreciable, demonstrable,*
except for most two-syllable words:
e.g. *debate—debatable, inflate—inflatable.*
Note *miserable.*

28d – **All the words ending in -ge add -able:**
e.g. *knowledgeable* or *knowledgable, unchangeable.*

Some words ending in *-ce* drop the *e* and add *-ible* (cf. rule 28g).

The following words keep the -*ce* and add -*able*.

-ceable		
balanceable	faceable	retraceable
danceable	forceable (able to	sacrificeable
defaceable	be forced)	serviceable
displaceable	ineffaceable	sliceable
disserviceable	irreplaceable	traceable
divorceable	noticeable	unnoticeable
effaceable	peaceable	unpronounceable
embraceable	pierceable	unreplaceable
enforceable	pronounceable	
experienceable	replaceable	

28e – **If you cannot find the -*able*/-*ible* word in this book, it almost certainly ends in -*able*,[5] as there are over 1,600 words ending in -*able*. The following -*able* words must retain the silent *e*.**

-eable		
chaseable	fireable	saleable
chokeable	handleable	settleable
delineable	probeable	unsaleable

Most -*able* words may drop or retain the silent *e*.

-able or -eable		
atonable or atoneable	immovable or immoveable
blamable or blameable	likable or likeable
citable or citeable	linable or lineable
confinable or confineable	livable or liveable
datable or dateable	lovable or loveable
debatable or debateable	machinable or machineable
dislikable or dislikeable	minable or mineable
drapable or drapeable	mistakable or mistakeable
drivable or driveable	movable or moveable
dyable or dyeable	namable or nameable
finable or fineable	raisable or raiseable
framable or frameable	ratable or rateable
givable or giveable	rebatable or rebateable
hatable or hateable	resalable or resaleable
hirable or hireable	ridable or rideable

---

[5] In American English, only *handleable* and *settleable* *must* retain the silent e. The following words *must* be written without the silent *e*: *mistakable, resalable, unmistakable, unsalable, unshakable*.

  As in other Englishes, most of the -*able* words may be written with or without the silent *e* in American English and the spelling without the silent *e* is the preferred one, except that retention of the silent *e* is the preferred spelling in *hateable, nameable, rideable* and *shareable*.

-able or -eable		
ropable or ropeable	smokable or smokeable
savable or saveable	statable or stateable
servable or serveable	stonable or stoneable
shakable or shakeable	swathable or swatheable
shamable or shameable	takable or takeable
shapable or shapeable	tradable or tradeable
sharable or shareable	tunable or tuneable
shavable or shaveable	unmistakable or unmistakeable
sizable or sizeable	unshakable or unshakeable
slakable or slakeable	usable or useable

– *-ible*

– Words which end in *-ion* also take *-ible*:
  e.g. *admissible, divisible, perfectible.*

Exceptions: *correctable, detectable, predictable.*

28g – Words or parts of words that end in an /s/ sound usually take *-ible.*

Note the difference between *forceable* (able to be forced) and *forcible* (having force).

The following words ending in *-ce* drop the *e* and add *-ible.*

-cible		
adducible or adduceable	forcible (having force)	irreducible
coercible	immiscible	miscible
conducible	incoercible	producible
convincible	inconvincible	putrescible
deducible	inducible	reducible
educible	introducible	reproducible
effervescible	invincible	seducible or seduceable
evincible	irascible	traducible

Exceptions: words ending in *-ce* can take *-able* or *-ible* (cf. rule 28d).

-ible

accessible
admissible
apprehensible
assertible
audible
avertible
 or avertable
coercible
collectable
 or collectible
combustible
comestible
compatible
comprehensible
compressible
concessible
condensable
 or condensible
connectible
 or connectable
constructible
contemnible
contemptible
contractible
controvertible
convertible
convictable
 or convictible
convincible
correctable
 or correctible
corrigible
corrodible
corruptible
credible
crucible
deducible
deductible
defensible
depressible
derisible
descendible
 (inheritable)
destructible

detectable
 or detectible
diffusible
digestible
dirigible
discernible
 or (rare)
 discernable
discussible
dismissible
dissectible
distractible
divertible
divisible
edible
eligible
emulsible
erodible
eruptible
excludable
 or excludible
exhaustible
expressible
extendible
 or extendable
extrusible
fallible
feasible
flexible
frangible
fusible
gullible
horrible
ignitable
 or ignitible
illegible
immersible
immiscible
implausible
impossible
inaccessible
inadmissible
inaudible
includable
 or includible

incompatible
incontrovertible
incorrigible
indefensible
infeasible
instructible
intelligible
invincible
invisible
irascible
irreversible
omissible
ostensible
perfectible
permissible
persuadable
 or persuasible
pervertible
plausible
possible
preventable
 or preventible
remissible
reprehensible
resistible
responsible
retractable
 or retractible
reversible
revertible
rinsable
 or rinsible
submersible
suggestible
suppressible
susceptible
suspendible
 or suspensible
tangible
tensible
terrible
thurible
transmissible
vincible
visible

Note that *-ible* is derived from the Latin word ending *-ibilis*. However, a knowledge of Latin is no help here because some of the Latin *-ibilis* words have come to us via French, in which language the *-ibilis* has been changed to *-able*.

Rule 29 – *aer-* or *air-*

Where an *o* follows the sound /air/, it is always written *aer-* as the combination *airo-* never occurs in English, e.g. *aeroplane*.
Note *aerial*.

Rule 30 *-ance* or *-ence* (or *-ense*), and *-ince* or *-inse*

In the exceptional cases when the accent falls on the ending, there is no problem, since the pronunciation indicates the spelling:
e.g. *advance, askance, glance, prance, pretence*.
Nor is there a difficulty when the ending is preceded by *c* or *g*, *-ance* producing a hard *g* and *-ence* producing a soft *c* (often *-sc-*) or *g*. The difficulty arises because in nearly all cases the ending is unaccented and *-ence* and *-ance* sound the same. Care is needed with words used infrequently.

30a – **Adjectives ending in *-ant* produce nouns in *-ance*** (*tolerant—tolerance*) **and adjectives ending in *-ent* produce nouns in *-ence*** (*prevalent—prevalence*).

30b – **If the ending is preceded by *c* or *-sc-*, it is always *-ence*** (*reticence, adolescence*), except for *significance* and *insignificance*.

30c – **Verbs ending in an /r/ sound which combines with one previous vowel and is accented nearly always produce nouns in *-ence*,** e.g. *adherence, reference*.

Exceptions: *assurance, insurance, perseverance, procurance*.

Note that the Latin vowel is not a sure guide here because many words were taken from French and ended in *-ance* and only *some* of them were later changed to *-ence* to accord with the Latin derivation. Thus *subsistence* is evidence of this change but *resistance* was not changed.
The ending *-ance* is sometimes added to Old English words:
e.g. *forbearance, riddance*.
(cf. OED under *-ance* and *-ence*)

The following lists are by no means exhaustive.

-ance		
abeyance	admittance	assistance
abundance	allegiance	attendance
acceptance	alliance	avoidance
accordance	ambulance	brilliance
acquaintance	appearance	capacitance
acquittance	arrogance	clairvoyance

continued

-ance

clearance
cognizance
comeuppance
compliance
concomitance
concordance
conductance
connivance
consonance
continuance
conveyance
countenance
dalliance
deliverance
deviance
distance
disturbance
dominance
elegance
encumbrance
endurance
entrance
extravagance
exuberance
forbearance
forbiddance
fragrance
grievance
guidance
hesitance
hindrance
ignorance
impedance
importance
instance
irrelevance
issuance
iterance
luxuriance
maintenance
nonchalance
observance
ordinance
parlance
penance
performance
perseverance
petulance
pittance
poignance
precipitance
predominance
preponderance
procurance
protuberance
provenance
puissance
purveyance
remembrance
remittance
remonstrance
repentance
resemblance
resistance
resonance
riddance
semblance
severance
significance
substance
sufferance
surveillance
sustenance
temperance
tolerance
valance
variance
vengeance

-ence

abhorrence
absence
adherence
adolescence
ambience
    or ambiance
ambivalence
antecedence
audience
belligerence
benevolence
cadence
circumference
competence
concurrence
condolence
conference
confidence
congruence
conscience
consequence
continence
convenience
convergence
decadence
defence
deference
dependence
deterrence
diffidence
diligence
divergence
divulgence
effervescence
effluence
eloquence
emergence
eminence
equivalence
existence
experience
impenitence
impotence
imprudence
inadvertence
incidence
incoherence
incompetence
indolence
lenience
licence n.
magnificence
negligence
offence

continued

-ence	opulence	providence	silence
	patience	prurience	somnolence
	penitence	recumbence	subsidence
	persistence	recurrence	succulence
	pestilence	redolence	transcendence
	precedence	reference	transference
	preference	residence	truculence
	pretence	resurgence	turbulence
	prevalence	sentence	violence
	prominence	sequence	

Some may confuse *-ence* with *-ense*.[6] The list of words ending in *-ense* is not large, as *-ense* is not a suffix, so it is comprehensive except for rare words.

-ense	condense	immense	prepense
	dense	incense	recompense
	dispense	intense	sense
	expense	license vb.	suspense
	frankincense	nonsense	tense

Note: only *expanse* and *manse* end in *-anse*.

30d — The sound /inse/ at the end of a word is usually written *-ince*.

-ince	convince	prince	since
	evince	province	wince
	mince	quince	

Note: *rinse* is the only word ending in *-inse*.

---

[6]In American English, *defense*, *offense* and *pretense*. For the rest, American English follows the non-American usage.

Rule 31   _-ant_ or _-ent_

– **These endings, when unstressed, sound the same but linking cognates can help** (cf. rule 30a):
e.g. _violent—violence, assistant—assistance._

As a last resort, learn a spelling pronunciation. As with rule 30, there is no difficulty if the stress falls on the last syllable or if the ending is preceded by a _c_ or _g_, as either the pronunciation or the hardness or softness of the _c_ or _g_ determines the _-ant_ or _-ent_, e.g. _fumigant._

In many words, the _-ent_ is part of the suffix _-ment._

These are the only words ending in _-mant_:
adamant, affirmant, claimant, clamant, counterclaimant, dormant, formant, informant, misinformant, reclaimant, transhumant.

If we exclude these categories, the main words ending in _-ant_ and _-ent_ are:

	aberrant	consonant	disputant
	abundant	constant	dissonant
	acceptant	consultant	distant
	accountant	contaminant	dominant
	adjutant	contestant	elegant
	annuitant	conversant	elephant
	anticipant	convulsant	emigrant
	antioxidant	coolant	entrant
	appellant	cormorant	errant
	appendant	covenant	exorbitant
	arrant	croissant	expectant
	aspirant	currant (fruit)	expellant
	assailant	declarant	or expellent
	assistant	defendant	exuberant
-ant	attendant	defiant	flagrant
	blatant	defoliant	flippant
	bouffant	deodorant	fondant
	brilliant	dependant n.	fragrant
	celebrant	depressant	fumigant
	coagulant	descendant n.	gallant
	cognizant	desiccant	germinant
	colorant	determinant	giant
	combatant	detoxicant	habitant
	complainant	digestant	hesitant
	complaisant	dilatant	hydrant
	compliant	discordant	ignorant
	concomitant	discrepant	immigrant
	concordant	disinfectant	important
	confidant n.	dispersant	incessant

continued

-ant		
incompliant	pennant	restaurant
inconstant	petulant	resultant
indignant	pheasant	retardant
inebriant	piquant	reverberant
infant	pleasant	ruminant
inhabitant	pliant	sergeant
insouciant	poignant	servant
instant	pollutant	sextant
intolerant	postulant	sibilant
intoxicant	precipitant	simulant
irritant	pregnant	stagnant
itinerant	preponderant	stimulant
libellant	propellant	suppliant
lieutenant	or propellent	surveillant
litigant	protectant	tenant
luxuriant	Protestant	tolerant
malignant	protuberant	toxicant
merchant	puissant	tremulant
migrant	pursuant	trenchant
militant	quadrant	truant
mordant (sarcastic)	radiant	tyrant
mutant	rampant	ululant
nonchalant	recalcitrant	undulant
obeisant	recusant	unisonant
obscurant	redundant	vagrant
observant	relaxant	valiant
occupant	reliant	variant
oxidant	reluctant	verdant
participant	remnant	vibrant
peasant	repentant	vigilant
pedant	repugnant	warrant
penchant	resistant	
pendant	resonant	

-ent		
abhorrent	apparent	concurrent
absorbent	ardent	confident adj.
accident	benevolent	confluent
adherent	bivalent	congruent
advent	cadent	consequent
afferent	client	consistent
affluent	coexistent	constituent
ambient	coherent	content
ambivalent	coincident	continent
antecedent	competent	convenient
aperient	component	convent

continued

-ent	corpulent	immanent	recurrent
	correspondent	imminent	redolent
	current (water; adj.)	impertinent	referent
	decadent	incident	repellent
	decumbent	incipient	resident
	delinquent	indolent	resilient
	dement	inherent	resplendent
	dependent adj.	insistent	respondent
	deponent	insolent	reverent
	descendent adj.	insolvent	rodent
	despondent	irreverent	sentient
	deterrent	latent	serpent
	different	lenient	silent
	diffident	mordent (music)	solvent
	dissentient	nutrient	somnolent
	dissident	obedient	strident
	dissolvent	omnipotent	student
	ebullient	opponent	subsequent
	effluent	parent	subservient
	eloquent	patent	subsistent
	eminent	patient	succulent
	emollient	penitent	talent
	erodent	permanent	torrent
	evident	persistent	transcendent
	existent	portent	transient
	expedient	present n.	transparent
	expellant or expellent	president	trident
	exponent	prominent	truculent
	fervent	propellant or propellent	turbulent
	flatulent	proponent	unguent
	fluent	provident	vehement
	fraudulent	prudent	violent
	frequent	prurient	virulent
	gradient	recipient	

The endings *-ant* and *-ent* denote mainly adjectives (*apparent, radiant*) and some agents (*coolant, student*). They come from the present participle in Latin usually via French and sometimes with subsequent changes in English. Thus the Latin endings are no sure guide, e.g. *defendant* (cf. OED under *-ant* and *-ent*).

Rule 32   *anti- or ante-*

– *anti-* means 'against' and *ante-* means 'before'.

anti- is far more common than *ante-*.

Here are nearly all the common words with *ante-* and a small fraction of the hundreds of words with *anti-*.

ante-			
	antecedent	antemeridian	anteposition
	antechamber	antenatal	anteroom
	antedate	antependium	
	antediluvian	antepenultimate	

anti-			
	antibacterial	antipathy	antithesis
	antibiotic	antipodean	antitype
	antibody	antiseptic	antitoxic
	antilock	antistatic	antiwar

Rule 33   *-ary or -ery (or -ory)*

33a   – *-ary* is used for agents, instruments, adjectives meaning 'connected with' and words meaning simply 'a place for'.

-ary			
	alimentary	customary	granary
	ancillary	depositary (person;	hereditary
	anniversary	store)	honorary
	apiary	dictionary	imaginary
	apothecary	dietary	incendiary
	arbitrary	disciplinary	infirmary
	armillary	discretionary	inflationary
	aviary	dispensary	insanitary
	binary	diversionary	intermediary
	budgetary	documentary	involuntary
	bursary	elementary	itinerary
	capillary	emissary	judiciary
	centenary	estuary	lapidary
	commentary	exclusionary	lectionary
	complementary	exemplary	legionary
	complimentary	formulary	library
	concessionary	fragmentary	literary
	constabulary	functionary	luminary
	contemporary	funerary	mercenary
	culinary	glossary	military

continued

-ary		
missionary	pituitary	secretary
momentary	plenary	sedentary
monetary	precautionary	sedimentary
mortuary	preliminary	seminary
notary	primary	solitary
obituary	proprietary	stationary adj.
ordinary	pulmonary	statuary
ossuary	quandary	subsidiary
ovary	reactionary	summary
parliamentary	recessionary	temporary
pecuniary	reliquary	topiary
penitentiary	rudimentary	vocabulary
pessary	salutary	voluntary
pigmentary	sanitary	

Note *dispenser* but *dispensary*.

33b — *-ery* is used for places and products of work, including places where animals are bred and plants grown:
e.g. *bakery, millinery, stationery, swannery, vinery*.

-ery is also used for words that have a collective sense or mean a 'state or condition':
e.g. *machinery, scenery, slavery*.

-ery		
archery	doddery	perfumery
bakery	drudgery	phylactery
bindery	effrontery	piggery
bravery	foolery	robbery
brewery	forgery	slavery
bribery	greenery	snobbery
buffoonery	grocery	stationery n.
butchery	hosiery	thievery
carvery	jewellery	treachery
cattery	joinery	vinery
chancery	knavery	washery
clownery	machinery	winery
cookery	millinery	witchery
deanery	nunnery	wormery
distillery	nursery	

The following root words sometimes cause difficulty:
cemetery, dysentery, monastery, mystery.

33c – *-ory* is usually either part of the root (*history*) or the adjectival ending denoting agency (*auditory*), especially after *s* or *t*.

Note *adviser* but *advisory*.

A selection of words ending in *-ory* is given:

-ory

accessory	depository	oratory
admonitory	(store; person)	oscillatory
advisory	depreciatory	preparatory
allegory	derisory	promissory
auditory	derogatory	provisory
capitulatory	desultory	purgatory
castigatory	dilatory	recapitulatory
category	directory	recriminatory
celebratory	discriminatory	refectory
chicory or	dissatisfactory	reformatory
chiccory	dormitory	regulatory
circulatory	educatory	repertory
circumlocutory	elusory	repository
commemoratory	emendatory	reprehensory
commendatory	expository	respiratory
confirmatory	extrasensory	retaliatory
conflictory	factory	revisory
congratulatory	fulminatory	rotatory
conservatory	illusory	satisfactory
consistory	interrogatory	sensory
conspiratory	introductory	signatory
contradictory	inventory	statutory
contributory	laboratory	stipulatory
corroboratory	laudatory	suppository
cosignatory	lavatory	suspensory
crematory	mandatory	territory
cursory	minatory	theory
damnatory	moratory	trajectory
declamatory	noncontributory	transitory
declaratory	nonobligatory	undulatory
defamatory	obfuscatory	unsatisfactory
delusory	obligatory	victory
depilatory	observatory	
depletory	offertory	

Rule 34   *-ce* or *-se*, *-cy* or *-sy*

– **When a word can end in *-ce* or *-se* or *-cy* or *-sy*, use *-ce* or *-cy* for the noun and *-se* or *-sy* for the verb:**[7]
e.g. *advice, device, practice* and *prophecy* are nouns. Change the *c* to *s* to make the verb, viz. *advise, devise, practise* and *prophesy*.
Mnemonic: *advice, to advise.*

No word ends in *-ensy* and only *pansy* and *tansy* end in *-ansy*. These sounds at the ends of words are written *-ency* and *-ancy*.
If a word ends in an /s/ sound followed by a short /i/, it is usually written *-cy*.
The following lists give nearly all the words ending in *-sy* but only the main words ending in *-cy*.

-sy	apostasy	geodesy	leprosy
	courtesy	heresy	pleurisy
	ecstasy	hypocrisy	prophesy vb.
	fantasy	idiosyncrasy	theocrasy (religion)

-cy	accuracy	illegitimacy	obduracy
	adequacy	illiteracy	obstinacy
	advocacy	immediacy	pharmacy
	aristocracy	inaccuracy	piracy
	bureaucracy	inadequacy	plutocracy
	candidacy	indelicacy	policy
	celibacy	inefficacy	prelacy
	confederacy	innumeracy	primacy
	conspiracy	inordinacy	prophecy n.
	degeneracy	intermediacy	racy
	delegacy	intestacy	reprobacy
	delicacy	intimacy	saucy
	democracy	intricacy	secrecy
	diplomacy	inveteracy	spicy
	effeminacy	juicy	supremacy
	efficacy	legacy	technocracy
	episcopacy	legitimacy	testacy
	fallacy	literacy	theocracy
	hierocracy	lunacy	(government)
	icy	meritocracy	
	idiocy	numeracy	

A few words end in *-cey*, viz. *chancey, dicey, pacey, poncey, pricey, spacey* and *wincey*. *Chancey, pacey, poncey* and *pricey* are alternatives to *-cy*.

---

[7]In American English, *advice* n., *advise* vb., *device* n., *devise* vb. and *prophecy* n. and *prophesy* vb. follow the rule <u>c</u> for the noun and <u>s</u> for the verb.
All the rest, except *practice* n. and vb., end in *-se*, viz. *defense, offense, pretense, vise* (clamp) and *license* n. and vb.

Rule 35 _-cede, -ceed_ or _-sede_

- Where the sound /seed/ occurs at the end of a word it is usually spelt _-cede_.

-cede	accede	concede	re-cede (cede again)
	antecede	intercede	recede (go back)
	cede	precede	retrocede

Exceptions: _exceed, proceed, succeed, supersede_ and the word _seed_ and its derivatives.

Note _proceeding_ but _preceding_.

Rule 36 _-dge + -ment_

- The _e_ in _-dge_ and _-ment_ may be lost or kept.
  Abridgment, acknowledgment, judgment and _lodgment_ used to be the only allowable spellings of these words and their derivatives. Now, however, there are alternative spellings that retain the _e_: _abridgement, acknowledgement, judgement_ and _lodgement_.

Words ending in _-e_ that add _-ment_ usually keep the _e_, e.g. _advertisement_, but _argue_ does not. It produces _argument_.

Rule 37 _des-_ or _dis-_ (or _dys-_)

- Is the word a negation (_e.g. discontent, discourteous, dishonour, disorder_) or a reversal (_e.g. disallow, disarm, disband, discharge_)? **If it is and you drop the sound /dis/ and are left with a whole word, the sound you dropped is spelt _dis-_ because _dis-_ is an English prefix meaning negation or reversal.**

The Greek prefix _dys-_ is the opposite of _eu-_ ('good', 'well', 'easily'). It conveys the idea of 'abnormal', 'bad' or 'with difficulty'. It is used mostly in medical language. The following may be encountered in non-medical literature.

dys-	dysentery	dyslexia	dyspeptic
	dysfunction	dyslexic	dystrophy
	dyslectic	dyspepsia	

Rule 38 *-ction* or *-xion*

- **The vast majority of words which end in the /shən/ sound preceded by a /k/ sound are spelt *-ction*, e.g.** *diction.*

However, the following words are always spelt *-xion.*[8]

-xion	circumflexion	flexion	prefixion
	complexion	fluxion	suffixion
	crucifixion	infixion	transfixion

Where there is a choice between *-ction* or *-xion*, *-ction* is always the preferred spelling except for *retroflexion.*

connection or connexion	reflection or (rare) reflexion
deflection or deflexion	retroflexion or retroflection
genuflection or genuflexion	solifluction or solifluxion
inflection or inflexion	

Rule 39 *-ed* or *-t*, and *-on* or *-en*

- **The past participles of some verbs sometimes end in *-t* rather than *-ed*.**

The following are always spelt with *-t*:
crept, dealt, felt, kept, left, meant, slept, swept.
Note that *bereft* is an adjective and *bereaved* is the past participle.

The following past participles end in *-t* or *-ed*:
burnt or *burned; dreamt* or *dreamed; knelt* or *kneeled; leant* or *leaned; leapt* or *leaped; learnt* or *learned; smelt* or *smelled; spelt* or *spelled; spilt* or *spilled; spoilt* or *spoiled.*

In the early 1900s, there was a tendency to prefer *-ed* but now there is a tendency to prefer *-t*.

39a — *-on* or *-en*

A work like this cannot give the huge number of endings in *-on* and *-en*, to distinguish, for example, *lesson* (teaching) and *lessen* (make less).

- **the ending *-on***

-on usually indicates a noun. If we leave out of consideration endings in *-sion* and *-tion*, the ending *-on* does not usually indicate the derivation of the word, e.g. *pardon.*

---

[8]Webster does not give *circumflexion* or *suffixion* in American English or the alternative spellings *connexion, deflexion, inflexion* or *reflexion.*

– **the ending** *-en*

The ending *-en* often indicates the derivation of the word. It is a suffix used in various ways:
- It makes verbs from adjectives, e.g. *cheapen, deepen, lessen.*
- It makes adjectives from verbs, e.g. *chosen, mistaken.*
- It makes adjectives from nouns, e.g. *earthen, wooden.*

Rule 40   How to spell /ər/ and /ərd/

Words with these sounds can be broken down into three main groups:
-er, -or or *-re* (or *-ure*);
-ar or *-our*, and *-ard* or *-erd;*
-ture, -tcher or *-cher*

The endings *-er* and *-or* can be confused because they both denote agent and both are usually pronounced the same. The ending *or* is the Latin suffix and *-er* is the English suffix.

40a – *-or* in technical cases

More difficult words use *-or*.
It is the ending used in words of Latin, French and legal origin. Lawyers and scientists use *-or* to distinguish these words from those words in common use ending in *-er*:
e.g. *payor; vendor; acceptor, resistor*

40b – *-er*

– **The ending** *-er* **is used with Old English words to denote profession or occupation** (*lawyer; baker, slater*) **and to indicate agents** (*blotter, imposter, poker, welder*). **It is also the comparative suffix for adjectives** (*farther*), **a noun ending** (*lavender*) **and a suffix for verbs which describe a frequently repeated action** such as *flatter, judder, shudder, spatter.*

The list of words ending in *-er* runs to thousands and the ending is usually correctly spelt. Here are a few examples:

-er			
	angler	father	lavender
	barber	fender	miner (job)
	blister	fever	pincers
	caliper	gander	proper
	canter	hanger (coat)	rafter
	copper	helicopter	trailer
	elder	holster	tumbler
	falter	larder	
	farther	lather	

It is also the ending for the *-grapher* and *-loger* of Latin origin, e.g. *biographer, chronologer* and endings in *-erer*, e.g. *murderer.*

– **If in doubt, the safer bet is** *-or* since the most difficult but least used words end in *-or*.

Avoid the tendency to simply add *r* to a verb ending in *-ate*: e.g. *decorate—decorator, indicate—indicator*.

Note *mare* and *mayor*, which sound the same.

Here is a list of *-or* words that may sometimes cause difficulty.

-or			
	abbreviator	attestor	conspirator
	abductor	attractor	constructor
	abettor	or attracter	or constructer
	abominator	attributer	consulter
	accelerator	or attributor	or consultor
	acceptor	auditor	contaminator
	accumulator	author	contractor
	activator	aviator	contributor
	adapter	bachelor	convector
	or adaptor	calculator	convener
	addresser	calibrator	or convenor
	or addressor	calumniator	converter
	administrator	capacitor	or convertor
	adulterator	capitulator	cooperator
	adviser	captivator	or co-operator
	or advisor	carburettor	coordinator
	aggressor	castigator	or co-ordinator
	alleviator	castrator	corrector
	alternator	celebrator	councillor
	ambassador	chancellor	counsellor
	amputator	cinerator	creator
	ancestor	circulator	creditor
	anchor	coadjutor	curator
	annihilator	collaborator	debtor
	annotator	collector	decorator
	anticipator	commentator	defector
	apparitor	competitor	deliberator
	applicator	compositor	denominator
	appreciator	compressor	depositor
	appropriator	conciliator	designator
	arbitrator	conductor	detector
	aspirator	confessor	detonator
	assessor	conqueror	deviator
	assimilator	consolidator	dictator

continued

diffuser
or diffusor
dilator
director
discriminator
disrupter
or disruptor
disseminator
dissipater
or dissipator
doctor
duplicator
editor
educator
ejector
elevator
eliminator
emperor
endorser
or endorsor
epilator
equator
eradicator
error
escalator
estimator
evaluator
exactor
exaggerator
excavator
executor
exhibitor
expiator
expositor
exterminator

extractor
facilitator
fornicator
fumigator
generator
gladiator
governor
hallucinator
hesitater
or hesitator
illustrator
impersonator
imposter
inaugurator
indicator
injector
inspector
instigator
interrogator
inventor
invigilator
junior
liberator
liquidator
manipulator
manor
mediator
minor (lesser)
mirror
moderator
monitor
motor
narrator
navigator
oppressor

percolator
perforator
perpetrator
persecutor
possessor
predicator
prevaricator
projector
promulgator
proprietor
prosecutor
prospector
protector
radiator
recriminator
recuperator
redactor
refrigerator
renovator
resistor
respirator
resuscitator
retractor
scissor
sculptor
segregator
selector
senator
simulator
solicitor
spectator
tractor
transistor
ventilator
visitor

40d – *-re*

– **Some words end in -re, about half of which end in -tre.**
Except for *genre* and *padre*, this ending *-re* sounds like the ending *-er* and is sometimes confused with it.[9]

---

[9]These words are spelt *-er* in American English except for *acre, cadre, chypre* or *chipre, genre, lucre, macabre, massacre, mediocre, nacre, ogre, padre, sucre* and *timbre*.

-re		
accoutre	lustre	piastre
acre	macabre	reconnoitre
cadre	massacre	sabre
calibre	meagre	saltpetre
centre	mediocre	sceptre
chambre	metre	sepulchre
chypre or chipre	mitre	sombre
fibre	nacre	spectre
genre	nitre	sucre
goitre	ogre	theatre
litre	padre	timbre
lucre	philtre	wiseacre

— *-ar* or *-our,* and *-ard* or *-erd*

— *-ar,* especially the *-ar* of agent, e.g. *burglar,* **can be confused with *-er.***

-ar		
altar	foliar	perpendicular
angular	friar	pillar
annular	glandular	polar
auricular	globular	poplar
beggar	grammar	popular
binocular	granular	rectangular
briar	hangar (plane)	regular
or brier	jocular	scholar
burglar	jugular	scimitar
calendar	lumbar (back)	similar
caterpillar	lunar	singular
cedar	modular	solar
cellar	molar	spectacular
cellular	mortar	tabular
cheddar	muscular	triangular
circular	nectar	tubercular
conciliar	nuclear	tubular
consular	ocular	uvular
curricular	particular	vascular
dollar	peculiar	vicar
exemplar	pedlar, peddler	
familiar	or pedler	

Note the difference between *lumbar* (back) and *lumber* (jumble).

— *-our*[10] (the earliest spelling of *-or*) **can be confused with *-or*.**

-our			
	arbour	enamour	odour
	ardour	endeavour	parlour
	armour	favour	rancour
	behaviour	fervour	rigour
	belabour	flavour	rumour
	candour	glamour	saviour
	clamour	harbour	savour
	clangour	honour	splendour
	colour	humour	succour
	demeanour	labour	tumour
	discolour	misbehaviour	valour
	disfavour	misdemeanour	vapour
	dishonour	neighbour	vigour

Note: words ending in *-our* change the ending to *-or* before the suffixes *-ate*, *-ation*, *-iferous*, *-ific*, *-ize* (and *-ise*) and *ous*, e.g. *humorous*.

Exception: *colourize.*

— *-ard* **or** *-erd*
These endings should prove no problem even though they sound the same when unstressed.

Apart from *halberd, herd, nerd, potsherd* and *sherd,* all the other words that end in *-erd* are compounds of *herd*, viz. *cowherd, goatherd, shepherd, swanherd, swineherd.*

Numerous words end in *-ard*. Here are some examples:

-ard			
	afterwards	downwards	standard
	backwards	mustard	wizard
	blizzard	scabbard	

---

[10] All the *-our* words end in *-or* in American English except for *glamour.*

– **The sound /chə/ at the end of a word can be written *-ture*, *-tcher* or *-cher*.** The ending *-ture* is the most frequent and only the main examples are given.

The few words ending in *-tcher* are the ones given and their cognates.

-ture		
adventure	indenture	puncture
agriculture	juncture	rapture
architecture	lecture	rupture
armature	legislature	scripture
candidature	ligature	sculpture
capture	literature	sepulture
cincture	manufacture	signature
conjecture	mature	stature
creature	miniature	stricture
culture	mixture	structure
curvature	moisture	suture
debenture	nature	tablature
denture	nomenclature	temperature
enrapture	nunciature	texture
expenditure	nurture	tincture
feature	overture	torture
fixture	pasture	venture
forfeiture	picture	vesture
furniture	portraiture	viniculture
future	posture	viticulture
gesture	prefecture	vulture
immature	premature	
imposture	primogeniture	

-tcher		
botcher	hatcher	snitcher
butcher	hitcher	stitcher
catcher	matcher	stretcher
dispatcher	patcher	switcher
ditcher	pitcher	thatcher
etcher	scratcher	twitcher
fetcher	sketcher	watcher
fletcher	snatcher	

-cher			
	archer	impeacher	reproacher
	attacher	launcher	researcher
	bencher	leacher	retoucher
	bleacher	lecher	scorcher
	broacher	luncher	screecher
	clincher	lurcher	searcher
	coacher	lyncher	sloucher
	coucher	marcher	smircher
	cruncher	moocher	squelcher
	debaucher	muncher	starcher
	detacher	peacher	stauncher
	drencher	percher	teacher
	encroacher	poacher	toucher
	enricher	preacher	trencher
	entrencher or	puncher	voucher
	intrencher	quencher	welcher
	filcher	rancher	wencher
	flincher	reacher	wincher

Note the sound /chune/ at the end of *fortune* and cognates like *misfortune*. Other words ending in *-tune* have the sound /tyune/.

 — *-ure*

Endings in *-ure* can be confused with endings in *-er*.

-ure			
	azure	embrasure	ordure
	brochure	enclosure	perjure
	censure	erasure	pleasure
	closure	exposure	seizure
	composure	failure	tenure
	conjure	figure	tonsure
	disclosure	fissure	treasure
	disfigure	injure	verdure
	displeasure	leisure	
	disposure	measure	

Rule 41   *-erous* or *-rous*

– **Some words form adjectives in *-erous* (*boisterous, slanderous*) and some form them with *-rous* (*disastrous, monstrous, wondrous*).**

If the word is pronounced clearly, there is no difficulty with the spelling, which follows the pronunciation.

Rule 42   *everyone* or *every one*

- **Write *anyone*, *everyone*, *no-one* and *someone* as one word when *anybody*, *everybody*, *nobody* or *somebody* can be used. Otherwise write the words separately,** e.g. Each person may take *any one* of the presents.

No one is an alternative to *no-one*.

Rule 43   *fore-* or *for-*

- ***fore-* means 'before' and is usually stressed:**
  e.g. *forecast, foregone, forehead, foreman, forewarn*

- ***for-* is usually not stressed and means 'away, out, completely' or indicates prohibition:**
  e.g. *forbid, forget, forgive, forgo, forsake.*

Note *forward.*

Rule 44   *in to* or *into*

- ***in* and *to* are written separately when they make sense when said separately,** e.g. He came *in to* his meal. He crashed *into* the wall.

Note that the same rule applies to *onto* except that, in many cases, a simple *on* is better.

Rule 45   *-ize* or *-ise*, and *-yze* or *-yse*

- ***-ize* or *-ise***

- **Nearly all words ending in *-ize* (e.g. *apologize*) have an alternative ending in *-ise*.**

These endings go back to the original Greek word ending in *-izo*, which in French changed to *-iser.*

Collins Dictionary favours *-ize* as the preferred spelling, e.g. *apologize, realize, recognize.* In this, it is supported by the OED, Fowler's Modern English Usage and the University Presses of Oxford and Cambridge. This also accords with American usage, which is having a progressively more powerful effect on English usage.

Note *stanza.*

- **In some words *-ise* is the only, or preferred, spelling.**

These do *not* originate from the Greek *-izo.*

A list of the more common is given.

-ise	advertise	disfranchise	nowise
	advise	or disenfranchise	otherwise
	apprise	disguise	premise
	arise	enfranchise	prise
	cerise	enterprise	revise
	chastise	excise	slantwise
	circumcise	exercise	supervise
	comprise	franchise	surmise
	compromise	guise	surprise
	contrariwise	improvise	televise
	demise	incise	unwise
	despise	likewise	wise
	devise	merchandise	

Note: the *-ise* in *premise* is pronounced /iss/, not /ize/.

— -*yze* or -*yse*

— Note the following words, which end in -*yse*.[11]

-yse	analyse	dialyse	overanalyse
	autolyse	electrolyse	paralyse
	breathalyse	hydrolyse	psychoanalyse
	catalyse	lyse	reanalyse

Rule 46   *-lely* or *-ly*

— *-lely*

— Like words ending in *-l*, words ending in *-ile* follow the normal rule and add *-ly* to form adverbs, as do *pale*, *sole* and *stale*:
e.g. *accidentally, actually; vilely; palely, solely, stalely.*

-ilely	agilely	futilely	puerilely
	docilely	hostilely	senilely
	ductilely	imbecilely	servilely
	facilely	infertilely	sterilely
	fertilely	inutilely	tensilely
	fragilely	juvenilely	versatilely

Exception: *whole* becomes *wholly*.

---

[11] In American English, all of the words ending in *-yse* except *breathalyse* and *lyse* end in *-yze*.

- **Words ending in -ble, -cle, -dle, -fle, -gle, -kle, -ple, -tle and -zle all drop the e and add y to form adverbs and adjectives:**
  e.g. *crumbly, humbly; muscly, treacly; cuddly; sniffly; singly; tickly, dimply; subtly; drizzly.*
  Note that *brittlely* has an alternative *brittly.*

Note also that the preferred adverb from *supple* is *supply*. There is a variant spelling *supplely* which differentiates it from the verb (or noun) *supply*.

Beware of short words and words with double consonants, where there is more temptation to include an e. Almost all the words with double consonants and a selection of short words follow.

-bly	bubbly dribbly pebbly	rubbly scribbly stubbly	wobbly

-dly	cuddly fiddly	muddly puddly	waddly

-fly	sniffly	waffly	

-gly	giggly goggly jiggly jingly jungly niggly	shingly singly spangly squiggly straggly tangly	tingly waggly wiggly wriggly

-kly	crinkly freckly	knuckly prickly	tickly tinkly

-ply	crumply pimply	purply ripply	rumply supply

-tly	bristly brittly	gently nettly	rattly subtly

-zly	drizzly	frizzly	

Rule 47   – *-uly or -uely*

– **Where the *u* is silent the *e* is retained:**
e.g. *brusquely, grotesquely, obliquely, opaquely, picturesquely, sculpturesquely, statuesquely, uniquely, vaguely.*

Note: *due, true* and *rule* drop the *e* to give *duly, truly* and *unruly* but *blue* keeps the *e* to give *bluely*.

Rule 48   *un- or in-*

– **Always use *un-* with words ending in *-ing* or *-ed*.**

Exceptions: *indisposed, inexperienced.*

– Use *in-* (or *il-*, *im-* or *-ir*) with words ending in *-ance, -ate, -ence, -ible, -ion, ity* or *-tude*.
These endings all indicate a word derived from Latin.

Exceptions: *unregenerate, unintelligence; unfeasible, unintelligible, unsusceptible; unpremeditation, unsaturation, unsophistication.*

The exceptions for the ending *-ity* are more numerous:

uncivility	unconventionality	unpredictability
or incivility	undesirability	unprofitability
unaccountability	unemployability	unquestionability
unavoidability	unexceptionability	unreadability
unbelievability	unfamiliarity	unreality
unconditionality	unflappability	unscrupulosity
unconformability	unknowability	unsubstantiality*
unconformity	unmorality	unthinkability
unconstitutionality	unpopularity	
uncontrollability	unpracticality	

*an alternative to *insubstantiality*

Double consonants can cause difficulty, so they are given here and in rule 48c.

illegal	illogical	immense	immovable
illegible	immaculate	immiscible	immutable
illegitimate	immaterial	immobile	innocuous
illiberal	immature	immoderate	innoxious
illicit	immeasurable	immodest	innumerable
illimitable	immediate	immoral	innumerate
illiquid	immedicable	immortal	innutritious
illiterate	immemorial	immotile	irreclaimable

continued

irreconcilable	irregular	irreplaceable	irrespirable
irrecoverable	irrelevant	irrepressible	irresponsible
irrecusable	irrelievable	irreproachable	irresponsive
irredeemable	irreligious	irresistible	irretentive
irreducible	irremediable	irresoluble	irretrievable
irreflexive	irremissible	irresolute	irreverent
irrefragable	irremovable	irresolvable	irreversible
irrefutable	irreparable	irrespective	irrevocable

48c – **Nearly all other words take *un*-.**

Note that *in*- is the Latin negative prefix and *un*- is the Old English one. So *un*- is preferred except where a Latin form is established. Even where this is so, an *un*- form may be used to express a simple negative where an *in*- (or *il*-, *im*- or *ir*-) form has connotations beyond simply negation:
e.g. *immoral* and *unmoral, insoluble* and *unsolvable, inhuman* and *unhuman*.

un- produces a double letter with words beginning with *n*.

unn-	unnamed	unneeded	unnerve
	unnatural	unneedful	unnoteworthy
	unnavigable	unnegotiable	unnoticeable
	unnecessarily	unnegotiated	unnoticed
	unnecessary	unneighbourly	unnurtured

GLOSSARY

adverb: a word which qualifies a verb, adjective or another adverb.

agent: someone or something that performs an action.

attribute: a quality or condition.

attributive: indicating an **attribute** by placing one word near, usually before, another, e.g. *the green book*, as opposed to *the book is green* (**cf. predicative**).

blend: two or three letters that mingle to form a new single sound with all the letters recognizable in the sound, e.g. *-bl-*, as opposed to **digraph**.

cognate: a word that is related to another word in form and meaning, e.g. *wish* and *wishing*.

colloquial: used in informal speech and not strictly correct in formal or literary language.

combination: the same sequence of letters occurring in a number of words.

compound word: a word made by joining other words.

derivative: the same as **cognate**.

digraph: two letters which combine to form a new sound in which all the letters are not recognizable, e.g. *-ch-* or *-ea-*, as opposed to **blend**.

diminutive: a noun with a suffix indicating that it is small, e.g. *statuette*.

homonym: one of two or more words which are identical in sound or spelling but which have different meanings, e.g. *made* and *maid* or *lead* (metal) and *lead* (go before).

loanword: a word adopted from a foreign language, e.g. *gateau*.

mnemonic: an aid to memory, often a sequence of words or letters in a verse or sentence (see rule 6a and 6b for examples).

monosyllabic: consisting of one syllable.

phonetic: when the pronunciation follows the sounds of the letters used.

phrase: a group of words without a verb which forms a small unit of sense in a sentence.

possessive case: a change made to a noun to indicate possession, e.g. *Jane's book*.

predicative: following verbs like *be, seem, appear*, e.g. *the book is green*, as opposed to *the green book* (cf. **attributive**).

prefix: a unit of meaning added to the beginning of a word.

preposition: a word indicating relationship to a noun or pronoun, e.g. *in the box*.

Received Pronunciation: thought to indicate education and/or social standing; it is the accent represented in the phonetic transcription of words in dictionaries.

root word: the word which carries the main part of the meaning in a compound word or simple word, e.g. *board* in *blackboard* (*black* is an attribute) and *rich* in *superrich*.

schwa: the phonetic symbol /ə/, which indicates the indeterminate sound of the *a* in *again*.

sibilant: having the hissing sound of /s/, /z/, /ch/ or /sh/; the letters *s* and *z*.

suffix: a unit of meaning added to the end of a word.

'sympathy' sound: an expression coined by the writer to describe the sound /aw/ (phonetic symbol /ɔ:/). It occurs not only in the vowel digraphs *-aw-* and *-au-* but also in a number of other vowel combinations especially with *r* and *l*.

REFERENCES

The following publications were found helpful:

Cotterell, G. *Phonic Reference Cards*, LDA, 1975

Crystal, D. *The Cambridge Encyclopedia of the English Language*, Cambridge University Press, 1995

DfEE *The National Literacy Strategy: Framework for Teaching*, DfEE, 1998

Gowers, E. *Fowler's Modern English Usage*, Oxford University Press, 1978

Hornsby, B. and Shear, F. *Alpha to Omega: The A–Z of Teaching Reading Writing and Spelling*, 4th edn, Heinemann, Oxford, 1993

Jones, D. *Everyman's English Pronouncing Dictionary* 11th edn, J. M. Dent, London, 1960

Leonard, W. J. *Classified Spelling*, Schofield and Sims, Huddersfield, 1972

* Lewis, N. *20 Days to Better Spelling*, Harper and Row, 1953

Metcalf, J. E. *The Right Way to Spell*, Elliot Right Way Books, Tadworth, 1994

Robin, G. and Watson, C. *The Usborne Book of English Spelling*, Usborne, London, 1983

Sansome, R. *The Oxford Junior Dictionary*, Oxford University Press, 1978

* Spalding, R. B. and Spalding, W. T. *The Writing Road to Reading: The Spalding Method of Phonics for Teaching Speech, Writing and Reading*, Quill William Morrow, New York, 1990

Weiner, E. S. C. and Delahunty, A. *The Oxford Guide to English Usage*, 2nd edn, Oxford University Press, 1993

Wright, W. D. *Learn to Spell*, James Nisbet, Welwyn Garden City, 1975

The following publications were also used:
The Shorter Oxford English Dictionary, 3rd edn, 1985, sometimes referred to in the text as OED
Webster's Third New International Dictionary.
Footnotes indicate where these rules differ from the rules for American spelling. Any other footnotes would be out of place in a book such as this. Therefore I acknowledge here my indebtedness to the above works.

All the books listed above follow UK (Australian and Canadian) usage except for the three marked with an asterisk, which follow the rules for American spelling.